LIGHTHOUSE

By the same author

THE COURAGE OF HIS CONVICTIONS

THE UNKNOWN CITIZEN

THE PLOUGH BOY

FIVE WOMEN

A MAN OF GOOD ABILITIES

PEOPLE OF THE STREETS

THE TWISTING LANE Some sex offenders

THE FRYING PAN A prison and its prisoners

IN NO MAN'S LAND Some unmarried mothers

THE MAN INSIDE (ed.)

THREE TELEVISION PLAYS

THE PEOPLE OF PROVIDENCE

SOLDIER, SOLDIER

LIGHTHOUSE

TONY PARKER

ELAND, LONDON
&
HIPPOCRENE BOOKS, INC., NEW YORK

Published by
ELAND
53 Eland Road, London SW11 5JX
&
HIPPOCRENE BOOKS INC.,
171 Madison Avenue, New York, NY 10016

First issued in this edition 1986
© Tony Parker 1975

First published by Hutchinson & Co. (Publishers) Ltd 1975

British Library Cataloguing in Publication Data

Parker, Tony
Lighthouse.
1. Lighthouses—Great Britain
I. Title
387.1'55'0922   VK1057

ISBN 0–907871–66–6

Photoset, printed and bound in Great Britain by
Redwood Burn Limited,
Trowbridge, Wiltshire

Cover illustration © Tony Ansell
Cover design © Patrick Frean

For Tim
from his father
with love

BIOGRAPHY

Tony Parker was born in Manchester in 1923, and grew up and was educated there. A pacifist, he was a conscientious objector in the 1939-45 World War, and worked underground in a coal mine for 18 months before being discharged on medical grounds after he was injured in an accident.

He has written many books of a documentary nature, all of them based like this one on tape recorded interviews – a technique he has pioneered and made his own, and which was described by the *Times Literary Supplement* in a review of contemporary literature as "the one genuine new art form of the past decade". He and his wife, a former Medical Social Worker, now live in Suffolk. They have five grown up children.

He has recently been awarded a Simon Senior Research Fellowship by the University of Manchester.

CONTENTS

CONTENTS

The Corporation of Trinity House,
Trinity House,
Tower Hill,
London E.C.3.

Dear Sir,
    Thank you for your letter. I regret it is not permitted for visits to be made to off-shore lighthouses owing to difficulties of access.

Yours faithfully,
(Signature indecipherable)

The Corporation of Trinity House

Introduction I

The old man lived on a remote small island, on his own in a tiny bungalow he'd had built ten years earlier when he retired; it was on top of a cliff so he could have an uninterrupted view from his sitting room window out as far as the horizon, over the endless unbroken miles of rolling and constantly mood-changing Atlantic Ocean.

He was tall, white-haired, and with twinkling bright blue eyes. His face was tanned by the weather and wrinkled with age. He was wearing a thick dark blue fisherman's pullover, navy serge trousers and slippers. His stance was straight-backed and his handshake firm, his voice strong and his smile direct and welcoming.

– Come in young sir, come in! Are you the gentleman who wrote to me? You couldn't have come at a better moment, I've just got the kettle on for a cup of tea. Certainly I'm sure I'm not busy! Good heavens, what would I be busy with at my time of life? All I've done today is a few hours in the garden, too cold outside to stop there for long. I hardly do a stroke these days, only sit by the window there, twiddling my thumbs and watching the sea. Bone idle, that's what I am! A lazy old good for nothing now, not like I used to be, can't think what's got into me.

– That's absolutely true, yes sir, that is quite correct. I am a

retired lighthouse keeper. Which one was I on? Why that one
there on the horizon, where else? Why would I have a house
built for myself in this exact spot here, if it wasn't so I could look
out of my window and see her every morning, and her light
every evening, and be satisfied however hard the wind blows
and the sea rages she's still there?

A long time ago that was though, that I was out there; a long
long time ago, sixty years or more when I was only a lad of
nineteen or twenty. Then I had to leave the Service on account
of my brother getting married and going away, and me the only
one left to help out my father who was getting too old for his
farm. I never really feel I've left it though. There's part of me
still there and always will be. That's the way it gets you with
lighthouses, once you've been a keeper on one it stays in your
memory because it was your home, or that's how you looked
on it at least.

From all I've heard about it since I'm led to believe it's not
changed all that greatly inside of it, even now after all this time.
Nearly a hundred years she's been out there so far, think of that!
The men who built her must have been very fine craftsmen
mustn't they, that she could stand up so long against the sea?
It's because those who designed her, they had the knowledge of
the sea and the respect for it which you've got to have before you
start you see. Not like these rich oil companies you read of
nowadays in the papers that build oil rigs, and no sooner have
they spent millions of pounds putting them up than the sea
knocks them down. They haven't got the knowledge and respect.
You've got to have those to start off with, otherwise the sea'll
treat you how you deserve.

If you're interested, why don't you write to the Corporation
of Trinity House up in London and ask them if you could go
and have a look for yourself? Ah well, you don't surprise me,
not one little bit. Lighthouses don't change and neither does the
Trinity House. They were just exactly like that towards en-
quirers in my day; and they will be for ever more I shouldn't

wonder, though Heaven alone knows why. I've never been able to understand it myself. They've a lot to be proud of and nothing to hide so far as I've ever known. It's just they're concerned with their traditions, you see, they're set in their ideas. They go about their business in their own way and have no truck with outsiders. It's the Navy they call 'The Silent Service' isn't it? My good grief, compared with Trinity House the Navy's a bunch of chattering monkeys in a monkey house, it is.

*

A swarthy-featured young Cornishman sitting alone in a corner of a pub one night smiled, as he talked wrinkling his brow from time to time and staring thoughtfully into his beer in the hope he'd see words in it.

– That's right my handsome that's what I am, a lighthouse keeper, yes.

How to tell you what it's like . . . honestly I wouldn't know where to start. It's a different world you see out there, a totally different world; you couldn't imagine it for yourself and I couldn't explain. When you come to think of it, three men living their lives marooned on a rock sticking up out of the sea. Bloody ridiculous isn't it when you come to think about it?

The only way you could really find out what it was like would be to come off there a few weeks to live with us, have a proper chance for each one of us to talk to you, wouldn't it? Only not in the summer like the visitors when they come out in the pleasure boats to take pictures of us like we were performing animals in a circus; in the winter so you'd get the proper picture. Yes of course we'd have you, it'd make a change for us not having only ourselves to talk to all the time. Why don't you write up to Trinity House in London again, ask them if you can come and stay with us for a bit? That'd be the way.

*

The Corporation of Trinity House evolved from a medieval mariners' Guild which some historians believe developed from a Fraternity founded by Stephen Langton, an Archbishop of Canterbury at the beginning of the thirteenth century. The Fraternity consisted of:

Godley disposed men who do bind themselves together in the love of Lord Christ in the name of the Masters and Fellows of Trinity Guild, to succour from the dangers of the sea all who are beset upon the coasts of England to feed them when ahungered and athirst, to bind up their wounds and to build and light proper beacons for the guidance of mariners.

It is probable it was known as 'Trinity' Guild because seamen traditionally placed themselves under the protection of the Holy Trinity.

In 1512 this Guild of mariners presented a petition to King Henry VIII asking for a Royal Charter. He granted it in 1514 'that they or their heirs, to the praise and honour of the most glorious and undividable Trinity and St Clement may establish a Guild of perpetual Fraternity of themselves in the parish of Deptford Strond in our county of Kent'. (St Clement, who was reputedly martyred in the first century A.D. by being dropped into the sea with an anchor attached to him, was a patron saint of sailors and fishermen.)

By the terms of the Charter the Guild was to be controlled by a Master assisted by twelve wardens. It would be responsible:

for all and singular articles anywise concerning the science and art of mariners; [and its members] had power and authority for ever of granting and making laws or ordinances and statutes amongst themselves for the relief, increase and augmentation of the shipping of this our realm of England. All which laws, ordinances, and statutes, those offending to punish and chastise at their discretion according to the quantity of the offence.

The Charter was confirmed in 1547 by Edward VI, after the Guild had changed its name to 'The Corporation of Trinity

House of Deptford Strond'. In 1566, during the reign of Elizabeth I, an Act of Parliament authorized it to erect 'such and so many Beacons, signs and marks for the sea in such place or places of the seashore and uplands near the sea coasts or forelands of the sea whereby the dangers may be avoided and escaped and ships the better come unto their ports without peril'.

A Coat of Arms was granted by the College of Heralds in 1573. This was in the form of St George's Cross on a shield, with an Elizabethan galleon in each quarter, a crowned lion holding a sword above, and the motto *Trinitas in Unitate* on a scroll beneath. James I extended the Charter in 1604 to include powers concerning the compulsory pilotage of shipping and the exclusive right to license pilots in the River Thames; and in this Charter for the first time the controlling administrators were referred to as the 'Elder Brethren'. Trinity House built a lighthouse at Lowestoft in 1609, but the Corporation's right to erect lighthouses was not exclusive; the Crown retained power to grant patents to do so in return for payment of rent, to individuals who were then permitted to charge fees to passing ships. Incomes derived in this way frequently developed into large fortunes.

Oliver Cromwell was uncertain of the Corporation's allegiance and suspected it of Royalist sympathies. Its Charter was dissolved and its administration put in the hands of a Commission; but the Charter was renewed by Charles II after his restoration to the throne in 1660. The following year Samuel Pepys recorded that he had been offered one eighth of the subsequent profits if he would support a Captain Murford's application for a lighthouse patent. Whether he did so or not he became one of the Elder Brethren of Trinity House in 1672, and after the accession of James II in 1685, its Master.

Authentic details of the early history of Trinity House are scarce: there are extensive gaps in its records as a result of the Civil Wars between 1642 and 1648, the Great Fire of London in 1666, another fire in 1714, and the bombing of London in December 1940 during the Second World War.

In 1822 a Parliamentary Select Committee recommended that all lighthouses in private ownership should be purchased by and brought under the control of Trinity House; an Act in 1836 empowered the Corporation to do this and granted it a State Loan for the purpose. A further Act of 1854 decreed that Light Dues should be paid into the Mercantile Fund, and in 1898 the Merchant Shipping (Mercantile Marine Fund) Act diverted them into a specially created and separate General Lighthouse Fund. This is now administered by the Department of Trade and Industry and is used to finance the Scottish and Irish Lighthouse Services as well. 'Light dues' are charges levied on nearly all ships, based on their size, using ports in the United Kingdom and Ireland. They are collected by H.M. Customs and currently amount to about £13 million a year.

The work of Trinity House is controlled by ten Active Elder Brethren and a Secretary, assisted by administrative, engineering and marine staff. They operate in the manner of a board of working directors, consulting daily and meeting once a week formally to deal with policy matters and supervise the activities of the Corporation. These include, as it is the Principal Pilotage Authority of the United Kingdom, the licensing and examining of pilots and the exercise of disciplinary control over them; the marking and disposal of wrecks except those within harbour limits; and the administration of charities, estates and almshouses. Trinity House is represented on a number of committees and councils connected with maritime affairs, including several Harbour Boards such as that of the Port of London; and Elder Brethren sit as Nautical Assessors in marine causes in the Admiralty Division of the Royal High Court of Justice and, if required, on the Judicial Committee of the Privy Council.

One of the principal executive subcommittees of the Board is the Light Committee, responsible for the administration and operation of the Lighthouse Service of England and Wales and with certain statutory powers over aids to navigation maintained by the Lighthouse Authorities for Scotland and Ireland. It is composed of three of the Elder Brethren appointed annually in rotation from among the ten Active Elder Brethren, and supervises the work of the Trinity House Lighthouse Service. Trinity House has sole responsibility for all fixed and floating seamarks and visual, audible and radio aids to navigation. Members of the Board make an annual inspection of all lighthouses, light vessels, beacons and buoys under its control; and once every three years inspect all other sea-lights and beacons in England, Wales and the Channel Islands. Within its jurisdiction are 93 lighthouses, 27 light vessels and nearly 700 buoys of which over half are lighted.

A Trinity House historian describing the work of inspection of lighthouses sixty years ago wrote:

Any man who has been picked for duty as a keeper must be of unimpeachable precision. All brasswork has to be cleaned and polished until it gleams like burnished gold, while the rooms must be washed and kept in the pink of condition, free from the smallest specks of dust. The necessity for extreme cleanliness and spotlessness is emphasised, and the Inspector has a highly trained and quick eye for detecting carelessness. He has one instinct developed peculiarly – the discovery of dust. He draws his finger over everything, and squints quizzically at every object from all angles. Woe betide the keeper if the slightest trace of dirt is detected, for if a man permits a door knob to become sullied he is just as likely to overlook the polishing of the lenses, or to perform some other vital task in a perfunctory manner.

No later description of demanded standards has yet been written.

Trinity House possesses a fleet of lighthouse tenders, pilot cutters, fast launches and ancillary craft. The Committee Ship on which the Elder Brethren make their voyages serves a dual purpose: it is a working vessel and is also used by them on ceremonial occasions when they exercise their privilege of preceding the reigning Sovereign whenever he or she goes afloat in British waters.

The ten Active Elder Brethren are men who have had long experience in command of ships in either the Merchant or Royal

Navy; they are authorized to use the title of 'Captain' and wear uniform similar to a Royal Naval captain's with distinguishing marks, and frock-coats and morning waistcoats for special occasions. A small number of 'Honorary Elder Brethren' are, in the words of a Trinity House publication, 'selected by invitation'; they include the present Master of the Corporation H.R.H. Prince Philip, and among others the Duke of Norfolk, the Duke of Gloucester, Admiral of the Fleet the Earl Mountbatten of Burma, the Rt. Hon. Harold Wilson and the Rt. Hon. Edward Heath.

The Active Elder Brethren themselves, again in the words of Trinity House, 'are selected when a vacancy occurs' from 'among the ranks of the Younger Brethren, numbering approximately three hundred, who are all Master Mariners or Senior Naval Officers'. Younger Brethren can only become Younger Brethren by invitation from the Trinity House 'Court' under the supervision of the Active Elder Brethren.

*

– And a very good day to you too young sir! So you've not forgotten your old friend then? Good, splendid, come in, yes of course come in and sit down. Thank you for that history thing. Are you still writing those books of yours? Well I suppose it's a way of making a living isn't it, much the same as anything else? It wouldn't suit me though, I'd sooner be out and about doing something useful.

Is that idea still in your head about trying to get out on a lighthouse or two? You wrote to the Trinity House again but still had no luck with them? Yes I can well believe that, I can.

A book, you've put that out of your mind have you? No, I didn't think you would, somehow. You've brought your infernal tape-recording machine with you I see. You be setting it up then and arranging things how you want them while I'm making us the tea.

– The sea can be very frightening and it can be very beautiful as well. But you have to give it the respect it deserves; because whichever it is at its different times if it comes to a choice between the strength of man-made things and the strength of the sea, there's only one answer. The sea's the master.

If a young man came to me now and asked me what I thought for him joining the lighthouse service, there's many questions I'd want to ask him. The first one would be had he ever been out on the sea in rough weather and if he had how did it make him feel? Not watching it from the safety of the land, but in a small boat actually upon it: had he felt the strength of it, did he think he could experience being face to face with it without it shattering his nerve? I wouldn't expect him not to be frightened by it; but I'd ask him to consider if he could put up with that regular feeling of being afraid.

I'd want to know if he thought he could deal with the long periods of loneliness without making himself a misery to himself and to the other two keepers who were out there with him? I'd ask him if he could turn his hand to this and that, mechanical things and ordinary simple everyday household occupations like washing-up and cooking for himself? Was he self-reliant, was he patient, would he have discussions but not arguments, was he even-tempered, could he rely on himself to always keep a civil tongue in his head? Had he got one or two hobbies he could pass his time with, because sometimes the other keepers'd want to be left on their own so it's essential he should know how to occupy himself? And most of all would he be conscientious about keeping the hours of the watch, take his turn without complaining whether it was the middle of the day or the middle of the night, that being the principal reason for him being there to ensure that the light always shone?

If he could satisfy himself and me about all those kind of things and it was still his ambition to do it, I'd think if he was so determined then the only way for him to find out if he really had it in him what was needed would be to go ahead and see. I'd tell him when he saw a lighthouse keeper walking around ashore in his uniform, with his buttons and bows and all the rest of it, and he looked at those smart Trinity Cottages they give to the men these days to live in with their families, that was only the best side of it. But out there on a tower in his overalls with only the washing-up bowl to have a bath in and nothing but a tin bucket up under the lantern for a lavatory, then he'd find it very different. No one could tell him if it was the sort of life for him; nor could he tell it himself until he'd been there to try.

– It's not one gale, it's not two gales, it's not twenty gales tied together by their tails that frightens you. It's what comes after, when the wind's had two or three days to put a thousand miles of ocean into motion and turn it into what's called a heavy ground sea. That's what it is makes you afraid. It rolls the boulders along with it that are down there on the sea bed; and when it strikes them against the base of your tower the whole place quivers from its top to its toe. You can hear them, you can feel them: thump, thump, thump, being thrown like that under the water against the foundation, rolling into it one after the other and making the tower shake: and you shake with it too, like all your teeth are going to be rattled out of your head. On and on it goes, on and on. And each one you feel you think it can't take one more thump like that, the next one for certain will be the one that'll bring the place down with a crash, and that'll be the end. He'll have to have that experience to teach him to know the meaning of fear.

*

– Well yes, said the six foot two inches tall fifteen stone Principal Keeper, I suppose you could say it was a bit like that sometimes if you wanted to, yes. Specially if you were the sort of person who has a tendency to let little things worry you a bit. But very few towers actually fall down you know; we don't lose a great number of keepers, least not in a normal week. Christ those cigars of yours stink; I'd worry more about dying from suffocation if you were with us on our tower than I would about being smashed to buggery by the sea.

Our tower's only a small one; it'd have to be wouldn't it otherwise I'd never fit! Looking at the size of you I reckon we could squeeze you in somewhere if you wanted to come, so long as you wouldn't mind sleeping in the cage with the budgie. So what if Trinity have turned you down a couple of times? That was last year and the year before wasn't it? People come and people go; it was only a few weeks ago I heard they'd got someone new in there who's breaking the news gently to them now that the twentieth century looks like it's here to stay. Buy me another drink and I'll tell you some more; and if anyone reprimands me for inviting you to come on our lighthouse I'll say I was under the influence of alcohol. I'll have one of those cigars in self-defence. Fucking hell, I thought I was a hard man; you mean you actually smoke those for pleasure? Jesus Christ.

*

– What? They've actually given you permission to do it? Well I'll be jiggered! Here's me been telling you the last three years you'd never get it, you hadn't a hope. You've been persistent all right, that's for sure; all the same things have changed a bit since my day, I can tell you that and no mistake. Anyhow good for you and good for them: I've always thought Trinity kept itself to itself too much, I could never see what for or why.

How'll you make a start then, where'll you begin? Here with me you say, talking to me? Heavens above, I'd have thought you'd heard enough of an old man's chatter to last you the rest of your life. Of course I will, yes with pleasure; I'll give you any amount of help you want in any way I can. I'll tell you what to start with, I've got an information sheet somewhere, in that drawer I think; one that Trinity House sends out to people writing to them enquiring about becoming lighthouse keepers.

Would you like to have a look at it if I can find it, make a few notes from it? Copy the whole thing out if you want while I make us some tea. Now let's have a search and see if I can find it, I'm sure I've got it somewhere here.

Trinity House Lighthouse Service
'Candidates for appointment as Lighthouse Keepers must be of British nationality, medically fit, have full normal vision with or without spectacles, and be between the ages of 18 and 32 years. No technical knowledge is required as preliminary training is given in how to operate and maintain different types of equipment for lighting, fog signalling and radio, and in weather reporting.

Thereafter a successful candidate enters the Service as a Supernumerary Assistant Keeper (SAK) for a period of approximately twelve months' probation, during which he will serve at a number of different lighthouses to gain practical experience and, when necessary, be posted as Relief for keepers absent through sickness or on leave. In addition to pay an SAK receives a daily allowance for quarters, and is entitled to seventeen days' paid holiday a year plus one week for each month of service on a rock station.

On satisfactory completion of the probationary period, he will then be promoted to Assistant Keeper (AK), and be appointed to a particular lighthouse: rent-free married quarters are provided or a housing allowance is paid in lieu. An AK's salary increases by annual increments for seven years after appointment.

As and when vacancies occur, promotion to the position of Principal Keeper (PK) on a higher salary scale will follow, with annual increments for a further five years. All posts as Assistant Keeper and Principal Keeper are permanent, and pensionable at current Civil Service rates.

Uniform clothing is provided free each year; and in addition to basic pay and rent-free accommodation or housing allowance in lieu, for keepers appointed to rock stations a daily rock-money allowance and a daily victualling allowance is paid while the keeper is resident on the station.

AKs and PKs appointed to shore lighthouses have twenty-eight days' leave a year; those at rock stations are granted four weeks free from duty on completion of each period of eight weeks on the lighthouse.'

– Here's our tea then; does that put you in the picture on some of the background? You'll know what people mean now will you, when they talk about SAKs and AKs and PKs? Good. Right; after that how should we go on? Would it help if I was to try and tell you a bit of the basic what do you call it, the basic terminology so you'll be familiar with it when people are talking to you?

All right then. Now that piece of paper you've been reading, anyone that didn't know any different would think there were just two kinds of lighthouses wouldn't they? Those on land that they call 'shore stations', and those out at sea they call 'rock stations'. Theoretically as you might say, as far as pay and allowances goes that's correct. But if you're mixing with lighthouse keepers as you will be you'll find in general conversation none of them hardly ever refers to 'lighthouses' or 'stations'. The word they use is 'lights'. And as far as they're concerned there aren't just two kinds, there are three. Which is land lights, rock lights and tower lights.

Let's see if I can make the difference clear. We'll start with the sort that's officially called a 'shore station' but that ourselves we always call a land light. That's one that's near the sea, perhaps on a cliff; but built on the actual mainland, do you follow? It'll be there to mark a specially dangerous piece of coastline, say on the tip of a jutting-out headland or something like that. To define it simply: you don't have to cross water to get to it.

But even though it's on the mainland, of course that's not to say it mightn't very probably be in a very out of the way sort of place. A lot of them are, a great lot of them: very remote and inaccessible indeed some of those land lights. A long way from main roads and bus routes and things, isolated right out on the coast miles from anywhere. I know one that's a good fifteen miles or more from the nearest town; and another that hasn't even got so much as a village within two miles. So a land light even though it might be on the mainland, well it could easily be much more isolated in a lot of respects than a lighthouse in the sea but perhaps only a few hundred yards offshore from a town.

But as far as keepers are concerned, the big difference between a land light and any other sort is that it's got accommodation. For keepers and their families, built together with the lighthouse in one unit so they all live together. A keeper appointed to a land light doesn't have to go away from his home to work; he lives all the time in the ordinary normal domestic situation. I think you'll find to be posted to a land light is the ultimate aim and ambition of most keepers, leastways the married ones. There's no doubt their wives prefer it of course. Whatever the difficulties of living in an isolated place, getting the children to school, shopping, little chance to go anywhere for social life, that sort of thing: they'd still much sooner have a home life where they live with their husbands all the time. Like it says in that paper the keepers get less leave, only twenty-eight days in the year because there's only three of them stationed at a land light to share the duties. All the same they're there all the time with their families.

So there you are then, that's the sort of place we mean when we talk about a land light. Understand that do you now all right?

Now we go on to the other kind, what the Trinity paper calls 'rock stations'. These are what most people have in mind I suppose, when they're talking about lighthouses in general: somewhere out at sea, that water has to be crossed to get at and where keepers go and work and live without their families. Well that's true, that's what they all are: and they don't have accommodation for families attached to them. A man working on one has quarters there, but a house or accommodation provided for his family on the mainland. So when he goes off to work he leaves them. As far as they're concerned he's away on the lighthouse for his two months' tour of duty. The rock stations have a complement of four keepers; at any one time three of them'll be off on the lighthouse, and the other one'll be having his month's leave ashore.

In general terms, but only in general terms mark you, then so it's true there's only two kinds of lighthouse: land lights where a keeper lives with his family, and rock lights which he has to leave his family for and go off to work on his own. To keepers themselves as far as the actual working conditions are concerned it's still not as simple a matter as that though. There's one big additional difference; which is whether he's on what we call a rock light or whether it's one we call a tower.

A rock light in his language is a lighthouse that's built on an island. Whether it's a small island or a big one like some of them are isn't important. As far as a rock light's concerned the thing about it is whatever the size of it there's land of some kind round the lighthouse that's never covered by the sea. If you're on a rock light, if you feel like it whenever you want to you can get outside the lighthouse and walk round for a bit, stretch your legs, do a spot of fishing, get some fresh air and so on. You're not cooped up inside the lighthouse every minute of the day and night during your stay. So remember when keepers talk about a rock light, they're talking about a kind of place like that.

The other kind is very different and is what they always refer to themselves as a tower light. The sort like that one out there on the horizon that I was on. That's a proper lighthouse; I think you'll find every keeper in the Service will agree with me on that. It doesn't have any dry land round it, none whatsoever at all. It's a lighthouse sticking straight up out of the sea; and it's one you can't ever get outside of at all. Once you're in it you're in it. Your only exercise'll be running up and down the stairs, or walking round the gallery if the weather's fine enough outside the lantern at the top. And that's it; that's where you are for your entire eight weeks' stay. That's the sort of place we mean by a tower light; not the same thing at all as a rock light.

Does that sort it out for you? Land lights, rock lights, tower lights; got them all clear? So long as you keep those differences in your mind you'll have a proper picture what lighthouse people mean when they use the expressions.

While I remember to mention it, there's one other little thing. When we say 'on' and 'off', we don't use the words the same way you do. If a keeper's on a lighthouse, we say he's 'off'; meaning he's offshore. We talk about 'going off', not 'going on'; so a spell of duty is called a turn 'off'. Coming ashore we express simply like that; 'coming ashore', not 'coming off'. More or less all the time what to a land person would be 'on' is 'off' to us. Just a matter of habit, but I suppose it could get a bit confusing for you if you weren't used to it. So there you are then, I expect the rest of it you'll pick up as you go along.

The Land Light

Connie Preston

A Very Peaceful
sort of an Existence

2

Very remote and inaccessible indeed, some of those land lights, he said.

'Trinity House Property. No Unauthorized Admittance.' Round a sharp curve of neat gravelled roadway towards a huddle of low buildings dimly visible in outline at the foot of a slender white tower. High above them from the top of it a broad band of light turned slowly round and round, illuminating the enclosing basin of the wet black sky.

At the end of the nearest building a porch light was on; inside it the freshly painted olive-green front door and a shining brass knocker, and the small fair-haired woman in an oatmeal trouser-suit who opened it had a smile. The Principal Keeper's wife.

– I've made coffee and a few sandwiches, these are salmon and cucumber, those are potted shrimp. Shall I leave the plate by you on this table so you can help yourself? Please do, I made them specially; I knew it'd be a long journey for you to make to get to us, we're such a long way off the beaten track, aren't we?

George isn't on watch till midnight so we've plenty of time to talk. I'll be waking him round about half past eleven, but he only has just a cup of tea when he gets up; nothing to eat so don't worry about leaving any for him, he'll not want it. He might have a piece of the cake but I doubt it, usually he prefers nothing else but his cup of tea. We had our evening meal earlier on so I won't have anything either. No please don't mention it, it was no trouble, it's a great pleasure.

It's a big event for us to have a visitor out here, especially in the winter time. How long will you be staying? You're very welcome indeed, stop for however long you like. We thought it'd be best to give you the room we put an SAK in when we have one stationed with us. It's off a corridor between two of the cottages, its own washbasin and so on, a separate entrance door so you can come and go as you please. Will that be all right?

You won't have been able to see much what the place looks like arriving in the dark. Have a wander round tomorrow in the daylight, you'll soon find your way about. There are three cottages with storage buildings between them built in a block together round the lighthouse with a paved yard in the middle: the dwellings are at angles to one another so their front doors face different ways. All three are more or less the same size and shape and layout; but because of the way the buildings are arranged you don't get a feeling you're all on top of one another and haven't any privacy. It might sound strange, but you can go two or three days without seeing anyone from the other cottages unless you go out of your way. That's a good thing I think: you've got neighbours when you need one another but you're not forced into one another's company all the time.

This is Number One where we live; if you go out of the front door, in the opposite corner of the yard is Number Two which is Mike and Sheila's house. Number Three where Tom and Stella live, their front door is round the back facing the other way. It sounds a bit complicated, but in the daylight you'll get the hang of where we all are.

It's a very peaceful sort of an existence here. Very quiet, an uneventful sort of life; I enjoy it, I'm happy and contented with it. We've had our worries and troubles, our movings about over the years, but now we're settled for a while. We've been here just over two years so far and as far as we can tell nothing will

change now for a few years. I'm enjoying the stability of it and
the peace and quiet.

George and I have been married for over twenty years. No
let me see, now you ask it must be getting on for nearer twenty-
five. What a long time ago it was when I was a girl and I first
met George. I'd be eighteen or nineteen I suppose. To marry
a lighthouse keeper: who'd have thought that, I certainly didn't?
Such a thing hadn't even crossed my mind.

It came about because I was on my holidays staying with my
sister. Her husband worked for Trinity House, he was an electrician at one of their maintenance depots. She lived in a small
seaside village; and a few miles offshore from it was a lighthouse.
There was this young keeper from it who wasn't married; he
had his quarters in a house next door to my sister's, and while I
was there he was ashore on his shore leave. He was a friend of
my sister and her husband, and he was always popping in and
out of their house. Trinity's very much a one great big family
sort of an organization, nearly everyone in it knows everyone
else.

During the time I was there for my holidays I more or less
took him for granted: I mean we didn't go out together or anything like that. The end of my holiday coincided with him going
back to the lighthouse, or perhaps he went back a day or two
before; I've forgotten exactly but it was something of that sort.
He'd said would I write to him and I'd said yes, though to be
perfectly honest I'd no intention of writing regularly. Perhaps
now and again like you would to anyone you struck up a casual
friendship with on holiday but no more.

But anyway a few weeks later I was back staying with my
sister again. I'd decided I wanted to get a job there, I fancied the
idea of living near the sea. So I paid another visit to her to see
if I could find myself something. Up till then I'd been a shorthand
typist: I'd lived all my life in a city but I was getting fed up with it.

I'd not been at my sister's again above a day or two when I
had to go to the village post office and general stores place to

get something. I'd hardly opened the door when the woman behind the counter said 'Hello, aren't you Elizabeth's sister?' I said yes, and straight out she said to me 'Well why haven't you written to that nice young man on the lighthouse yet? Don't you know he's expecting a letter from you every day?' I was so flabbergasted I couldn't think what to say: I turned round and ran all the way back to my sister's, blushing like mad I should think.

It was so funny I didn't feel annoyed about it, I was just absolutely astounded. As soon as I got back to the house I said to Elizabeth 'How on earth does anyone know I said I'd write to George? And what's more since he's off on the lighthouse now, how can they tell I haven't?' Elizabeth stood and laughed at me, it was the expression on my face I suppose. She said 'Well that's how it is in a village; and that's how it is in Trinity too. So if you're going to have anything to do with a lighthouse keeper you'd better start getting used to it.'

What had happened was that George had gone back off on the lighthouse, and whenever it was his turn to do the radio test, talking to the coastguards on the shore, he'd slipped in a remark that he was expecting a letter, and asking if one was waiting to come out for him on one of the boats that go out round lighthouses nearly every day in the summer. People on shore nearby listen in to these tests on their own radios if they know the right waveband, especially if they're connected with Trinity, so they can keep up to date with what's going on. Everything always gets round like a flash between lighthouses and keepers ashore at the time and everyone else.

Well, to get back to me and George. When I realized how seriously he'd taken it that I said I'd write, and how much it meant to him I should, of course I did. Then he wrote back to me, I wrote to him again and so on. There wasn't anything serious about it to start with though; he was just an acquaintance really, I hardly knew him.

I did get myself a job, so I was living permanently with my sister by the next time he came ashore. From then on the friendship just sort of developed; after a while I found I was missing him a lot when he was off on the lighthouse, and looking forward to each time for him to come ashore. It went on like that for I suppose a year or more.

Every rock light has four Trinity Houses, they always call them cottages, that are allotted to the keepers. Because he was single George was in the quarters in the house next to my sister's and one day we heard one of the married keepers was going to be transferred in the June to another lighthouse. That meant there was going to be a cottage vacant for an AK who was married. So that was it. There wasn't any doubt in either of our minds we were going to get married before long, we took it for granted.

So did everyone else in the village too. As soon as it was known there was going to be the vacant cottage, people didn't ask questions about what we intended. It was simply 'Oh that'll be nice, you and George'll be able to have a summer wedding, won't you?'

I've been very very happy ever since. This one great big family atmosphere that everyone connected with Trinity feels, I'm happy being part of it. It gives you a real sense of security and belonging. The organization's small enough for you to know nearly everyone in it and for them to know you; wherever you go when your husband gets posted to different lights over the years, you'll find somebody there you've already been with before, or you've heard about them through other keepers. Even if somebody joins the service as an SAK and has been through his probationary period, even in that short time you'll either come across him yourself or meet somebody else who has.

An important aspect of it is that favouritism doesn't enter into the promotion side. Nearly every SAK does about the same length of time before he gets made up to AK; and the AKs, they know when they can expect promotion up to PK. It's automatic, it's based entirely on the length of time a man's been an AK, not on examinations or reports. After he's been an AK around twelve to fifteen years he'll be made up to PK when the next vacancy occurs; and it's taken strictly in turn. Every man knows how many there are before him to be promoted to PK; and as each one gets there, he knows he's getting higher up the list himself. I think that's a good system; it's fair and it doesn't make for bad feeling.

All this I've been telling you will qualify me for being what they call 'Trinity minded'. You'll hear that said by a lot of people about a lot of other people. I don't mind it: it doesn't seem to me a bad thing to be. If your husband's job's his life as it has to be in the lighthouse service, you've got to have a certain frame of mind if you're going to fit in with it. I'd say to anyone that I'm happy; I like the life, I'm glad to be part of the family, and I wouldn't want to change.

After George had done nearly five years on the rock there, we heard he was going to be transferred to a land light. I remember looking forward very much to it, thinking how much nicer life was going to be having George at home and him not having to go away. That much at least, having him at home, it was much nicer. But the land light, goodness me I didn't enjoy living there not one bit. It was one of the very isloated ones: much much more isolated than this is, it was three miles even from the nearest main road. What's more it was built right on the very edge of a cliff; and all the land behind it was all up and down every few yards. I shouldn't think there was fifty yards anywhere along the path to the main road that was even what you would call a gentle slope, never mind flat. Whenever I went out shopping I was eternally struggling up and down everywhere with the pram. The lighthouse itself and its cottages were all enclosed behind a great high wall you couldn't see over. It was exactly as though you were living in a prison. So I couldn't say I enjoyed my first experience of living on a land light. It was lonely, it was bitterly cold in winter and usually wet and raining in the summer, really it was a dreadful place.

Altogether we were there about three years. Then George got

transferred to another land light that was a much nicer one. It was this one here. Isolated a bit perhaps, but compared to the other one it was paradise. While we were here that time we had our second baby, another boy, Andrew. He's eleven now and going to school in the town. It means a lot of travelling on the bus for him, he has to leave home in the morning about seven o'clock to walk to the village to catch it, then he doesn't get back again until towards six o'clock in the evening. But he doesn't mind it, he likes living out in the country and by the sea. I asked him the other day if he'd like it if we moved and he said he wouldn't.

That time we spent nearly three years here, with George as an AK. Then he was transferred again, to another land light up in Norfolk. That was a really beautiful one; it was on the outskirts of a very pretty seaside town. We were very happy indeed there; we stayed nearly five years.

Then came the time we had to make the decision every AK has to make when he's been in the service about fifteen years and he's offered promotion up to PK. It's inevitable when you go up from AK to PK you find yourself having to go back on rocks again. Some men get so settled on land lights that when their turn for promotion to PK comes, rather than take it they decide they'd sooner stay on as they are as AK. When they offered George to make him up to PK, we had a talk about it: we knew it'd mean he'd have to move from a land light and go back on rocks for a few years, but we decided that was all part of the life, so he accepted.

The station he got wasn't a very good one from the family's point of view, because it didn't have a Trinity house to go with it. That's how it usually is when you're first made up to PK: in a sense it's almost like starting at the bottom of the ladder again as far as stations go. Some rock lights have their own houses ashore, but that particular one didn't; so instead we had a council house in a town that was inland, a good fifty miles away from the light George was on.

So you find yourself with two small children, in the middle of a council estate among strangers who don't think you've any right to be there; and your husband's away for two months at a time off to the lighthouse. That's not very easy. The local school Richard had to go to was a very big and rough one too, he wasn't happy there either. I can remember him coming home very upset one day because some of the other boys had been tormenting him. He wouldn't tell me what it was about at first. Eventually he said they knew his father wasn't at home much, and they kept asking him where he was, what he was doing, why he kept going away. When he told them his dad was a lighthouse keeper they didn't believe him; they said he was in prison or he'd left home and gone off with somebody else. They can be very cruel sometimes, other children, Richard was very upset about it. They kept it up so much I honestly think he must have started wondering about it himself. He'd never even seen the lighthouse where his father was, so I suppose he wasn't really sure if it existed. So it wasn't so good, that period.

But anyway we were among the fortunate ones compared with some other PKs, because George was only on rocks for about five years. He got sent to another rock first but then he got another posting, which was back again to here. Which is where we've been now for the past two years, and as far as I can tell unless something unusual happens we can settle down to staying here for the next few years. If George gets another posting, it's not likely he'll be sent back off on rocks again. The next'll almost certainly be another land light, and so on till he retires. Unless he specifically asks to go back, and I shouldn't think George'll be likely to.

There is just one thing when you're talking to him. I wonder if he'll mention it, I don't really know . . . No, I'd better not say anything more, I'll leave it to him. He might want to talk about it or he might not; you'll have to see.

Principal Keeper George Preston

An Open Door

3

In his late forties and slimly built, with light brown eyes in a thin face under neatly combed wiry dark hair.

– Well, someone to talk to on the middle watch, that's a new experience. I'd bet there isn't another keeper anywhere this very moment finds himself with company. They'll all be on their own now, starting their middle. Yes exactly this minute, in every lighthouse all over the country there'll be a new keeper just beginning his turn on watch. You understand our watch system do you, anyone explained it to you? We'd better begin with that then hadn't we? Perhaps the best way'd be if I set it out in like a sort of a table.

There's three keepers stationed at every land lighthouse; I'll put them down as A, B and C. Twenty-four hours round the clock, every day of the year including Saturdays, Sundays, Christmas Day, Bank Holiday and everything else, there's always got to be one keeper on watch. He's on duty in the lighthouse to make sure the light's lit and working when it's supposed to be, or maintain and service the machinery during the daytime. The duty periods for the three keepers are divided up on a rota that repeats every three days; so using the twenty-four-hour clock system it looks like this:

Time	Day 1	Day 2	Day 3
00.00–04.00	A	C	B
04.00–12.00	B	A	C
12.00–16.00	C	B	A
16.00–20.00	A	C	B
20.00–24.00	B	A	C

Then the fourth day it starts back at the beginning again and so on. It works out you have the same hours of watch every fourth day. The number of hours' duty you do varies over the three days but comes out at the end the same total for each keeper. A does eight hours on the first day, B does twelve hours and C does four; on the second day A does twelve, B does four and C does eight; the third day A does four, B eight and C twelve. So each man's done all together twenty-four hours' watch over the three days. If a keeper's on leave or off sick, they bring in an SAK to replace him and he takes his turn on watch in the same order as the one he's standing-in for.

The one we're on now, midnight till four in the morning, is always called the middle. How it got that name I couldn't be certain, perhaps it's to do with being the hours of the middle of the night or something of that sort. It seems right when you think of it though it'd be beyond me to try and explain why. It certainly does feel like the middle of something. as though it's like sort of halfway between one day and the next, I'm not good at putting something into words. Even on a land light the middle watch is the one you feel you're absolutely on your own. I'm used to it, so's every lighthouse keeper. And I suppose every man feels the same; sometimes it can get well not exactly oppressive but the sort of time you find your thoughts beginning to ramble. If there's anything on your mind you'll find yourself thinking about it. Sometimes you just sit and stare, other times you'll get weird ideas and funny feelings come into your head. Perhaps like that somehow you're the only person left in the world, everyone else has disappeared; there aren't any other people anywhere,

no one else alive but you. Things like that sort, stupid things.
I suppose if every fourth night of your life you find yourself
awake when everyone else is asleep it's not surprising. Sitting
on your own looking out of a lighthouse window; it's a funny
sort of existence.

Over twenty-five years in the Service, how'll I tell you much
about that? How I got into it at the beginning was I was eighteen
or just a bit younger when I joined. I wanted to go in the army
originally. My father always had a big influence on me; he
wasn't a skilled man, most of his life he'd had a hard time finding
jobs, he was in and out of work. There was seven of us children,
I was the eldest; and he's always used to tell me to try and get
in something decent when I grew up. Not to be dependent on
other people for work, try to find something I could get in and
stay in and have security in life. There wasn't a big choice what I
could do, not being clever at schooling. I asked him one day
what did he think of the army, if I tried to sign on long-term in
something like that? He said it was good and permanent all right,
but had its drawbacks like it was for fighting so there was always
the chance you'd end up getting shot. He said have a bit more of
a look round, see if there was anything better before I com-
mitted myself.

What happened then was I saw an advertisement in the paper,
asking for people interested in being lighthouse keepers to write
and find out more about it from Trinity House. I liked the
sound of what I got back in the way of information so then I
went up to London for an interview. They accepted me straight
off and that was all there was to it.

I was taken on as SAK, and there wasn't a lot of training; you
only had a couple of weeks at Harwich or Blackwall depot, then
you were sent off on different lights to pick up the rest on the
job as you went along. A funny thing happened: after I'd done
my training the first light I got sent to was the Eddystone. That
was a very big thrill for me and I'll tell you why. When I was
a boy of around nine or ten one of the places we lived in was a

village near a big stone quarry. I remember one day talking to one of the men who worked there and asking him what they used their stone for. He said it was a granite quarry, which meant the stone from it was very hard. It was so strong he said, that they'd once used it to build a lighthouse with it called the Eddystone; and the lighthouse had stood in the middle of the ocean over fifty years and however rough the seas they'd never been able to knock it down.

Most of my SAK time was on rocks and towers, like it usually is. But I only stayed SAK for something under twelve months; which was unusual, or would be nowadays. It was only I was lucky, it wasn't I was specially brilliant; it just happened there was a lot of vacancies for AKs then and so young men got made up pretty quickly.

My first post as AK was another rock light. I wasn't married so I didn't have the house that went with it. I lived in quarters in a village on the coast and I'd been there about two years when one day I met Connie who'd come to stay with her sister there. We started writing to each other, then about a year later there came chance of one of the Trinity cottages so we got married. Odd how that worked out too, it was like there was something inevitable about everything. As soon as I got on the Eddystone I knew the lighthouse service was what I was meant for, from the moment I met Connie I knew she was the girl for me. The important things that happen for you, somehow it's almost as though someone's planned it for you when you come to look back.

We'd been married a few years, then we had our first child, then I got a posting to a land light. Connie was very excited about it, we both were until we actually got there. It wasn't at all a good place to live in for a young woman with a small child. Connie stuck it out; she would, she's that sort of person: and we were together all the time so it had its compensations. When we look back on it we say we've known the worst as far as land lights are concerned; but we came through it all right, so everything after can't be quite as bad.

We had a move eventually and the next seven or eight years were all on other land lights and were good. The next difficult time was when we were up in Norfolk and I got the offer of being made a PK. It meant me going away again, but I don't think either of us had much doubts. If you're happy in a job obviously you want to get on as far as you can.

It doesn't make much difference as far as the amount of work's concerned; everybody on a lighthouse does more or less the same. The PK doesn't do less work than the others or just sit around giving the orders. He does the watches and work duties like anyone else. Whatever different jobs need doing he doesn't take the attitude the PK's a cut above the others and doesn't have to do certain things. There's none of that, you don't behave any different in any way. Being the PK only means you're the one who carries the can.

But if anything does go wrong, the PK's responsible and there's no escape from that. Even if it was something he'd no control over, when it comes to it he's the one who's looked on as being responsible for it, because he was the man in charge. On his station whatever happens has to come back to him in the end. That's what you accept when you accept being a PK. That's been what I've chosen, to accept the responsibility. Look, getting on to almost three o'clock now. Have to break off a bit while I go up and check the light.

*

At the end of the corridor a glass-panelled door and beyond it an iron staircase spiralling up through rooms with rumbling generators, to one at the top with banks of control panels and switches. A short metal ladder in the middle of it: up through a hole in the roof to the light with its lenses revolving round and magnifying it to the powerful beam which swung round the sky. Out through a heavy metal door, and on to the gallery.

Drizzle, blackness, unbroken dark; the west wind blowing

steadily, and far below the surge and crash on the rocks of the unseeable sea. He leaned on the gallery rail for a few moments staring out at it, turned in a circle and looked up, then down at a thermometer fixed to a stanchion, and then went back inside. A quick check on the light and the lens machinery; then down the ladder and spiral staircase again, not touching the hand rails but putting his hands up occasionally instead to the low ceiling to steady himself in descent. At the bottom in the corridor he smiled.

– We never touch the brass railings on the stairs: no keeper does because he's the one who's got to polish them. Right then, now what I've got to do is enter the weather in the logbook. It has to be recorded every three hours by whichever keeper's on watch. Mike did it at midnight before he came off duty, I do it now, Tom'll do it at six o'clock, nine o'clock and midday, then Mike again and so on.

The first four columns in the book are for visibility: there are four marks, other lights visible from here if the weather's absolutely clear. When I was up on the gallery I had a look which I could see, and now I enter them accordingly. One's twelve miles away; I could see that all right so I put a tick under it. The next is twenty-five miles off, that one's visible too. The third's only twenty miles away but it's a red light and not very strong so it doesn't carry far: I couldn't see it, so in that column I mark it invisible. The fourth one's forty miles off and I couldn't see that either tonight.

In the next column I put the outside temperature you saw me have a look at: 49 Fahrenheit, 9 degrees Centigrade. In the next barometric pressure from the barometer on the wall here. 30.25. Still dropping, it's come down in the last twelve hours from 30.34 so there's definitely worse on the way.

Weather conditions O/D. That's for overcast and drizzle. Wind direction sou' southwest. Wind Force 5, that's about nineteen knots, something like twenty-two miles an hour. How do I tell, well the direction I got when I looked up at the weather vane on top of the lantern and the force I judged from the feel of it on my cheek when I was out on the gallery. It's something comes to you with experience; you notice the difference between Five and Six without really having to think about it.

The wind force number is its speed according to the Beaufort Scale; that's the accepted method of measurement pretty well everywhere. I think Beaufort was a nineteenth-century Admiral, he worked it out for wind speeds at sea. There's a copy somewhere here, in one of these manuals should be.

Speed in knots	Force	Description	Sea condition
Nil	0	Calm	Like a mirror
1– 3	1	Light air	Gentle ripples
4– 6	2	Light breeze	Small wavelets
7–10	3	Gentle breeze	Wavelets with crests
11–16	4	Moderate breeze	Small waves and 'white horses'
17–21	5	Fresh breeze	Moderate waves, many 'white horses'
22–27	6	Strong breeze	Large waves with some spray
28–33	7	Near gale	Waves heap up and foam
34–40	8	Gale	Wave crests break into spindrift
41–47	9	Strong gale	High toppling waves and spray
48–55	10	Storm	Surface broken up and tumbling
Over 56	11	Violent storm	Chaotic: rarely experienced
	12	Hurricane	Ditto

1 knot = 1.151 m.p.h.

If you ever want to work out the equivalents for yourself inland, it'd be roughly like this. Force 0, smoke rises straight up in the air. Force 1 would be if the smoke drifts a bit. A Force 2 you could just about feel on your face and there'd be a bit of rustling of leaves in the trees. Force 3 would put small twigs of trees on the move, Force 4 would blow paper about and raise the dust, and in a Force 5 leafy trees start to sway. When you can hear the wind whistling in telegraph wires that's Force 6. Force 7 makes it a bit difficult walking against the wind. A Force 8 will be when twigs are actually breaking off trees. Force 9'll blow off chimney pots and slates, and Force 10 will uproot trees. Force 11 or 12, well by then there'd be too much going on for you to be spending time taking much interest in the exact wind speed. Those are only rough guides, but they'll give you a kind of picture in your mind.

Well now I've done my weather as they say. Sign my name here opposite the 03.00 hours entry, then the book stays here on the desk for Mike to enter it up at 06.00.

– What we were talking about before we broke off and went up top, I was saying how when you get to PK you accept you're responsible in the end. Whatever happens on any light you're in charge of: it's a thing, a kind of something for me I'm not ever likely to forget...

You'll hear mention of it almost certain. Maybe since it was me who was the one there it's better that if anyone tells you about it it should be me. Earlier on I said I'd go back on a tower if I had to; but in the middle watch your thoughts wander. I think about this; I don't talk about it much but I think of it, I suppose I always shall.

I was made up to PK and first went away again about eight years ago now. The first rock I was on was a station on a fair sized island and you could walk round a bit; when the weather was good you could go for a swim if you wanted to or lie in the sun. I was there three years, then I got moved to one that was a tower. It was very cramped, no sitting room and the only two rooms for the keepers to live in were the kitchen and bedroom;

the other floors were store rooms and service rooms. A rough light too it could be for the weather: a lot of storms even in summer, and nearly always a swell on the water because you were far out from the land.

I'd been PK there about a year and a half, and the AKs under me were good men. Then it happened one month we had to have a young SAK off out there: one of the AKs had gone sick so the SAK was brought to take his place for a few weeks, and be on a tower to get experience of what it was like. He hadn't been in the Service long; a nice young lad of about twenty or twenty-one. He seemed to be settling in, he got on well with Danny who was AK and with me. He was a great reader and an entertaining sort of chap as well, always one for showing us card-tricks and things like that. His name was Ginger, that was what they called him because of the colour of his hair.

This day I'd been on the morning watch, four o'clock until midday. When we were sitting in the kitchen after we'd had our middle of the day meal, Ginger started asking me what I thought his chances would be of catching fish with a new rod he'd brought off with him. He went to get it out of the locker under his bunk to show to us and ask our opinion. We were pulling his leg and laughing at him because it was a light rod an angler might use in a stream, not the sort that'd be any good for fishing in the deep sea. Danny got his own and told him that was the kind to use if he wanted to have any hope of catching something.

You know how it is; a good-natured chap Danny, he said if Ginger was thinking of trying to fish he'd better use it. There's only one place you can fish from on a tower light and that's the entrance doorway. Like it is on most towers, the door's about thirty foot up above the water with an iron ladder leading down. If the sea's low when the relief boat comes you might use the the ladder to jump off; but not often, it's more than half under water most of the time.

It was a calm sort of day, not much wind, not much swell on the sea. Ginger asked me it I thought it'd be all right for him to try his luck later from the doorway. I said I was fairly sure it would; the sea was nowhere near coming up to it, I said so long as he didn't do anything daft like going out on the ladder he'd be all right.

We did the washing up and went up and did a repair on one of the generators; and by then it was getting on for four o'clock in the afternoon. My next turn on watch was the middle starting at midnight, so I said I was going to turn in and get a few hours' sleep beforehand. I went up to the bedroom and got in my bunk and had a bit of a read for about twenty minutes or so; then I closed the curtain that was round the bunk and lay down and shut my eyes. I'd not been lying down more than three or four minutes when I heard somebody come in the bedroom and start rummaging about. I pulled the curtain back a bit to see who it was, and it was Ginger. He said he was sorry, he hadn't meant to disturb me; he was looking for a book he wanted to read, he asked me if I'd seen it lying around. I said no, and I made some daft joke to him about how he couldn't be very optimistic about catching much if he was going to read a book and fish at the same time. He couldn't find the book, and a few minutes later he went out.

I pulled the curtain to again and closed my eyes. I wasn't very sleepy, I always find it hard to get off in the daytime. I was more or less dozing in a sort of half-sleep I suppose when I suddenly felt a hand come through the curtain and start shaking me by the shoulder. It was Danny; he was whispering, at first I wasn't properly awake and I couldn't make out what he was saying. Gradually it sank in he was telling me Ginger was missing. I looked at my watch; it was ten to five.

You can't think at first. I remember saying something stupid to Danny like that he couldn't have gone far. I was feeling a bit annoyed; I was sure Ginger was playing a joke on us, that he'd hidden himself behind one of the generators on one of the floors higher up or something. I got dressed and Danny and I started to search the tower: we went up to the top out on the gallery, then we came down it floor by floor shouting and looking every-where. There wasn't a sign of him.

We went down until we came to the entrance floor. All there was there were a few ropes and bits of tackle. The doors were open and fastened back, but there was no water on the floor so the sea hadn't come up suddenly there. By regulation there has to be an iron bar kept across the entrance, fixed into metal slots in the wall each end: but the bar wasn't across the doorway and there was no sign of it.

We'd come all the way from the top of the tower down to the bottom: so then we started again at the bottom and went back through the tower up to the top searching every inch. We couldn't believe it. We refused to let ourselves believe it, I suppose that's the truth of the matter. But after the second search that was it; we had to face he'd gone. There was only us two there and an open door.

I got on the r/t, I put out a Pan message saying we'd lost a keeper overboard. Then there wasn't another thing we could do; Danny and I just sat in the kitchen looking at each other, trying to think what could have happened.

The last time I'd seen Ginger had been when he'd come in the bedroom. The last time Danny had seen him was a minute or two after that: he'd come into the kitchen, picked up the fishing rod and gone out making a joke to Danny to get the big frying pan ready on the stove.

About a quarter of an hour after that Danny made a pot of tea and went down to see if Ginger wanted a cup. He saw the open doorway, but he thought Ginger had perhaps decided not to bother with fishing and had gone up to one of the machinery rooms. It was only when he'd looked in them all and not found him he decided he'd better come and wake me up.

Five minutes after I'd sent out the Pan, we started getting radio messages back. All ships near the area were coming to make a search, the Trinity House tender was coming out to us as fast as she could. Two hours later she was standing off us and the

Captain was talking to us on the radio. But by then it was evening and pitch dark, and the sea had got up as well. There was nothing anyone could do. The body was never found.

I was the PK of that light when that happened, it was the station I was in charge of. Still when I go to bed in the afternoons I can't ever settle to sleep till I've looked at my watch and made sure it's gone ten to five.

Letting the Sun take over 4

The weather was beginning to clear by ten-thirty in the morning. The drizzle had stopped: in the sky patches of pale blue were widening between the overhanging grey cloud. In the yard between the cottages a burly man in a boiler-suit, in his thirties with black curly hair and deep-set blue eyes; he was briskly brushing the concrete round the entrance to the white pillar of the lighthouse tower and whistling the habanera from *Carmen*.

– And good morning to you too; Sheila's just brought over a couple of cups of coffee, she's left them waiting on the desk inside for us, come on in.

George showed you round in here on the middle last night did he? The only difference now's you can see it in daylight, look out of the window at all that expanse of empty sea. Grumpy it looks too, doesn't it? Reckon the weather'll not improve much for a few days yet.

It's a bit like being on a ship in here on watch in the daytime with nothing to look at but water. It's not like a proper lighthouse though; you can't go out and sweep the yard down when you're on one of those. I remember a couple of years ago I was on a tower, when I was ashore once a woman came up to me, she said 'Excuse me, somebody's told me you're a lighthouse keeper, isn't it frightfully dangerous? I mean what do you do if it's rough weather out there and the lighthouse sets on fire?' I said 'Well the safety precautions are very good madam, there's a fire-exit on every floor.' She said 'Oh I'm glad to hear it, it's something I've often worried about; thank you, that's set my mind at rest now.' You meet some funny people, you know: things they ask you, things they say. They think there's something strange about lighthouse keepers, you must be a peculiar sort of person to be one. I suppose they could be right.

I'm a happy one: that's how I'd sum myself up, it's as simple as that. This is the life for me. Not exactly all that happy at the moment where I am now, but I will be when I get shifted from here. Back on rocks and towers again, back to proper lighthouses. A land light's definitely not a proper lighthouse, no. That wasn't what I joined the Service for, to be stuck on land lights. Somehow I seem to have had more than my full share of them so far. Anyway sit down, make yourself comfortable; let's have a natter and a fag, there's nothing else to do. That's one of the troubles with land lights, the time goes slow. Pass the sugar tin over, it's on the shelf there behind you.

– I'm thirty-three, I've been in the Service nearly five years so far. It took me a bloody long time to get round to it: far too long, when I think of all those years I wasted beforehand. I was one of those people who never knew what they wanted to do right from leaving school. I didn't even know what I wanted to do during all the time I was at school, never had an idea in my head. I didn't work at school, didn't try to; there was nothing I wanted, nothing that made me want to try. If you haven't got any object in view when you're a kid it's difficult for you to see any point in schooling.

My parents had separated when I was little; I was farmed out to live with my auntie and her husband, they'd got other children of their own. I suppose I was a bit of a problem to them; they never seemed to take much interest in me, at least that's how it looked from my point of view. It wasn't they were unkind, just didn't seem to have the interest to give me a push in any particular direction; even to ask me if there was a direction I'd like to go in, come to that.

I left school at fifteen without an 'O' level or even a single C.S.E. All I knew was that I wanted to earn my living for myself and stand on my own feet. There was another boy at school I was friendly with, he was going to get himself a job as cook on a ship. Cooking was something he was good at, apparently this job was there ready for him to start in, through a friend of his father's. He said there might be other jobs going on this ship, why didn't I go with him and see if I could sign on it too. It sounded a good idea so I went down to Southampton with him. We went to see the man who looked after the ship; he said he could use a strong lad as a deckhand, there was a job if I wanted it, so that's what I did.

I'd got the idea in my mind it was going to be some kind of cargo ship in the Merchant Navy, so the job'd lead to me getting a qualification, a seaman's ticket. Well it was nothing like that at all. It was a private motor yacht, belonged to an earl or duke or someone; my job was dogsbody and general helper. It was nothing to give me any qualification of any sort. My pal from school didn't do what he thought he was going to do either. He ended up in the galley washing-up: he never did cooking of anything more elaborate than potatoes.

It was a funny sort of set-up altogether, that ship. There was a crew of all different nationalities: Poles, Spaniards, Indians, Chinese, everything you could think of, about thirty or forty altogether and that was just the deck crew. The owner must have had a lot of money, he never seemed to work for his living; he spent his time going round the Mediterranean having different people on board as his guests. Big parties, fifteen or twenty guests at a time for as long as ten days or a fortnight: then we'd stop at some place like Malaga or Ancona or somewhere and they'd all get off and another lot'd come on.

I never found out what he did or who he was. Come to think of it I don't even know where he came from. All I know is he lived on his boat all the time. He had nothing to do with the crew; that was all done by managers and under-managers and people. It was a bit like a big country house, only floating.

The strangest thing about it was after we'd left Southampton for five or six years we never came back to England. All our time was spent in the Mediterranean. I didn't get much in the way of wages, only my keep. Sometimes when we were in a port I could go ashore for a couple of days; then I'd be given a few pounds in whatever the local currency was for pocket money. My school pal who signed on as a cook got fed up after a year, he went ashore one day and didn't come back; but I stayed on, it was an easy-going sort of life and I was quite content with it.

When we did come to England once we docked at Bristol; but that was only for a few days before we went back to the Mediterranean again for another five years. England didn't seem like home to me, it was just another port of call; I don't think I even went ashore. It seems hard to believe looking back on it I spent ten years of my life like that, never giving a thought to what sort of a future there was for me; which was none.

One day it suddenly came to an end: we were near Gibraltar at the time. The owner of the boat died, and the crew were paid off because it was being sold. We were given a few pounds to get to wherever we said was home. Different people in the crew went back to their different countries, and I said my home was England so that's where I came to.

My home wasn't really here at all though. I didn't know anyone and I hadn't kept in touch with my auntie and uncle. And I'd still got no more idea then what I wanted to do than I had ten years before when I left school. The only difference in the position was I'd wasted ten years of my life. I was twenty-five. It was more than time I tried to better myself.

All I'd got to earn a living with was my bare hands, good health, and the fact I was physically strong. I went labouring on building sites for a while, mostly round the Midlands. Then I got my one and only qualification for something: I learned to drive. There was a truck driver in one of the firms I worked for who taught me. About a year after that I got a job as a long distance lorry-driver for British Road Services. I didn't mind the life; it suited me working on my own and staying in different places on overnight stops. I didn't feel I wanted to be a lorry-driver for ever, but there was nothing else I could think of.

One night I stopped at a transport caff on my way up to Northumberland. There was a girl there helping behind the counter; she was very pretty and I really fell for her. So that was how I came to meet Sheila, and whenever I got the chance then I always went on that route. We were like each other in a lot of ways; about the same age, neither of us had proper parents or belonged anywhere. After about a year we decided to get married and set up together.

We lived in furnished rooms, and I went on with the long-distance driving and she went on working in the caff. I had a feeling there was some other kind of job I wanted to do if I could only come across it. But I'd no idea what. One night I got home, it was about eight months after we were married and I'd just come back from a long trip down to Exeter. While she was giving me my evening meal Sheila said 'Had you ever thought of being a lighthouse keeper?' She said it like that out of the blue, no leading up to it or anything.

I just burst out laughing. Anyone would wouldn't they if their wife suddenly came out with a question like that? I said no I'd never thought of it, whatever put that idea in her head? She said there'd been a driver in the caff the night before who she'd got talking to and he'd told her his son was in the lighthouse service. She said it sounded like a good job; they trained you for it and if you decided to stay on permanently you got a house given you as well, and a pension at the end. She said I'd have nothing to lose if I wrote up to Trinity House and found out some more.

I did it more as a joke than anything. But the information I got back from them, I don't know why but there was something about it that really intrigued me. Sheila egged me on to put in

the application form they sent, and then about a week later I got
a letter asking me to go and see them. When I went for the
interview they asked me what sort of qualifications I'd got; I said
all I could do was drive a truck which I didn't suppose would
be much use on a lighthouse. They said that didn't matter: they'd
give me a little written examination and so long as I passed it
they'd be prepared to give me a try.

Two or three days after that I got a letter saying they were
willing to take me on as a Superannurery Assistant Keeper, no
Supernuminary Assistant – well I never have found out what the
bloody word is, anyway as an SAK. I was delighted, so was
Sheila too. We were prepared for it to be a bit difficult during
the training, because it'd mean being away from home a lot. But
I was used to being away as a lorry-driver. We knew after I was
trained I'd have to be away from home two months at a time all
the year round as well, but we didn't mind that either. I could
see being a lighthouse keeper and having a permanent job was a
lot better than what I'd been doing all my life up till then. I
was going in late in age, which would put me at a disadvantage
compared with younger men when it came to promotion. But
there again I couldn't see myself getting much promotion as a
lorry-driver.

I went to Harwich for my training. It was mostly things to
do with different types of lights and how they work, and general
machinery maintenance. They also taught you practical things
like basic carpentry: how to repair furniture, rehang a door, do
glazing and painting and that sort of thing. And they showed
you how to cook too: nothing fancy, but how to bake bread for
instance. What they do is turn you into a good all-round handy-
man so that you can put your hand to anything that crops up.

After the month at Harwich came the start of the period of
being sent to different lighthouses. That was the part I'd been
looking forward to. I can't tell you how disappointed and really
bloody disgusted I was when I found myself on my first one. It
was a land light slap in the middle of the main bloody shopping

street of a town at the seaside. I was so angry when I got there I could hardly speak to the PK; the first thing I said to him was I hoped I wouldn't stay. I told him I wanted to go on a proper lighthouse, not work on a bloody street lamp.

I was there a few weeks and then he told me he'd had a message saying I'd got to report to another light. I was so pleased I hardly stopped to tell him good-bye; I rushed round packing my things up and I was off as quick as I could go. If I'd given him time he could have told me something that would have stopped me getting excited. But I didn't, so the result was I was even more furious than ever when I found the next one was another land light too. I nearly went potty.

And that's how it went on: a whole series of land lights one after the other, a few weeks here and another few weeks there, all round the country. I had no leave in between, I never got home for so much as a day; they shunt you round like a railway truck while you're an SAK. I kept writing to Sheila and ringing her up saying I was going to chuck the job in, I felt they were doing it deliberately to spite me. I wasn't really exaggerating much, I was absolutely bloody fed up to my back teeth.

They say everything comes to someone who waits, but it was a hell of a long wait for me. I think if it'd gone on much longer I'd have packed it in. Altogether I did over six months on land lights. But then eventually at last they sent me to a tower. Then I was happy, it was just like I thought it'd be. I had a bit of luck that first time too: I was only supposed to be there a month as relief for a keeper who was sick. But one of the other keepers went sick as well, so I was able to do a full two months. Then after that it was back to another land light again.

As it got towards the end of my year as an SAK I wrote to Trinity and asked them if they'd postpone appointing me to a permanent station till they could put me on a rock or a tower. I stayed SAK for nearly eighteen months before I was offered AK to a tower station, so it was worth waiting for.

That'd be three and a half years ago; up to last year I never looked back, I was very happy indeed. Then I got posted from there to here. Another bloody land light. I suppose I've got to face it that I'll have to stay another year or two before they'll move me again. I've written in twice since I came to say will they put me back on a rock or a tower as soon as there's a vacancy; so I might be lucky, you never know. I don't think Trinity are bloody-minded, it's just that they have a rota system of some sort. This is just the way it's happened in my case, but I wouldn't stay on if it means another land light after this.

– You ask some bloody hard questions but I'll try. Fundamentally I'm a loner; I always have been, I suppose that's what's at the bottom of it. When I was a child living with a family I wasn't really part of and all the time feeling I was different from them. And then at school, not being good at anything; not passing exams and not feeling I belonged in the school system.

Then all those years on the ship, that seemed to continue it somehow. Nowhere was home except the ship; that was home but it kept moving about from place to place. A continuation of the feeling of not really belonging anywhere; I think it must have carried on what I felt as a child. And coming back to England after that and still not having a home; being a long-distance lorry-driver, all the time on the move. My whole life had been one long not belonging anywhere.

I might have gone on for ever if Sheila hadn't asked me about the idea of being a lighthouse keeper. While I was waiting for the particulars to come I went in the local library to look at books about lighthouses. They'd only got one, I think it was called *The Modern Book of Lighthouses* or something. It wasn't all that modern, it must have been thirty or forty years old; the photographs in it were that brown colour old photographs used to be. But all the British lighthouses it showed were proper ones, towers sticking up out of the sea. It was looking at the pictures that really started to get me interested and feel excited. I felt it was like learning the secret of what it was I wanted to do. That was why I was so bloody angry when they kept sending me to land lights when I was SAK. I felt they were cheating me.

I'll always call those the proper lighthouses; and they're the only ones that appeal to me. It must be because they're on their own: they're loners and so am I, so we suit each other. I'm lucky I found a girl like Sheila, she's a lot like that herself. It doesn't mean we don't love each other or we don't get on; we both understand the other person. Because we're alike the separation side of it doesn't affect us like it might do other people.

My happiest time so far has been the two and a half years on the tower. I was never lonely. I enjoyed coming ashore every two months for leave, but by the time it came to go back again I was always looking forward to it. Other keepers say when they go back to a tower they need a day or two to settle in; but I didn't, the first second I was back it was like I'd never been away.

I used to do a lot of reading out there: I even began to give myself some sort of beginning of an education. Books about the stars, I used to spend a lot of time studying those and then going out on the gallery at night when it was clear, seeing which I could recognize and put names to. I got interested in ships too: they never came all that close to us, but I could see them going by in the distance. I got so I could tell at a glance what sort they were, I'd know if a ship was a fast cargo liner or a banana boat even if it was miles away.

It never made any difference to me whether it was winter or summer, I liked them both. And when you live out there, you can't help it that you get very fond of the sea. I got to feel really friendly towards it, like it was a personal friend. I still do even though I can't swim. I know I'll never die by drowning because the sea's a friend, it knows I like living on it. Out there if I ever fell in it'd throw me up again back on to the tower.

I never had a moment's unhappiness out there with the life, I wouldn't have known if you'd asked me what the feeling was. Only when I was ashore and the weather blew up so I was overdue for my return; that was what unhappiness was. I hated being stopped from getting back. Sheila'll tell you I was downright unbearable. There was a Christmas once that was the worst Christmas there's ever been.

Most people wouldn't understand it, I suppose. They'd think you'd have to be very unhappy with your home life to enjoy going away and leaving it. All I can say is it's not like that for me. It might be in a few years, because we've a baby girl now and when she gets older I might change my ideas. But I can only say how I am now, and how I'll be in the future I don't know.

My main thought at the moment's to get through my time here; I'm keeping my fingers crossed the next posting won't be too long and that it'll be back to a tower.

– It's coming up to midday; I'll go up on the gallery and then come down and enter the weather in the log; and then that'll be the end of my favourite watch. The morning one's my favourite, four o'clock to midday's best because you see the dawn. You extinguish the light at sunrise and every time it's my watch and I do it, it gives me a thrill. It's like you're in charge of starting the day; the light's done its job so you're letting the sun take over. It feels really good.

Sheila Longman

What's Important
is the Attitude 5

After the washing-up was done and he'd gone to bed, she sat
at the kitchen table smoking and drinking coffee out of a mug.
Thirty-two, soft-voiced, small and slender with long dark hair,
a pale complexion and large green eyes in a high-cheekboned face.

– Annette'll probably drop off to sleep, she usually does after
dinner; she's no trouble, she never has been. Connie says I
don't know what it's like to have a baby; she told me neither of
hers gave her a moment's peace when they were small. Perhaps
it's because Annette's a girl: a friend of mine's got a boy about
the same age, I had a letter from her the other day and she said
she'd hardly had a decent night's rest since he was born. Perhaps
the parents' temperaments have got something to do with it too:
Mike and I are both quiet sort of people, maybe Annette's going
to be the same.

In being a lighthouse keeper's wife what's important is the
attitude. I'd say it was the most important thing of all, the
attitude. You've got to be a self-contained person, someone who
isn't miserable as soon as they're on their own, not needing the
company of other people all the time. You've got to be able to
do things for yourself, look after yourself. I've always been like
that, so I don't have to make a lot of effort to change myself
into somebody different. I should think it's because my parents
both died by the time I was sixteen; I was the youngest of three

girls, the other two were married and had families of their own, so I had to learn to stand on my own feet.

I lived with one or other of them for a few months after mum died. I was a shorthand typist working in an office in London, then after a while I teamed up with another girl and we shared a flat. When she got married I shared the flat with another girl who worked there, and after that I went to work in Manchester as a typist in a hospital. Then I worked in a florist's shop and a dress shop, I went in a cosmetics factory for a bit, I was on the switchboard of an engineering firm, did some waitressing, more shorthand typing: I had a whole succession of jobs all in different places, I was a real rolling stone.

I had different boy-friends from time to time but none of them serious. By the time I was twenty-five I'd more or less made up my mind I was too old ever to get married, but I can't say it worried me. I liked not being tied down in one place with one person. It was quite a shock to me when I met Mike and started going steady with him. The main surprise was to find we were so alike in our outlook on life: up till then I'd thought men wanted wives who'd be completely dependent on them and not have any outside interests of their own. For instance one of my hobbies used to be fencing; wherever I was living the first thing I always did was join the local fencing club. I was good at it and I liked to have two nights a week at it. That never bothered Mike at all; if he asked me out and I said I was going fencing he'd ask me out for the next night instead.

After we got married he was just the same. Friends'd invite us somewhere and he'd say we couldn't come on a Tuesday night because it was my fencing night, we'd go another night instead. He was never jealous about it, he never ever suggested I should give it a miss. I do think that's how it should always be between husbands and wives. It very often isn't from what I can see. I don't think I could be married to someone who wasn't like that; and I don't think there are all that many husbands like him.

When we met he was a lorry-driver, I expect he's told you. I'd got myself a job at a transport caff which was owned by a girl I knew and her husband. It was a rather rough sort of place, I don't expect I'd have stayed long there if I hadn't met Mike. I only saw him once or twice a week because he used to go on long runs; but over a period of a year we got to know each other well enough to know we suited each other and got married.

At first we lived in furnished accommodation; I moved out of the transport caff even though I went on working there. Mike was away a lot because he was still driving, but I'd accepted that was how it would be when we decided to get married. The only thing that worried me was he was so restless in his job; it wasn't he didn't enjoy it so much as the fact that I thought he could do something he'd like better.

It was a pure fluke I heard about the lighthouse service from a man in the caff, but as soon as I did I thought it sounded just the sort of thing Mike'd like. It was different from an ordinary job and I knew that'd appeal to him. I knew the loneliness side of it wouldn't worry him; and I knew him being away from home wouldn't worry me. When I suggested it I could see the thought of it intrigued him straight away and I was delighted when he decided to apply. I had to laugh that they kept sending him to a whole series of land lights one after another while he was doing his training as SAK. He used to write to me or ring me up and when he did he was using the most dreadful language about what was happening. Normally he's very patient and quiet and hardly ever loses his temper; I could hardly believe he'd got it in him to get so worked up about something.

I kept telling him to hang on but I must admit there were times when I began to doubt if he would. There were times as well when I began to wonder whether I'd done the right thing in suggesting it to him. My idea of lighthouses had always been of places out in the seas too: it was that sort of romantic side of it I thought'd attract him. I felt if he was going to be away stuck on land lights all the time it would be just like him being a lorry-driver only worse. He was away much longer periods, he

never got even so much as a day off for months; and on top of
that the money was terrible, it was far less than he'd been earning
driving.

But after they sent him out to the one in the sea for the first
time things were much better then, he calmed down. He liked it
as much as we both thought he would. We knew it would only
be a matter of time before he was made AK and got on the
permanent staff, and we had the house that would be given us
then to look forward to as well.

One day it suddenly occurred to me he might get appointed
AK to a land light, and how awful it would be if he did. But the
thought had already crossed his mind too; he told me he'd written
up to say he didn't want to be an AK until they could give him
a tower. It meant he had to wait a bit longer than most people
for it to happen; but once he'd actually been and seen what it
was like he didn't mind.

He was delighted when he got it at last, I've never seen him
so excited, he was like a little boy. And I was relieved too, I
know there'd have been trouble if they promoted him and then
sent him on a land light. Anyway they didn't and we moved into
a nice cottage, one of the Trinity cottages for that particular
light in a nice seaside place.

The thing that struck me most was how nice the other keepers'
wives were when I moved in. They knew I was a new girl as far
as the lighthouse service went; but they were very helpful and
friendly all through the two months every time that Mike was
away. They were always asking me in for cups of coffee, or
popping in when they were going shopping to see if there was
anything I needed they could get. The PK's wife, Mrs PK as
she's always called, she was particularly nice; a lady called
Mrs Vincent, Margaret Vincent, you might come across her,
you'll like her if you do. It's the PK's wife most of all who makes
the difference in the atmosphere in the cottages. Margaret was
like a mother to us, and the other wives made me feel really
welcome too. Then when Mike came ashore for his leave they

dropped out of the picture while he was there; then as soon as he'd gone off again they made sure I wasn't left on my own.

I didn't mind it at all when he went away. Well I say I didn't mind, but obviously you do for the first day or two. You've got used to having him around, the house feels a bit empty when he's not there but you soon get over it. Mike and I have always been self-contained people, we can live together without each one wanting to know what the other one's thinking all the time and that sort of thing.

It's been a much better life for me altogether since he went into the service. While he was on the tower people said to me how did I stand it, they wouldn't like it, they couldn't live that sort of life having their husband going away all the time. That wasn't really anything to stand that I could see. I suppose it's a case of what suits some wouldn't suit others. I didn't even bother if the weather was bad and he was overdue coming ashore, I knew he'd come eventually. You just have to be patient; if you're going to let that sort of thing affect you then you shouldn't be a lighthouse keeper's wife.

What was ten times worse was when there was an overdue the other way round: when he was ashore due to go back on the light and the relief was delayed by the weather and he had to hang around waiting. He'd have all his things packed and then couldn't go; he hated those times. Mike likes to live according to a routine, he can't stand it if things don't go according to plan. He likes to know exactly where he is and what's going to happen. If I'm going to be out on a certain night or we make arrangements to go somewhere on a certain date he likes it to stay like that and not have any chopping and changing.

He said to tell you about a Christmas we had. That'd be two years ago last Christmas; it really was terrible, I'll never forget it. He was supposed to go back on the light about December 21st or 22nd, I know it was a Tuesday. Some friends of ours asked us to go over and see them for the day on the Monday and have a sort of early Christmas Day. They'd got a chicken and Christmas pudding, a couple of bottles of wine and crackers and things, they'd done it all really nicely and we had a marvellous time. When we came back Mike packed all his things for going off; and I'd bought him a frozen chicken to take with him and baked him a Christmas cake as well. I remember he'd got the paper hat out of his cracker from our friends and he stuck that in his bag too; he said he was going to wear it all day on Christmas Day on the lighthouse.

The other wives at the cottages were Valerie, and Alice whose husband was due to come ashore at Christmas; she'd got two children and they were running round like mad decorating their house for their daddy coming back. Mrs PK had said to me and Valerie whose husband was already off there for Christmas that she'd do Christmas Day for the three of us; we'd all spend it in her house and then go in and have a drink with Alice and her husband in the evening.

When we got up on the Tuesday morning, the morning of the relief, the weather had blown up very bad; it was obvious it wasn't going to be done that day. Next day Wednesday was just the same; and the Thursday which was Christmas Eve as well. Alice was getting more and more upset because her preparations were going to be spoilt; her children kept running in our house every few minutes asking Mike did he think the weather was improving, and Mike was getting more and more impatient and bad-tempered. I can laugh now talking about it but I didn't then: it was really dreadful. The wind still kept up and then the next day was Christmas Day morning. Mike got his paper hat out of his bag and tore it up and he chucked the frozen chicken in the sink and told me to throw it away because he wouldn't eat it. We'd already given each other our Christmas presents on the Monday so all that side of it was over; all he did was sat around in an armchair looking out of the window and swearing at the weather.

Alice came in, she was doing her best to keep her spirits up. Her kids were crying, Mrs PK was telling her to try not to mind, to come into her house for Christmas dinner with the children and Mike and me and the other girl. Then Alice suddenly started sobbing 'I want my husband', and her kids went right off, wailing 'We want Daddy, we want Daddy'. I lost my temper and shouted at Alice, 'I don't want my husband in the mood he's in, I can tell you that; you can have him'. Mike exploded and started cursing and saying 'It's not my bloody fault, I didn't want to be here for bloody Christmas'. And then to cap it all Valerie whose husband was out on the light and not due to come ashore burst out crying too, saying never mind me and Alice complaining, what about her; her husband was out there and she just had to put up with it, nobody was giving a thought to her feelings at all.

So there we all were on the morning of Christmas Day in the kitchen of our house. We were shouting and swearing and crying and rowing, it was absolute pandemonium. What anybody would have thought about life in the lighthouse service if they'd come in in the middle of it I can't imagine. Mrs PK disappeared out of the back door to go back to her own house; and two minutes later she came in our kitchen again and put two bottles of sherry down in the middle of the table with a thump. She said 'Right now, we'll all sit down and we're going to go on drinking both these until they're empty.' So we all sat drinking sherry out of mugs for an hour until we got good and tiddly, and then gradually we all started laughing about it because it was so ridiculous.

I think it was about another two days still after that before the weather calmed down sufficiently for Mike to go. I know I felt a complete idiot when friends kept ringing up to talk to me because they thought I'd be on my own, and having to tell them Mike was still there. They kept saying 'Oh how nice for you'; the first one or two asked to speak to Mike as well and said 'Aren't you lucky?' He could hardly contain himself. Finally he told me he wasn't going to speak to anyone in case he said something he shouldn't; after that I told anyone who rang up he'd gone out for a walk.

If it hadn't been for Margaret bringing the sherry in, I should think none of us in the cottages would have been talking to each other after that Christmas. That's what I meant when I said if was the PK's wife who makes the difference to how things are. It's a very closed community, a block of lighthouse cottages for a sea light; four women with one of them's husband at home and the other three away.

When Mike was home we didn't go out a lot; we used to spend most of our time reading or talking or watching the telly, or perhaps going out for a meal sometimes in the evening with friends. It was nice, and the thing we enjoyed most of course was having a home of our own. Another good thing about that sort of existence is when your husband's at home and you know he's only going to be there for four weeks before he goes off again, you don't seem to have arguments or disagreements. Rather than open your mouth to say something you think to yourself he's only there for a week or two so nothing's worth having a row about, nothing's all that important. In those circumstances whatever it is really isn't important; it gives you a sense of proportion, I think it keeps your marriage happier in a way.

To be frank about it, I do find living on a land light a bit of a strain: you're so much on top of each other all the time. When you're on an out of the way one like this and you can't often go out anywhere, somehow you seem to rub up against each other more. Now we've got Annette she gives us something else to think about; perhaps as she grows up she'll be a new interest for us. I hope we'll have another baby or two as well, I don't think only children are a good thing. But we're both a bit old to be starting on a family; and I think when Mike gets another sea light I'll find it restricts me more too and keeps me tied down. But I want a family so it'll work out I expect.

I hope it's not too long before we move on; and I certainly hope when the next move comes it'll mean Mike can go off again. But we can't rely on it, Trinity appoints keepers where they're needed to suit them, not how keepers themselves want. If the next one's a land light too, Mike couldn't refuse to go; he'd have to put up with it or else hand his resignation in. I'm sure he'd never do that because there's always the hope the one after that will be what he wants. But he won't be happy until he gets back on to what he calls proper lighthouses, I know that. And I know I'll like it better too when he does.

It might sound a peculiar thing to say but I dislike being the wife of a keeper on a land light almost as much as he does being one. I accepted that being married would involve him being away a lot, not in a sense of resigning myself to it but because I've always thought of myself as a person who could stand on her own feet. That's been my attitude all through life; I resent it if other people intrude on me too much. To me if someone has got that attitude then being married to a lighthouse keeper is ideal.

If you try to explain that you didn't mind your husband away a lot, I suppose some people jump to the conclusion you don't get on well. We do and we always have done; but we don't think we're odd not wanting to be together all the time every minute of every day and every week in every year, because that's how we are. When Mike does eventually get a posting to another sea light, I know some people'll be very sympathetic towards me and feel sorry for me. That'll really annoy me. We'll both welcome it: we'll feel much better able to settle down.

Assistant Keeper Tom Whittaker

The Years have gone   6

For several days little of Tom was to be seen. Stockily built and going bald, a brief glimpse of him now and again as he passed in the yard. But always with his head kept down, muttering an offhand 'Morning' or 'Dafternoon' before disappearing quickly into the lighthouse tower or the door of his house with a look on his face conveying he was busy. Once unavoidably meeting by the gate as he was bringing back his black and white mongrel dog from a walk, he gave a cursory nod and then turned away abruptly and went hurriedly off into the distance along the path by the edge of the cliff.

An elaborate wooden model of a Swiss chalet stood on top of the china display cabinet in the dining-room. In a corner an old grandfather clock ticked pedantically. From another room the distant rumble of wagon wheels, the rattle of gunfire and clatter of horses' hooves: a television Western, above it the shouting and laughter of children. He sat on a dining chair by the table with his tobacco tin, cigarette papers and ashtray beside him, constantly click-clicking his lighter to relight unsatisfactorily drawing cigarettes, cupping them in the fingers of one hand and abstractedly touching the folds of skin of his throat inside his open-necked shirt with the other. Harsh-voiced, from time to time he grimaced at what he was saying, apologetically and almost self-mockingly.

– I've been a bit rude towards you since you come, keeping out of your way and that. Nothing personal, just I haven't felt like talking to no one the last few days. Neither's the wife, all we've wanted to do is keep ourselves to ourselves until we got over it. I've had a shock you see, it shook me up a lot, Stella as well; something that'll take a bit of time for getting used to. I can't say I'm over it yet, but there's no point in going on hiding away. My worries are my worries, and nothing to do with others. Stella said it might do us good to talk to someone outside the service; so if you want to ask me about being a lighthouse keeper and things, fire away and I'll do my best.

I come in the service almost exactly fourteen years ago. Fourteen years ago next April the first to be exact: a very appropriate date for joining, it hadn't struck me till now. I was just a few months under thirty-two; I only got in at the last minute as far as age is concerned, if you're older than that they won't take you.

I never really intended joining the lighthouse service at all. I wasn't long married, I'd been working ten years in a firm that made radio sets and electrical equipment. Not on the technical side, I'd no knowledge of that sort; I was in the packing and despatch department. Then the firm sold out to one of the big companies or was taken over by them, I forget exactly which it was. Anyhow I was made redundant and out of a job.

I'd half a mind to go back to Manchester where I originally come from; I wasn't a skilled man, in East Anglia where we were living there wasn't a lot of work going. But Stella, that's the wife, she was a Norfolk girl, she'd lived in that part of the country all her life: she didn't fancy the north, and her family were round where we were. I'd had different jobs of all sorts before I met her; in a car factory, on a farm, bus conductor, working for a wholesale greengrocer, furniture removing, in a flour mill. It was near enough a case of you name it I'd done it. When the firm packed up we'd been married a year and we'd just got our first baby coming. When you lose your job at a time like that it's not a good thing, you get frightened, panicky almost. You get to the state you think you must take the first thing that's offered you, the main thing above all you've got to try and get is security.

We'd been to Clacton for our holidays earlier that year, or I'm not sure it mightn't have been the year before on our honeymoon. We went up the coast one day as far as Harwich, and we'd seen the Trinity House depot there; all the buoys and gear and stuff, we wondered what it was all about but thought no more of it at the time. Then this time I'm telling you of that I was out of work and thinking what I should do, Stella reminded me of the Harwich place; she said she wondered if it was worth me going there to see if they'd got any work.

When I went to see them I was thinking of work in the stores or something of that nature. They said no they hadn't any to offer. Coming out I got chatting with a chap in the yard, he told me Trinity House had its own labour force called the DLF, the Direct Labour Force. He said that was a very good job if you could get into it. So back I went into the office again, I asked them if they had any vacancies going for the DLF? The man inside said they hadn't, but he said like a kind of joke 'You seem keen on getting with Trinity; if you're all that keen why don't you put in for lighthouse keeper or on one of the light vessels?'

I said 'No thanks I'm not that daft.' I told Stella about it when I got home, she took it as a joke too. Another week or so went by, and I still hadn't found work. One day I said to her I thought it might be worth finding out some more about the subject because things were beginning to look pretty desperate then. I wrote up and asked them to send me particulars about working on the light vessels. It's always the same, things either don't turn up at all or they come together: the same day I got the reply back from Trinity I had another letter from an advert I'd written to, asking me to go for interview to a firm that made furniture you buy in pieces and assemble yourself; they wanted someone for their despatch department.

I'd only written enquiring about light vessels, but Trinity sent me information about the lighthouse service as well. Me and Stella both read it all through; it was the security side of it that appealed to us, that seemed to be the most attractive part. What I'd read about light vessels didn't appeal to me: I'm not a good sailor, I'm the sort who gets seasick in a rowing boat on a paddling pool, I didn't fancy the idea of bobbing up and down on the sea four weeks at a time. The lighthouse service sounded better: even though it meant being away from home a lot, there was the promise of a house and a pension and the knowledge that once you were in you were in. In our position we felt that'd certainly take a big weight of worry off our minds.

I filled in the application and sent it off, and I went to see the furniture firm at the same time. They offered me the job there and then, but I asked them could I have a few days to think about it. Trinity were very quick with their reply asking me to go for a test; which I did and passed it. So there I was then with the choice of two jobs, where two or three weeks before I couldn't see myself getting any. On the one hand the furniture-making firm was offering me a good salary but there was the danger something could happen in a year or two like with the radio factory; and on the other hand there was the offer of being a lighthouse keeper. The starting pay was very poor, in those days I think it was something only just over about three hundred pounds a year plus allowances; but you knew you'd have security.

We ummed and aahed about it, and finally on balance we decided for the lighthouse service. So there it was, I made the choice. I've often wondered what would have happened if I'd gone to the furniture company: in view of the fact I once nearly took a job with them I've kept my eyes open over the years for things about them in the papers. There's been quite a bit from time to time. They're about the biggest manufacturer of that sort of thing there is in the country now. I'll need say no more about that.

As SAK I went through all the usual business like everyone

else, getting sent here there and everywhere. It was hard going for a year or more, but harder for Stella than it was for me what with having the baby and everything. We'd so little money we ended up living in a caravan on a caravan site; but all the time we kept telling ourselves it'd be worth it in the end.

Our first disappointment was when I finished the training and was made up to AK. I was appointed to a rock station, but it wasn't one of the ones that had houses, so we had to go looking for a place ourselves. Trinity have got a pull with some of the local councils so we got a council flat. It wasn't what we'd hoped but at least it was a place of our own and we didn't have to pay no rent. Its main trouble was it wasn't anywhere near the light-house I'd been appointed to so there was a lot of travelling for me to do.

All the same it was a start of sorts. We had our second baby, and went on hoping I'd get moved to a better station where there'd be a house. I was somewhere about just over two years there before I got a transfer. This time it was to a tower light, and once again we was unlucky from the housing side. That one'd got no shore accommodation to it either, so it was more council accommodation for us again. That was nowhere near the light again either. By then we'd got our third child, Richard: the other two were girls, Debbie and Janice.

I did three years on the tower nearly. That was five and a half years altogether of being away from home. But always we were hoping one day I'd get a station with a house attached, and then perhaps eventually a land light to follow.

I can't say I liked my time on the rock; but I liked the tower even less. I'm not one of those sort of people that likes being separated from his wife and children. To me it was part of the job and it had to be done, but I could never wait to get ashore quick enough when my turn off was finished. One of the things about being a keeper is that whenever you get ashore for your leave, the first thing people you know say to you as soon as they see you is 'Hello – when are you going back?' It really used to get irritating, that did. I used to hate it when I was at home as it got towards the date for me going back.

I'm not romantic about the sea either, like some people. I never had any kind of liking for it whatsoever: to be on it made me sick, I don't think I ever did a single journey either out to the light or back from it in the relief boat when I wasn't sick, unless it was a real exceptionally calm day. As for being stuck out in the middle of the sea, I never looked on that as anything but uncomfortable and dangerous. It's as treacherous as a vicious dog, it's not safe to turn your back on it for a minute.

That's probably because I had a nasty experience once on the tower. I was down on the set-off, that's the sort of narrow concrete platform running round the outside below the entrance door, with another keeper one day; the Trinity House supply boat had just come to top us up with diesel oil supplies for the engines. It was an ordinary calm day, no wind or anything and we were thirty feet or more up above the water. Suddenly this tremendous wave came up out of nowhere and swamped us. We were hooked on to the safety harness so we were all right and all we got was soaking. But if we hadn't been hooked on that'd have been the end for us; it came up so unexpected like from behind the back of the tower, no one had time to shout us a warning.

I've seen men working on that set-off, it's usually the young ones; they'll take one look at the sea on a fine day and not bother to hook themselves on the harness like you're supposed to. I've even seen men sitting on the set-off fishing. If you say anything to them they laugh at you; they don't believe that a wave could come up like that. But once you've had it happen to you, it puts a different complexion on it after.

I didn't ever get used to that tower at all. It was a dark and dismal place inside of it, small windows, no daylight hardly, and because of the seas you had to have the door shut most of the time. It never got any fresh air in it, it was full of oil fumes and cooking smell all day long. I've often thought how the Trinity

House Elder Brethren and the Superintendents and people who come out for their annual inspection to the towers, what a false impression they get from a quick visit like they make on a calm summer's day. The whole place has been cleaned up for them coming, all the windows and door open to make it nice and fresh and get rid of the smells: they can't have any idea what it's like in winter when you haven't had so much as a window open for a week.

It does something to you, being cooped up eight weeks on there and no exercise; you were like a tired old woman when you come ashore, you couldn't hardly exert yourself for anything. The first day or two on land it hurt you to walk even half a mile on the flat; it was like someone had been kicking at the back of your knees, because all your leg muscles was used to was going up and down the stairs.

I never got used to the loneliness of it either. Sometimes when I was on middle watch in the middle of the night I used to switch on the radio transmitter and sit and listen to ships talking to one another, just so I could hear the sound of people's voices. A lot of them were foreigners, I couldn't understand a word of what they were saying; but at least it made me feel there were other people somewhere around and the world hadn't come to an end, which is a feeling you can easily get when you're stuck out there.

One thing that makes the biggest difference of all as far as rocks and towers is concerned, in fact I'd say it's the most important thing of the whole lot, is what sort of crew you're off with. On the whole people in the lighthouse service are very easy going and easy to get on with, you have to be a fairly placid sort of individual otherwise you'd never stick the life. But now and again you come up against some character or other who's got an absolute gift for making everyone else miserable. To my mind that sort of person shouldn't be in the Service: if he is then he shouldn't be on sea lights because he makes life unbearable for the other two who've got to put up with him.

That was the main reason I hated being on that tower so much, because of the PK who was there most of the time. There aren't many like him. He's notorious in the Service for being just about the worst one there is. Any SAKs we used to get out, he'd give them a dog's life; put them to polishing the brass and cleaning the lens, then when it was done he'd go up and have a look and come down again and tell them it wasn't good enough, and to go back and do it again. He did that just for the sake of doing it. I asked him about it one day and he said 'That's how I was treated when I was an SAK, it's the only way you can teach them who's in charge.'

A right so and so he was, even when he'd got AKs off with him and neither of them kids. After the first few turn-offs I got to know what he was like: for the sake of peace and quiet I fitted in with his ways and didn't do anything that'd provoke him. You can't live at close quarters with people and be perpetually having a row with them about stupid petty little things, so you try to avoid anything you know'll lead to aggravation.

There was a new AK came off once, the first afternoon he was there he sat down in the kitchen to have a cup of tea just like you or I would, or like you would anyway since you didn't know any different. There were three ordinary kitchen chairs there that were all the same; and this AK sat down in one. Two minutes later the PK come in for his cup of tea and said to him 'That's my chair you're sitting in. That one's AK Whittaker's, and that one's yours there.'

He drank his tea without saying another word, and then he went out again. This new AK looked at me and he said 'Where's he come from then, Trinity House museum?' You could understand how he felt, he'd been an AK about four or five years and he'd never come across a PK like that one before. He was a special case all right; if he could report you for leaving a pair of pliers lying around he would. The way he saw it, he was the boss and his word was law, and everyone had to be made aware of it. He even carried it on into everyday conversation when you were off on the light with him: it didn't matter what it was, politics, something you'd read in a book, any kind of discussion about anything. If you disagreed with him he'd start to go red and he'd say 'I'm in charge of this station, there's going to be no more arguing, we'll change the subject.' That was it then and you had to shut up.

I only ever got the better of him once. I can smile about it now: I smiled about it then, only not so he could see me, I had to pretend I was taking him seriously. It was once when I'd been on morning watch; I'd entered up the six o'clock weather in the log as O/M, which is overcast and misty. He got up about half past eight, and after his breakfast he looked in the log. Then he looked out of the window and he said 'That's fog, not mist.' I said 'Maybe it is, but at six o'clock when I did the weather it was overcast misty, so that's what I entered.' He said 'Well it was wrong: cross that out and put down F for fog.' I said I'm not going to cross it out, I was on watch, I did the weather and I entered what it was. If it's like it is now in another half hour when it's time to do it again, I'll put it down as F for fog.'

So he took his pen out, he crossed through what I'd written and he put in F instead and initialled it. He said to me 'An experienced AK you're supposed to be, and you can't even get the weather right.' If it hadn't been for his remark I think I'd have left it, but it really got my goat that did. So I said 'All right then, if you feel I don't know my job, then there's only one thing to do about it isn't there? Next time I'm on watch in the middle of the night and you're in your bed asleep, before I enter up the weather I'll come and get you up to look at it so you can make sure I've got it right.'

There wasn't really an answer for him to that. At least he had the sense to back down and say all right perhaps he'd been a bit hasty, he'd accept my word for the weather in the future. He still wasn't the sort of man who'd do it with a laugh though. It all had to be very serious even up to the point of him saying his apology. It's little niggles like that can make life difficult for everyone on a light. When you've got a crew not hitting it off it adds a lot to the strain of being there, makes the time seem longer. But I don't think it was just me being sensitive about him. You'll hear about that particular PK from other people; I think you'll find most of them think him hard going.

For all I know he's still there. But everything comes to an end, and my time on the tower did too; I was transferred after just almost exactly three years. Everything that happens to me seems to happen in twos: like when I'd lost my job and was out of work, then suddenly found myself with two jobs in prospect. This time I got transferred from the tower light to my first land station as AK: and we got our first Trinity house to go with it as well. That was seven years ago: the land light I was posted to was this one, and we've been here ever since. They've been the seven hapiest years of our life. Our two eldest children, Debbie's fourteen now, and Janice is coming up to thirteen next month. Our boy Richard is nine, all three of them are at school in the town and doing very well. We've saved a bit of money, managed to put enough by to buy ourselves a car, and that makes a big difference to living somewhere like here.

But as the years go by and you're in one place for such a long time, you can't help it, you start taking things for granted. Which is why this thing that's happened has come with such a shock like a bolt from the blue. It'd never crossed my mind it could happen. When it does it makes a man start thinking about what he's done in his life and whether he should have done something different with it.

It's too late now, the years have gone. But if I could have them back again I'd see to it I'd turned myself in a different direction that day fourteen years ago when I joined the Service. If I'd known then what I know now, I wouldn't have joined; I think it was a very bad mistake.

What's happened is that a few days ago I had a letter telling me I'm going to be transferred. It's hard for me to talk about it and keep control of my feelings; I've thought it must have been a dream, I couldn't believe it was true. But it is and I've got to face it. It's very hard though.

The time I've been here on this station is longer than both Mike and George's time put together. That's what I'd forgotten; I ought to have been keeping it in my mind and taking it into account. You hear of shifts and postings and all the rest of it, and usually you have a fair idea when your time for a move is coming up. Four years ago, even three years ago, I'd have been mentally prepared for it; normally after you've done three or four years in one place you can expect to be moved because that's about the average length of time for anyone to stay somewhere. But as time went on and nothing happened to me I reckoned they must have decided to leave me where I was. Fourteen years in the service, twelve and a half of them as AK; I've been taking it for granted they'd leave me here now till it came due to offer me promotion up to PK.

I know that always carries with it going back on rocks again for a few years. You have to start at the bottom again as far as stations are concerned, go back like George did; then if you're lucky, a few more years after that you get a land light. I wasn't sure what I was going to do when my turn came, since we'd been so happy so long here. Our first proper home, the kids settled in at their school, not wanting to disturb them; I wasn't all that sure I ever wanted to go up to PK.

That's the way my mind had been working, turning towards thinking of things like that. When they tell me now they're transferring me from here and putting me on a rock again, still as an AK not as a PK, well I'm in a turmoil about it. It's another rock station without a house too, which means back to council accommodation again. Stella and the kids will have to start living in a strange town, the children will all have to go to new schools. That's going to be bad for them all, but specially Debbie since she's got her O levels coming up next year. All the breaking up of everything we spent all those years waiting for: it's a hard thing to happen to someone, a very hard thing.

For a man of my age, I'm over a year older than George is, I'm forty-eight; it's a lot to ask someone to face at this time in his life, to uproot himself and his home and his family and their whole way of living.

To put him back on a rock that's a station with no house to go with it, and not to offer him any promotion for it either; I don't think no one wouldn't feel they were being hard done by. I think they could well have left me here after all this length of time till my turn for promotion came up. They could have sent someone else if they wanted a man for a rock. What's wrong with them sending Mike for instance? From all he's said to me at different times he can't wait to get back on one. He doesn't know yet I'm going to be moved; but I'll bet any money when he does he'll put in a letter right away asking why he can't have the vacancy. When they get it they'll have two letters then; they've already got one straight back from me saying I don't want to go.

It won't make no difference though, I've heard of this kind of thing happening before; it's not common, but it's not all that unusual either. No one's ever yet got them to alter things around to suit keepers. As far as Trinity are concerned transfers are to suit their own decisions: they make them, and once they're made it's for the keepers to obey them like they were sheep, not start complaining or asking them to reconsider. That's one of the problems after you've been in for a long time; you stop thinking, you let Trinity take care of you and you let them do all your thinking for you as well. Then when you suddenly come up against the consequences like this, you find you can't think for yourself any more. To be realistic there's nothing I could do now except send in a letter resigning from the service all together. That wouldn't be a very good prospect for someone at my time of life; putting himself in a position where he'd have no job and nowhere for his family to live.

We were having tea yesterday, young Richard said his teacher'd been asking them all at school what they were going to do when they grow up. He said he told her he was going to be a lighthouse keeper like his dad. I couldn't help it, I wasn't thinking, it just slipped out; I said 'The sooner you get that bloody daft idea out of your head the better.'

Stella was shocked, she told me last night it was the first time she'd ever heard me swear in front of the children. I don't think I ever have before, never.

Stella Whittaker

That Bloody Bloody Sea

A small woman of forty with short dark hair and a round face and circular pink framed glasses, in a fawn jumper and a brown tweed skirt. In the late evening when her husband was sleeping and the children had gone to bed, she moved a toy dumper truck and an empty liquorice allsorts box off the deep armchair and sank comfortably back into its cushions. Relaxed, she lit a cigarette and sipped at a glass of sherry, and stretched her legs out in front of her, thoughtfully frowning and gently tapping together the toes of her slippered feet. The litter of magazines and newspapers and Monopoly accessories scattered over the carpet caught her eye: she smiled, unconcerned.

– Always the same awful clutter every night after they've been watching the telly. What my mother would say if she could see it I can't think, she was always on at me for being untidy when I was a girl. Maybe that's what made me determined not to be like that when I'd children of my own. When Tom and I used to talk about what we'd do when we got our own house at last, sometimes I wondered if it'd affect me that way when we did; you know, make me very particular and house proud. I needn't have worried on that score; look at it. But I think a home should be a place to live in, somewhere you can do what you like, not try and make it a kind of show piece all the time.

It's not bad this sherry is it even if it is Cyprus, shall I fill our glasses up again before we start?

It's difficult to know exactly what to say to you really. We're upset, naturally; but there you are, these things happen, they're part of the job. Nobody likes having to move, particularly from somewhere they've been such a long time. I think Tom's every right to feel sore they're putting him back on a rock but not offering him promotion to PK. I know it depends on length of service not on age; but starting like he did when he was thirty-two means there are some PKs who are nearly ten years younger than he is. I think they could have been a bit kinder to him after fourteen years. They should have either left him where he is until he was promoted or made an exception and put him up to PK: he's had enough experience as an AK by now. Still there it is, that's the system and we've known it all along. When he does get offered PK in three or four years that'll mean still more rock time ahead of him after that; it's going to be very hard for all of us.

But there's nothing else for it, I mustn't be bitter about it. We've got to try and put a brave face on it when we tell the children. They're going to be upset, it won't be any help to them if they see we're taking it as though it was the end of the world. Just at the moment I have to admit it feels like it. I keep telling myself and telling myself it isn't. I've got to pull myself together, both for Tom's sake and the children's. It's difficult though.

I've tried all along to bring them up to accept that with their daddy in this job they'd always be likely to be living in different places every few years, and sometimes he'd have to keep going away from home. I think Debbie and Janice are old enough to remember what it was like when he was on a rock before. Debbie was six or seven then, Janice a year younger, so possibly they'll remember and not find it too strange. The one who'll have the worst time of it is Richard: he was only two when we came here, I'm sure he won't have any recollection at all of his daddy going away.

All I can do is tell them it won't go on for long, in another few years we'll be back together again. Whether it's true or not I don't know. But I've got to make myself believe it; and them, and Tom. That's the only thing, to try and think about the bright side and keep looking at that; otherwise we'd all start getting very sorry for ourselves indeed. We'll have the problem of finding a house to rent again, probably a council one. I can't help thinking a better idea for us now might be to try and buy one somewhere, perhaps in East Anglia where my family are. If you do that, Trinity'll lend you the money for the deposit at a low rate of interest, and you put your rent allowance towards paying the mortgage.

If we did, at least it'd mean we had a permanent place; there'd be no more of the children possibly having to change their schools yet again after this. It'd give us the opportunity to settle once and for all in a place and make some new friends. We've talked once or twice about the idea in the past, about that's what we might do if we had to move. In a few days maybe Tom'll feel like bringing it up and considering it. He's always told me there are big disadvantages to it: I'm not sure I understand what they are properly though.

One thing I'm certain will be good from the children's point of view, whether we buy our own house or whether we don't, is that wherever we do go to live it won't be as out of the way as this, so that'll give them more chance to make friends with other children. It's always been difficult for them to do that here: if they ever wanted to have anyone home for tea or to play it was always such a palaver to arrange it. Other children had to be brought all the way out here by their parents and then collected again, or Tom had to take them back in the car. So up to now they've not had much chance to get to know many other children, seeing them only during the day at school. All the travelling too: at least they're not going to have that long journey back and forth every day to school. Wherever we go to live it's bound to be much nearer a town.

I think if you look at things you can always find some advantages to set against the disadvantages. It'll be nice too that when Tom's ashore he's home on leave and his time'll be his own, not like it is here. On a land light even when a keeper's not on watch he's always standing by on call for the rest of the day except for his four weeks' holiday a year when he can go away and they bring in an SAK. With the watch rota system like it is, you can hardly ever go out even for an evening. Your husband's either on duty at eight o'clock or midnight, or else he's been up the previous night till four in the morning and doesn't feel like doing much else except going to bed. So we've all that to look forward to: a lot more time on leave for him, and being able to do what we like with ourselves then.

I shouldn't complain though, the one it's going to fall far the hardest on is Tom. He's the one who's got to go and do the job. He hates rocks and being away from home. I know he'll make the best of it: I expect after he's got back into the routine of life out there he'll start on his hobby again that he used to do when he was there before. He did a lot of wood carving and model making; he made that lovely big model of the Swiss chalet we've got in the dining-room, didn't he show it you? It must have been ten or eleven years ago he did that and brought it ashore for me one day. He never even told me he'd been making it. He's very very clever with his hands; very patient, it took him months and months to do. I do hope he'll take it up again, it must be so boring out there. It might help him a bit to stand the loneliness of it. I feel bad about it, guilty in a way. After all, if it hadn't been me wanting security so much he might not have joined the service and he wouldn't be in this position now.

I shall be lonely again too but at least I've got the children with me all the time. Now they're getting older the girls are real companions for me; it'll be nothing like as bad on my side as it was before. For myself I'll just have to try and get back into the routine of him being away. I've done it once, there's no reason I shouldn't be able to do it again. I'll miss living here, the friends

I've made, particularly Connie; but nothing could be as bad as the time before when he was away and the children were young. I survived that so I expect I'll survive this too.

The routine I had to get accustomed to was the same all keepers' wives have to: being eight weeks or more on my own, living without him and taking all the decisions about the family; then having him home four weeks when he was head of the household, then eight weeks without him again, and going on living like that.

Even though I did it for seven years, I never got used to saying good-bye to him at the end of his leave. The last few days before he was due to go back I had to help him start packing his things, I used to really hate that. It wasn't made any easier by having to try and keep cheerful because he was so miserable about it himself. It can get a bit difficult sometimes; you don't want to let someone see you're so wretched inside you're nearly sick with it. But on the other hand you can't overdo pretending you're cheerful or else he starts to think you don't care: it has to be a very fine balance indeed.

One thing I was determined about was I would never let him see me cry. Leaving a weeping woman behind you isn't going to do anything but make it ten times harder for you to go. I always used to manage to keep control of myself till after he'd gone. Then I'd be crying for the rest of the day and night. After that I'd put a ring round the date he was due back on the calendar and start looking forward to it. Count the Sundays, that was the way I used to measure it. Only seven more Sundays before he's back, only six more, five more, four more; like that. Then in the last week I'd let myself start counting the actual number of days.

Overdues were something I'm afraid I was very bad about indeed. Not overdues at the end of his leave of course; I was always delighted if the weather was too bad and he couldn't go back. I knew it meant another keeper was overdue coming ashore and his wife couldn't have him. But it's no use pretending I wasn't pleased Tom was still with me because I was. When he was overdue out on the light trying to get ashore himself though, that used to drive me round the bend. It went on for days and days sometimes: once it was two and a half weeks, I got in a real state about it.

That's something I must remember now this time; wherever we go to live, it's not got to be anywhere near the sea. The last house we lived in was only a few hundred yards away from it: from the beach on a clear day you could see the lighthouse on the horizon. It was only just about as big as a matchstick, but you could see it. Every time, a few days before his relief was due I couldn't help it, I used to go down on the sands for a walk to look at the sea and listen to the wind. The lighthouse was a very difficult one to get on or off if the weather was rough, and it always had far more than its share of overdues.

I really hated the sea then. I suppose it can't have been as bad as my memory of it or happened as often as it seemed to; but my recollection is of I don't know how many times going down on the beach to look at the water, and actually seeing it begin ruffling itself up while I was watching it and feeling the wind start to blow on my cheek. I'd go back home until the next day, then I'd go and look again. Sure enough it'd be getting worse; and worse again the day after that. When it came to relief day, I'd be standing there on the sand knowing there wasn't going to be a cat in hell's chance of him getting off. I used to feel the sea was doing it deliberately, and I'd curse it and swear at it out loud because I knew there was absolutely damn all I could do to make it go down. It was so indifferent and arrogant, so powerful, so much stronger than me; it decided for itself it wasn't going to let him come ashore, and I got this feeling it was doing it to show me how insignificant and unimportant I was.

In the weeks between the reliefs I never went on the beach; even if the weather was nice. I couldn't stand the sight of the sea. But with the house being so near the shore you couldn't get away from the sound of it: you were always conscious of the noise of it in the background, then every so often it'd start building up and crashing its waves on the shore just to let you know it was always there.

About a mile inland there were some hills and a lovely green valley where I used to go to for walks whenever I could. There were wild daffodils and trees there and birds singing in them; song birds, not those damn awful seagulls that do nothing but squawk all the time. There was a stream too, and when the weather was nice you could sit down and play with the children or read a book. It was the only place I knew where you could go and get away from the sound of that bloody bloody sea.

I don't care where we live now, but I don't want to be anywhere near it that's certain; the further inland I can get the better. The next few years that sea's going to be controlling our lives for us again. I'm not going anywhere where I have to listen to it reminding me of the fact every day.

Tom won't be able to avoid it though, he'll have no choice. He'll have to think back like I'll have to, to the seven happy years we've had here. They say being on a land light's a test of a marriage, particularly when it's an isolated one because you're thrown on each other's company such a lot. It is, and all I can say is I'd sooner it could go on being put to the test. But it isn't going to and there it is. What we must do now is be thankful for the time we've had here, and keep reminding ourselves how much luckier we've been than such a lot of other people. That's the only way to get through.

The Rock Light

Assistant Keeper Paul Bailey

Winds make Weather 8

Nine miles outside a small seaside town, alone on a cliff side and sheltered by its curve, a terrace of four smart white painted cottages faced towards the sea. Out in the water a mile and a half offshore, the rock was a massive granite boulder, bare and barren with precipitous jagged sides a hundred feet high. Seven hundred feet long and three hundred broad, its top flattened into a small plateau about the size of a football pitch, with the lighthouse tower in the middle and the keepers' quarters and engine rooms built round it in a low-roofed square.

They were barely discernible in the late afternoon against the lowering storm grey sky. The wind was roaring in from the south-west unremittingly; Force 8 as it had been for three nights and two days it was hurling the waves frenziedly at the rock with a violence that sent clouds of spray rocketing a hundred and fifty feet in the air and pluming over the buildings, almost completely obliterating them from sight under an enveloping white shroud.

Rock stations have a complement of four keepers he'd said; three of them'll be off on the lighthouse, and the other one will be having his month's leave ashore.

Thirty, small and slightly built, fair-haired and clean-shaven with pale blue eyes, he stood looking out at the rock from the sitting room window. The room had two colourful modern abstract prints on the walls, and three photographs of lighthouses; well-designed comfortable modern armchairs, a white carpet, a big stereo record player, shelves crammed with books and records, and two ships in bottles in a display section on their own. He was quietly-spoken, relaxed in manner.

– I'm afraid there's no hope for you getting there yet, the relief won't be done tomorrow; nor the next day nor the one after that by the look of it. The landing steps are round the other side, with a thirty-foot gully between them and a rock we call 'The Ramp'. With the wind in this direction the sea'll be thundering through there between them like a bloody express train. The relief keeper you'll be going out with, Alf, he came up this morning to see what the chances were: he took one look at it and turned round and went straight off back down into town again.

So you may as well sit back and put your feet up with us for a couple of days at least. There's nothing to be done about it except wait as patiently as you can. It's part of everyday life to us, waiting for weather to change so you can get off out there and start your tour of duty, or if you're already there come ashore for your leave. Frustrating and irritating if you let it be; since you can't do anything about it though you might as well put up with it.

It's always been part of the enjoyment to me; it's the weather playing its little game, teasing. As relief day gets nearer you get up each morning and wonder what the chances are going to be, you listen to the wind in the night, wondering if it's starting to change direction and if it is whether it's for better or worse. I've always found a kind of excitement in it; the thought the wind's deliberately having you on, letting you know it's deciding if it'll let you go or not. It never seems malicious; I think of it being a kind of schoolboy practical joker playing pranks. A poem I read once, I'm not sure who it's by, that sums it up for me. Auden I think it is, I like a lot of his things.

> Winds make weather; weather
> Is what nasty people are
> Nasty about, and the nice
> Show a common joy in observing.

– I'd better fill you in on the situation here in the cottages
first I suppose; everything's a bit at sixes and sevens just now.
My month's shore leave ends tomorrow: but I'm not going back
to the rock again, I've been posted to a land light. Early next
week probably my wife Janet and I and our two children'll be
moving on from here to the new station. At the moment there's
an SAK out there for a month: he'll be coming ashore when Alf
goes off on the relief tomorrow or whenever it is.

Next door in cottage Number Three is Susie Archer. Her
husband Bob's off on the rock: when the relief's done, then he'll
be halfway through his two month tour of duty. Margaret
Vincent's in the cottage next to that, which is Number Two.
She's Stan's wife, he's the PK. He's off on the rock as well, and
he's also coming to the end of his first month. When they come
ashore next month another SAK will go out with the new AK
who's being appointed, and they'll make up the three there with
Alf. As the senior, Alf'll be Acting PK then, which he won't like.

The furthest cottage up at the end of the row, cottage Number
One, that isn't occupied. A couple of blokes from the DLF
come up to it every day, they're doing it out ready for the new
AK. The DLF will move in here then and redecorate this; I
suppose when it's done they'll put in another AK to take Alf's
place, and move him to somewhere else.

Alf doesn't live here, he doesn't have one of these cottages
because he's a bachelor. I'm not sure where his home is, I think
it's Leeds; he travels back and forth from there all the time. He
has to be here by the date the relief's due, but if it's delayed he
stays in digs down in the town. He could stop with us or Margaret
if he wanted to, but he'd sooner spend the waiting time on his
own. You won't see much of Alf until he gets word the relief's

definitely going to be done; then he'll turn up at the last minute down there at the harbour in a taxi with all his gear and boxes of food supplies.

As you'll have gathered he's a bit of an elusive character: he keeps himself to himself. I told him you were going to be around from today, so he'll not come back up here again. Don't hold it against him, it's not that he's standoffish or unfriendly. Let's say he's got his own ways, and leave it at that. You're going off to the rock with him; you'll have plenty of time to get to know him after you've got there, but he'll not want to meet you before. He's a nice bloke when you do get to know him; completely different off there to what he's like when he's ashore.

I've put in your order for your food supplies at the shop; they've got it all packed up in boxes ready for you, except for the meat and fresh vegetables. They don't put those in until they know for certain the relief is on; then they'll deliver it all to the harbour for you in their van.

The relief's done by a local boatman, Jacko. He gets up at seven o'clock in the morning tomorrow to have a look at the sea and decide whether he's going to do it or not. If he says you're going, you go: if he says it can't be done, you don't. It's as simple as that. So from now on you just wait; you're in the hands of the weather and Jacko. But it'll not be tomorrow anyway; that's certain.

You can talk to me tonight and Janet in the morning; we won't be here by the time you come ashore again. It'll be difficult for you to make any definite plans because you'll be hanging about waiting for the weather to go down. There might be a sudden improvement, the relief will be on and you'll have to go at only an hour or two's notice. Margaret and Susie'll still be here when you come back of course, but if you're still here waiting for the next day or two you might as well see them before you go. Anyway that's up to you.

My God, six o'clock: time I was putting the kids to bed, I give them their bath while Janet makes the supper. Put a record on if you feel like a bit of music: Mozart, Schumann, Beethoven, Bob Dylan, The Beatles, The Seekers. Take your pick, help yourself. After we've had our meal we'll settle down and have our chat, all right?

– Now I'm going to be transferred to a land light I'm going to miss not going off on that rock for eight weeks once every three months. I've had four years of doing it, I've got into a routine; I suppose you could say I was institutionalized. It's not really sunk in yet that I shan't be going back there any more. In a kind of way I feel a little resentful that my life pattern's going to be changed. I was on a land light for nearly three years before we came here: it wasn't a success, I asked for a transfer because rock life suits me better, and Janet too.

Every keeper on a rock moans about having to go back at the end of his month's shore leave. But the moment he gets there, he stops moaning and settles in to get on with it. In fact if we're going to be honest about it, most of us give a sigh of relief. It's 'Good-bye world' for a couple of months: no one can get at you out there, you're in a kind of retreat. Whatever we like to say or pretend to ourselves and other people, it is. When you come ashore it's for a month's leave; but just as true a way of looking at it would be that when you go off you're taking two month's leave from the world. I think you have to be in that frame of mind: if you were worrying all the time about what was going on back ashore you'd never be able to stick it. But once you have, I think anyone who makes out it's a strain isn't admitting the whole story.

Like you mentioned that keeper you met told you; it's true it's a different world out there. Sometimes you start wondering which is the real one, the one on the lighthouse or the one ashore. I said Alf was a different man out there; he is and so are the rest of us too, me included. To give you only a superficial example, if I was talking out there with you now instead of here in my own sitting-room, I wouldn't be talking like this. As soon as I get off on the rock my way of talking changes; I can't put two words together without a swear word in between. It might have something to do with being in all male company, it might be because everybody else does the same: it's a habit you slip into automatically, a kind of separate language, almost a foreign one, or perhaps the way I talk ashore is the foreign one and how we talk out there is more genuine.

Now I'm going to be ashore all the time I shall have to lose the habit and get back into the acceptable convention. Janet'll be glad, she says sometimes to hear me talk no one'd ever think I'd been educated, never mind at a public school.

That was in London where I was born and brought up. I've eight O levels and three A levels. O level English literature, Language, French, German, Geography, History, Maths and Physics; A level English, Geography and History. I was the only child of elderly parents; my father died when I was sixteen, my mother when I was nineteen. I was about to go to university when she died, I'd been offered a place at Birmingham. What exactly I was going to do when I got there I really don't know; take a degree and become a teacher I suppose. I wasn't enthusiastic about the prospect; like a lot of young people I'd no specific ambition to do anything. I was going to continue in the educational system because I couldn't think of anything else.

My parents weren't rich, my father had been an invalid most of his later years, so I hadn't much money. I could have gone on with my education and lived on grants if I'd wanted to, but the whole education thing had been much more their idea than mine. After they died I saw no point in going on with it since I'd only been doing it largely to please them. The money they left amounted all together to about three hundred pounds; I decided I'd go travelling with it and see how far I could get. Not in luxury, hitch-hiking; picking up work wherever I could find it, then moving on. The intention all the time was to keep as much of my money intact as I could.

I spent a pound or two on the fare for the ferry across the Channel. From then on I was lucky, I earned sufficient doing odd jobs to live on for about three months as I moved on across Europe. I can't remember how many different jobs I did or even half of them; working in kitchens of hotels, acting as an attendant and interpreter on camp sites, a driver's mate on lorries, working on ski-lifts, portering in fruit markets, I did everything.

I went through France, Switzerland, northern Italy; then I worked as a deckhand on a boat which went to Greece, and from there I got a job as a steward on another boat which went to Turkey. I had a stroke of luck then; I met up with one of those overland safari expeditions on its way to India. It was a group of English university students who were in a spot because one of their drivers had been taken ill and couldn't go on: they hadn't enough people with driving experience among them so they asked me if I'd join up with them as an extra driver.

That suited me fine: they didn't pay me anything, but they didn't charge me anything either. I got free food as well as free transport, right across Iran and Afghanistan and down as far as Bombay. I got very struck on a girl who was one of the students in the party; she was Janet, and by the time we reached India we decided we wanted to separate from the rest who were going to head back to England, and go travelling further on our own.

We used up some of our capital on our passage on a cargo ship to Singapore, then stopped there for a while to build up our finances. Janet worked as a chambermaid and a waitress and finally as a hotel receptionist, and I did some teaching in a posh private primary school that was run by an American company for the children of its executives. It only took us a couple of months to get together more than enough to take us on to where we were aiming for, which was New Zealand. When we got there, after having a look at Wellington and seeing a few other places in North Island we went on down to Christchurch in South Island.

Then we went up into the Southern Alps and had a wonderful time at a skiing resort for about six months. Janet had a well paid job as a receptionist in one of the tourist hotels, and I worked on the slopes as a so-called instructor for novices who wanted to learn to ski. As soon as they got proficient enough to stand upright, I passed them on to someone else who at least had got some idea of what he was talking about.

We'd got married by then, and we were very happy. For all I know we'd probably still have been there if Janet hadn't had a cable one day to say her mother was dying and asking her to come home. We had just exactly enough money to pay the boat fare home. It's a long journey, six or seven weeks; and by the time we got to Southampton it was too late, Janet's mother had been dead for a fortnight. Janet was an only child like me; and like my parents hers weren't wealthy either. So there we were back in England with about a hundred pounds between us; and by then Janet had started a baby.

What I was going to do for a job, I'd no idea. I suppose I could have got some sort of teaching work or work in an office, but after the sort of life I'd been leading for the previous three years I didn't fancy anything at all of the nine to five sort. It was obvious with a baby coming we wouldn't be able to go wandering round the globe again; but the whole idea of settling down into a routine occupation had no attraction whatsoever.

Even the thought of it made me shudder; and I know Janet certainly didn't want me to either. We're both rather independent sorts of characters: she knew she couldn't work for a while herself until she'd had the baby, but she'd no intention of living a conventional middle-class existence just because we were going to have a family.

We decided the only thing to do would be to sit down and take stock. Think about what I could do, what I had done, what I wanted to do; and then start looking round. What I could do and had qualifications for was something of the routine kind which neither of us wanted to get stuck in. What I had done was what I was happiest at: bumming around, going where I wanted, working when I felt like it, and not working but just enjoying life whenever I'd enough money to do it. I knew something else about myself too: I was happiest when I was doing things. They had to be of a fairly straightforward simple practical kind because I hadn't got it in me to be a skilled craftsman.

I went to the local reference library in north London where we were living, and I sat down at a table with a book called *Encyclopaedia of Careers* or something like that. I remember turning through the pages and shuddering more and more at each thing I read about; advertising, auctioneering, engineering, estate agencing, insurance. They all seemed to be concerned with nothing but making money. Or else there was only teaching of one kind or another, or things that required a lot of further study involving living for years on a grant. There was nothing about enjoying yourself or being happy; everything was about what's called 'getting on'.

I read the entry headed 'Lighthouse Service' without thinking, and then I went on. Mathematics, Milk Industry, Office Management . . . I got that far and then I thought 'Lighthouse Service', that's a funny sort of occupation. I turned back and read it through again. It sounded ridiculous so I put it out of my head and ploughed on through the rest of the book.

But on the way back home on the bus I kept returning to the idea, then telling myself it was crazy and thinking about something else; and then finding it kept coming back into my head again. When I got back to the furnished flat where we were living I remember Janet was doing the ironing. I went into the kitchen where she was and I said 'Do you think you'd like being married to a lighthouse keeper?' I suppose nine women out of ten would have said 'What's the matter, can't you put up with living with me any more?' But Janet didn't, she went on ironing and I could see she was thinking. Then she said 'Why don't you send for particulars? When we get them let's weigh-up what the advantages and disadvantages are.'

When the details came I read them through without saying anything and then I gave them to her. After she'd read them she said 'It sounds to me as though the first year's the one that matters, by the end of that you should have a good idea.' She was right, that's the whole idea of it of course.

I sent in the application and went for a medical: all it amounted to was to see if I'd got two arms, two legs and two eyes. Then a simple examination paper to make sure I could actually read and write and that was all there was to it.

I did my probationary year as a supernumerary; then we had another long talk about it, considering the advantages and disadvantages from my point of view and from hers. It had been rather hectic, getting pushed around land lights and rocks and towers one after another so quickly half the time I couldn't have told anyone where I was. But the opportunities I had for experiencing the different aspects of it left me in no doubt I liked it.

Janet had a tough time that first twelve months, on her own for most of it and with the baby being born as well. If she'd said she didn't want me to stay in the job, I wouldn't have done. But she said it hadn't been half as bad as she'd expected and she'd survived. From then on when I was made up to AK we'd have a house; and although she didn't like me being away much, she said if she knew she could look forward to me being home one month out of every three, she thought she could stand it.

That was nearly ten years ago now. We had another child; and I suppose as time goes by you get older and without you being conscious of it your ideas change. You start taking things for granted and settle down. I've been on a few towers but I never liked them, nor land lights; I've been on a couple of other rocks besides this one but neither of them were as good. I wouldn't have minded stopping here; after four years you get attached to a place. But going to a land light now, I don't really mind.

I've enjoyed nearly all of it and I think Janet would say she'd enjoyed some of it. She's looking forward to us being together all the time now. I can't say I'm going to stop in the service for ever, because I'm not certain I will. If somebody offered me an interesting job, I'd think very hard about it. At thirty with a wife and two children I couldn't pretend I'm not in a bit of a rut; but it's a comfortable rut, not one I'm in any hurry to get out of.

I may be kidding myself saying I might take it into my head to change my job one day. There are a lot of men in the service, you look at them and you know they're stuck in it for the rest of their lives. Even if they wanted to get out there's no other job they could do, they'd be out of work and starving. But I'm not in that position, if I put my mind to it I could make a change. At the moment I've no desire to, that's the long and the short of it. As jobs go it must be one of the cushiest anyone could find.

Life on a rock's pretty easy, especially one the size of that one out there. Each keeper has a room to himself, there's a kitchen, sitting room with television, a bathroom, a flush toilet; the light's worked with an automatic control panel, as long as it's on at sunset and off at sunrise that's about all you have to do apart from keeping the place clean and tidy.

I often wondered out there what I was being paid for. For being there, that's all I suppose. The light's a navigation mark primarily and secondly to warn ships to keep clear. They do, so the result's you hardly ever see any except far away on the horizon. It's like the man walking down Oxford Street tearing up bits of paper and throwing them in the air. A policeman stopped him and said 'What do you think you're doing?' The man said 'I'm keeping the elephants away.' The copper said 'There aren't any elephants in Oxford Street'; and the man said 'Yes, it's bloody effective isn't it?'

There's no hard work, so apart from taking his turns on watch a man doesn't have much to occupy himself with for the rest of his time. There are only two kinds of lighthouse keepers; one kind can go for eight weeks and do damn all except eat and sleep and sit in a chair, and the other kind who do something more.

Perhaps one's not better than the other, it merely depends on the individual. I do a lot of reading myself; I usually take out more books than I do food, weight for weight. Non-fiction chiefly, historical biographies, travel, sociology, psychology, politics, books on sea birds, the weather, oceanography, biology, anything.

When I didn't feel like reading and wanted to do something with my hands, I made ships in bottles. Those are a couple on the shelf there. It's a fantastically painstaking time-consuming occupation; but you get hooked on it once you've learned. Stan the PK taught me: it took me nearly a year but he was as patient about teaching as you have to be in actually doing it. It's an old craft among keepers; in the days when their pay was much lower some of them used it to make an extra income for themselves. If Stan put his up for sale in a shop they'd fetch fifteen or twenty pounds each, but he won't sell them, he only makes them as a hobby.

Any time he wanted to Stan could get himself a job as an arts and crafts instructor. He's started teaching young Bob how to do it now; and anybody who takes on the job of teaching Bob anything needs the patience of Job.

More than anything else it's people like Stan and other characters you meet that makes this job so interesting. You're living with them night and day for eight weeks or more at a stretch and you certainly get to know them under those circumstances in a way that'd not be possible in any other sort of job. You notice such minute details about people, you learn all sorts of things about them.

For instance having been out there at close quarters with Stan for so long, just by looking at him I usually knew exactly what he was thinking about. Margaret on her own ashore here, or if he's worrying about the station's stores list and whether it matches up with the actual stores themselves. I know his views about politics and religion, what sort of books he likes, his favourite programmes on the television. But I know all sorts of trivial other things too; like how many times he stirs his tea after he's put the sugar in, which days of the week he changes his socks, how long it takes him to shave and everything else. I don't doubt he knows as many things about me of the same sort. You can't hide anything of yourself.

If it's taught me one thing I never got from schooling it's how to make friendships; and with the sort of people that when I was a schoolboy I looked down my nose at as being uneducated and not worth knowing. There've been a few I haven't got on with; but on the whole I like lighthouse people and I'm glad I'm one of them.

It doesn't look like the wind's dropping. I'm always conscious of it, I think I always shall be. It's played such a big part in my life. It gets into you; I don't think I could ever live somewhere now where I couldn't hear it and everything was always quiet and still.

Janet Bailey

The Game that
suits You Best

9

Auburn-haired and hazel-eyed, precise and controlled in her
movements and gestures and her words; small and neat in a
bottle-green dress with white collar and cuffs she perched on a
kitchen stool with her elbows on her knees and her chin cupped
in her hands. Sometimes grave and sometimes animated, and
always self-possessed and calm.

– Paul's taken Judith and Anna down into town on the bus
this morning. Heaven knows what time they'll be back, I don't
need to bother hurrying to get lunch ready. He always fills them
up with sweets and ice-creams when he takes them out, so they
won't be hungry when they do get back. The way he spoils
them, it's ridiculous; his excuse up to now's always been he
doesn't see much of them. He'll have to change his ways now
he's going to be ashore all the time; but I don't suppose he will,
he's just like a kid himself when he's with them.
He was saying he seemed to have spent most of last night
talking to you about the weather; on a rock station you naturally
tend to get obsessed with it. It'll be strange not having to think
about it at all now for a year or two. I couldn't ever look at it
in quite the same light hearted way as he does, I've damned and
cursed it many a time when he was stuck out there and overdue
coming ashore. There's no point in swearing, you can't do anything about it, but it makes you feel a bit better yourself to let
off a bit of steam.

If the children are around I try not to complain too much for their sakes. I had to laugh once, he'd only been ashore a day and he trapped his finger in a drawer and came out with a very choice swear word. I was just going to say something to him about using language like that in front of the children when Judith said 'That's what you said yesterday isn't it, Mummy, when you looked out of the window and saw it was rough?'

Ten years married to a lighthouse keeper, if anyone'd told me when I was nineteen or twenty I wouldn't have believed it could be possible. I was as much a rolling stone when I was that age as Paul was, that was what brought us together. We've been lucky, we've both changed in the same way gradually over the same period of time; obviously you've got to adapt to the way of life or it won't work for either of you. I've a friend, Mary, it didn't turn out like that for her and her husband, they ended up divorced; but there's no way of telling beforehand, you can only try it and see.

Far and away the worst time was the first year while he was an SAK. If you're a woman and you can survive that, then I reckon afterwards you can survive anything. I hardly ever saw him more than about three days at once; sometimes it seemed no sooner had he set foot inside the door than the phone was ringing to tell him he'd got to go somewhere else straight away. I'd got a baby, I was doing typing work at home to earn a bit of extra money, it was hard going; but by the time he'd finished his probationary year and I could see how much he enjoyed the life, we both thought it'd be a terrible waste of effort if we gave up then. The worst was over, it could only get better and so we decided to go on with it. We're both used to it now.

Most of his time has been spent on rocks and towers, apart from a couple of years or so on a land light before we came here. That wasn't successful, neither of us liked it; we were glad when we came here, it's been a good station for him, and for me and the children to live at too, it's been one of the happiest times of our lives.

If I can't go roving round the world any more, which I can't, then this is as near to an ideal life as I think I'll ever get. I'm like Paul, I enjoy reading and listening to records, I don't greatly mind being on my own while he's away. Now we've got Judith and Anna, they're two marvellous children even if they are a bit of a pain in the neck sometimes, so I'm never really alone. The rock being so near to the shore where it is, I think that's good for the children too. They can see exactly where their daddy is; they know he's there not too far away, and I think that helps. In the summer when they have friends up here to play the first thing they always do is point it out to them very proudly and tell them their daddy's out there looking after that lighthouse.

We have games about it too; in the winter when they go to bed at night we flash their bedroom light off and on, we pretend we're signalling to Daddy. When the lighthouse light flashes back, you know how imaginative children are, they're convinced Paul's signalling back to them.

The worst time always is Christmas; Paul hasn't had a Christmas at home since we've been here, because of the way the rota's worked out. A couple of Christmasses he went off by about the middle of December which wasn't too bad; we knew he wasn't going to be with us, so the children had time to get accustomed to the idea. But the Christmas before last, he was due to go off about a week before Christmas Day but then the weather turned. The days went by, and by the time it'd got to the day before Christmas Eve it was beginning to look as though he was going to still be here. The children got very excited, they hid his presents in different parts of the house and started planning surprises for him; they even made up a little pantomime of their own they were going to perform for him. Then suddenly the weather went down again, and he had to go off on Christmas Eve morning.

They were very upset about it, naturally. I must admit I was too, particularly after they'd gone to bed and I went up to their room to hang their pillow cases up. It really hit me very hard, I was as miserable as hell all through Christmas Day. I couldn't show it, because I had to remember the children were even more disappointed than I was, so I had to try and keep cheerful for them.

Stan and Margaret, that's the PK and his wife, they were marvellous. He'd come ashore Christmas Eve on the relief that Paul'd gone off on; on the afternoon of Christmas Day he appeared through the front door wearing an old red dressing-gown and a red rain hood of Margaret's; he'd stuck a beard of cottonwool all over his face, and he had a sack on his back with crackers and sweets and a Christmas cake. The children didn't know who he was, they thought Father Christmas himself was paying them a special visit. They knew there wasn't a Father Christmas really, but they still didn't know it was Stan for a good half hour. They were talking about it for weeks afterwards.

It's the most important thing about any station, the other people who are on it with you, especially if it's like this one, a good way out from the nearest town and your only neighbours are the other wives. Margaret's wonderful; when Paul's away she's not making a nuisance of herself coming in and out all day long, but you know she's there to have a chat with if you're feeling fed up or miserable. Until last year the other keeper's wife was a girl called Liz who I liked very much; she and Margaret and I all got on very well indeed. She had two young children about the same age as Judith and Anna, they got on well with each other too so all in all it was a very happy situation.

She and her husband were moved to another light six months ago, and Bob and Susie came in their place. Somehow Susie and I don't hit it off, we're very different from each other. This makes things awkward, it completely alters the atmosphere as it's bound to. If you all get on well that's fine; but when you don't you get an atmosphere building up which is uncomfortable. I think Susie feels a bit of an outsider: she's bound to because Margaret and I have been here a lot longer than she has and know each other well. Margaret's better with her than I am; I'm afraid I tend to get very short with Susie sometimes, especially when she works herself up into a state as soon as there's so much as a day's overdue on the relief. We don't get many here, but when we do she comes bursting in crying and throwing fits about it, saying she wants her Bobbie and all the rest of it. Margaret's kind and sympathetic with her, but I just get sarcastic and rude.

I suppose it proves the point people in the service often make that you shouldn't have only friends from among other lighthouse people. That's all very well but it's difficult to avoid getting into that position. When you're out here as far away from the town as we are, a forty-five minute bus ride away and only three or four buses a day, you're bound to be a bit isolated. And the other people's lives outside the service are regulated by a different pattern to yours. You have two months on your own when you're at a loose end, then every third month your husband's home and you want to spend nearly all of it with him and the children, and don't want to see much of other people. So it's not easy to make friendships with outsiders.

If Liz had still been here, or I'd been able to get on better with Susie, I'd have been more unhappy about the prospect of moving than I am. If we'd been talking six months ago, I'd have said this was the happiest period of my life and I never wanted to move. If Trinity had told Paul they were going to move him to a land light then, we'd have done everything we could to try and get them to change their minds and let us stay. I think we might have succeeded. Most keepers want to get land lights; it's rare for someone to say he wants to go on a rock or stay on one, so I think our chances would have been good. When we did hear we were going to a land light we seriously thought of asking them if we could have another rock instead; but then we decided we wouldn't, we'd take the land light and have another try.

What I mean is that the previous time we were on a land light was very nearly disastrous. Everyone says it's a big test of a marriage: it was for us and we came close to failing it. The simple fact of the matter was that being together all the time we both got utterly bored and fed up and we weren't hitting it off at all. It got very near to the point when Paul would either have had to leave the service and get some kind of different job, or we'd have had to separate. We've always had a close understanding of each other, so we were able to sit down and talk it over sensibly and recognize the problem. We decided for the sake of the children we ought to do everything we could to try and make the marriage work; and maybe it'd help the situation if Paul went back on a rock again. He wrote to Trinity asking them if he could be moved, and it happened to coincide with there being a vacancy here. So we were lucky and within a couple of months we got the transfer.

I can't say why it was, it's very difficult to put a finger on it. We didn't get on all that well with the other two families for a start; and the land light was very isolated which didn't help. It must have been something in us, of course; I suppose it didn't have any excitement or adventurousness, that's about as near as I can get to describing why we felt bored and dissatisfied with life and with each other.

– To come here was the right thing for us, there was no doubt about that. As soon as we arrived everything changed to being like it used to be between us. Perhaps we're the sort of people who have to keep on parting and coming back to each other again to keep up our interest in each other. It reminds us of how much we like each other and miss each other when we're apart; each time he comes ashore it's like having a series of honeymoons. We court each other, we flirt with each other, we're blissfully happy, we never have a single quarrel or row.

It doesn't mean we approach it in the spirit of making the best of a bad job because we don't. We love each other and I miss him very much when he's off; as soon as he's gone I start ticking off the days until he's due back ashore. There's no question of putting him out of my mind or looking round for somebody else, I only want him. I write to him every day while he's gone: I can't send a letter out every day because you have to wait until a boat's going out with stores or extra supplies. So sometimes they get to be twenty or thirty pages long before he gets them, because I write two or three pages every night before I go to bed. There's plenty to tell him in them: about what the children have been doing or what one of them's said, a new book I've just read or something like that. And when it gets near the time for him coming ashore I get as excited at the prospect of seeing him again as I used to before we got married.

It seems I have to live a way of life in which I've always got something to look forward to; it's part of my basic personality. When I was a student at university I studied biochemistry, I remember the excitement of discovering things for myself in experiments rather than merely reading about them in books. It hasn't changed in me much, that feeling of wanting to find out more about living things and the excitement in doing it.

When he's away I get lonely and miserable some days like anyone else; but the moments of unhappiness pass, it's those days that make the time when he's ashore more enjoyable because of the contrast. It can be hellish when he's not here. Maybe that's got something to do with it; I seem to be a sort of person who can't be happy unless she has periods of suffering in between.

Have you read a book of Eric Berne's called *Games People Play*? I can't help thinking living's like a selection of different games, and you have a choice as to which one you're going to play. You try and choose the one that suits you best, that suits your personality and gives you the most enjoyment. So there's no doubt about it for me: being the wife of a lighthouse keeper who goes away gives me enjoyment and pleasure, and I wouldn't change it for anything.

I realize with a bit of a sinking feeling that it's going to change now. When we heard we were going back to a land light we both had our doubts, and we shall go on having them when we get there. It's not as isolated as the previous one so we can only hope we don't find ourselves in the same position as before. If we do we'll have to reconsider things. At the moment I'm being determinedly optimistic and telling Paul I'm looking forward to it; I may find perhaps this time it's different.

Maurice Oliver & Ray Flint

Two Men in Overalls

10

Although the wind had moderated a little the sky was still grey and surly, and the sea went on in a bad temper splattering the waves against the rock, giving it an unbroken white ruffled collar of foam. Above it a flock of gulls plunged and rose, whirling and scattering about in the distance like scraps of paper in the wind.

On the ground floor of the unoccupied end cottage the floorboards were up, bags of cement obstructed the doorways, planks were propped against the walls, and bare wire-ends protruded from holes in the ceiling. In one of the back rooms two men in overalls were sitting at a table thick with grit and dust, drinking tea out of tin mugs and smoking roll-ups. Ray Flint was young, tall and gangling and thin, with long hair down to his shoulders and nervy in manner. Plump and short with a full-moon face and large hands and short thick fingers, Maurice Oliver was about forty and loud-voiced and jocular.

– Mrs PK told us you were around, we were wondering if you'd think us worth a visit. No offence, but there's some doesn't pay much attention to the Direct Labour Force since we don't have white caps and collars and ties and posh uniforms and all that. Sit yourself down for a while, if you can find anywhere to sit. I've got some cementing to finish in the front, Ray'll talk to you while I'm doing it, I'll come back and see you later on.

Ray
– I've not been in the job long, I don't know there'll be much I can say. I'm twenty-three, married nearly three years, my wife and I've got a twelve-month baby and we live in a flat in Bristol. I've been with the DLF just under two years, I'm an electrician by trade.

We go round from station to station wherever Trinity puts us to work; sometimes land lights, sometimes rock lights, sometimes towers. We do repairs and maintenance on lighthouses and modernizations and alterations in the cottages. Sometimes Maurice and I are together or with two or three others, other times we're on our own, depending what the job is. It's a very good job to be in, because Trinity gives you security. You've no fears of ever being made redundant or your employers going out of business, which is more than a lot of people can say.

I came into it through one of my uncles; he's in the DLF himself, he told me a vacancy was going and to put in for it, and I think he put a word in for me himself. I'll stay in for the next few years. I wouldn't like to stop in it for good, I hope to set up on my own one day. While we've got the baby and not much money behind us, it's an opportunity to get a bit of capital together because it's well paid.

The thing I like most about it as well as the security is the variety of the different places you find yourself working in, and the independence. You have to use your own initiative; you think about the work and decide the best way of tackling it, then you go ahead and do it as you think best. On a sea lighthouse you can't ring up a foreman or a supervisor to ask him about something; and he can't come out every day to see if you're doing it right. You have to make your own mind up, in a way it's almost like working for yourself.

The other thing that's interesting is the places you go. For the next few weeks I'll be here in this house; after this I might be out on a tower in the middle of the sea, then I might be on an island for a while. If I was doing an ordinary electrician's job on land, one place is much the same as another, you wouldn't be getting this change of different scenery all the time.

The security, good pay, being left to work on your own, going round different places: those are the good things about it. I try and keep those in mind all the time, set them off against the things I don't like that are the definite disadvantages.

The biggest one is that you can never plan your life properly; it's not like an ordinary working man's week with fixed hours. When you leave home you usually reckon for a start you're going to be away for three to four weeks. But then when you get to the job you find it's going to take twice as long as you thought; or there's some vital spare part you discover you need halfway through so you've got to wait until it's sent out to you. In the end the job might go into six or seven weeks; and with the possibility as well that if you're on a rock or a tower the weather might turn bad and stop you getting ashore. It's not good having to tell your wife you'll be home in roughly three or four weeks but that's only as near as you can tell: it might be and it means you can't ever plan anything. There's always the tendency too if you're delayed for work to pile up while you're away. You get home, you're looking forward to a few days' rest, and you find instructions waiting that you've got to go off somewhere else.

Keepers know what their duty periods are, two months off and a month ashore. We don't have set working periods like that, we're on call all the year round except for holidays. Even then it can happen you're held up on a job and there's nothing you can do about it but cancel your holiday. With there being so few of us on the strength, less than fifty I think it is, there's always something waiting for attention. Our busiest working time is the summer, because the weather makes it easier for us to get on and off places then: this is another disadvantage, it means you always have to arrange your holidays out of season. It isn't too bad at the moment while the baby's young but it might get difficult later when he starts going to school.

Another thing that messes up your family and social life is because lighthouses are working all the year round so are you. Times like Easter and Christmas aren't holidays as far as you're concerned. If there's an urgent fault needs attending to somewhere, you have to go no matter what week of the year it is. I've already been caught once on a rock over Christmas; the weather came up bad as soon as I got there and stopped me getting ashore till the beginning of January. If I thought that was going to happen as a regular thing I wouldn't be prepared to put up with it long.

I don't find life easy on some of the rocks and towers. Maurice is always telling me lighthouse keepers are easy going sort of people and friendly; so far either I've been unlucky in the places I've been sent to or else I'm not the right type for the work. It might be because I'm young, but I've been on several places where I was made to feel I wasn't wanted. It can get miserable when it's like that and you've got to stay and put up with it.

Quite a lot of lighthouse keepers are very unfriendly except with each other: they put on superior airs and look down their noses at you because you're not one of them. They've got nothing to be superior about that I can see; I'm a skilled man and they're not, perhaps that's what they resent. They look on us as hired labourers coming in from outside and say we've got no official standing. If we had uniforms of our own or even Trinity badges on our overalls perhaps that'd make a difference. We don't work for anyone else but Trinity so there'd be nothing wrong with that, and it'd remind them we all belong to the same concern.

In the DLF we get a better daily subsistence allowance than keepers, that's another thing they resent. But they get theirs spread over a longer period of time, the whole of their fifty-six-day duty period; so when you come to average it out they get as much as we do in total, so I don't see why they feel strongly about it. But you can't be on a lighthouse more than two or three days before one of them'll bring it up and start moaning at you.

I have the most trouble either with the elderly PKs or with the junior AKs. It's either the men who are old and rigid, or the ones who haven't been in long and are wanting to throw their weight around. There's one particular light, something always seems to be going wrong there, I've been sent out to it four or five times now. The PK there's a miserable old devil, I loathe going. He doesn't maintain his equipment properly because he doesn't know how to: it's his own fault an electrician has to go out so often, yet he always tries to blame me and say I didn't do it right when I was there before.

Every time I arrive he starts by telling me to get the work done as quickly as possible and then get back ashore off his station and not hang around. I haven't gone there to hang around; it's no joy to me to be there with him; but he gives me the impression he thinks if he's not breathing down my neck I'll put my feet up and treat it as a holiday. He doesn't know the first thing about electrical work himself, but he behaves as though he was my foreman. He's watching me every minute to see if I'm working, and telling me I'm doing everything wrong.

I think he must be a bit mental: I can't think of any other explanation for the way he behaves. He insists you fold the dishcloth up and hang it on a bit of string over the sink: the salt's got to be put back exactly in the same spot on the same shelf every time, everything has got to be just so. If I do something he doesn't like he'll never tell me straight to my face. He writes out a notice on a piece of paper and sticks it up with a drawing-pin. 'Will the electrician not make a noise when keepers are asleep', 'This window is not to be opened without permission', 'No smoking in the bedroom' and stupid things like that. Another one he put up on the kitchen door once was 'Not more than three men in this room at any one time'. There were the three keepers and me, it was obvious what he meant; and I didn't think much of the other two for joining in with him either. He never talked to you, he sat in his chair in the corner as though he'd been there for a hundred years and said nothing.

Another light I was on, the keepers wouldn't cook for me while I was there. I was quite prepared to take my turn and be cook for the four of us together; but they weren't going to have that. I was told as soon as I got there I'd have to cook my own food separately every day. By the time they'd all had their dinner and washed-up and had a smoke and a chat and cup of tea, it was always half past three or four o'clock in the afternoon before I could start making my own meal.

Maurice says they're not all like that, it's only one or two stations. I've been on some that are different, so he might be right. Some keepers know you're there to do a job, and you're not used to being away from home; that sort will go a bit out of their way to make you feel welcome. They'll bake a loaf of bread for you if you're running short, perhaps even make you a cake; if you find you haven't taken enough food they'll help you out by giving you some of theirs. At the other extreme there was a keeper when I was low on food who gave me a tin of sausages and said I could buy it off him. When I asked him how much I owed him he said 50p: and he took it off me too.

I suppose anyone has to have a certain sort of mentality to be a keeper. They're an unsociable sort. I'd never want to be one. They're all right with each other; but they don't like outsiders and they keep it up when they're ashore. The one who's waiting to go off now, Alf: I saw him last night in a pub in the town; but he wouldn't have a drink when I asked him, he said he couldn't stop.

It might be because I've got long hair that they judge me by appearances and don't approve. Trinity's very traditional, they probably all jump to the conclusion I'm a junkie or something. They're all a very conventional lot. I think they're basically lacking in something, otherwise they couldn't put up with the life; the loneliness, the unreality, the abnormality of it all. No normal person would choose it: if he did, he couldn't stick it for long and stay normal, he's bound to get odd.

Maurice

– I've been with the DLF fifteen years; I'm a stonemason but I can turn my hand to carpentry and plumbing as well if required. I've a wife and three teenage children, two of them we adopted when they were babies. I'm basically a family man so it's the security more than anything else which appeals to me. For a skilled man it's a very good job indeed if he can get himself into the DLF; he's got security then for the rest of his life. I'm not much of a one for change, I never have been; this is only the second job I've had in my life.

I hope young Ray settles to it: it's a fine opportunity so long as he's content to earn a decent wage and not bother about making a fortune. Whether he will or not I don't know; at the present he's finding some of it a bit hard, particularly the being away from home so much. It's like a keeper's job in that respect, a lot depends on the sort of wife you have. It's the wives mostly the burden falls on; if they find they can't put up with it, it's usually because of them that their husbands leave.

I think Ray's thinking some of the keepers are hard to get on with sometimes as well, judging from what he's said to me from time to time. He's been unfortunate in being sent to some of the stickiest stations so early in his experience. That mayn't turn out to be a bad thing because as he goes round others he'll get a more balanced view. I've had the odd spot of bother now and again myself in my time; but I think once you know what it is you're going into, you're prepared for it and you can cope with it better after.

There'll always be the PK here and there who'll follow you around with a dustpan and brush all the time because he thinks you're making the place untidy. You have to try and look at it from the point of view that when you go to a lighthouse, you're going to somebody's home. They haven't invited you: they've been told you're coming and they've got to put up with you. So it's up to you to be careful about the way you behave, and try and see it along the lines of how you'd feel if someone uninvited came into your home. It's the trivial things that cause the trouble; like making sure you empty an ashtray after you've used it or put a chair back in the same place you found it. Things like that annoy a PK if he's got a sort of housewife mentality.

I know nearly all of the keepers in the service these days, having been in it myself so many years. But even now when I go on a station, the first thing I do is sit down and have a chat with the PK. I tell him what I've come to do and how long I think it's going to take. I always tell him a bit longer than I know it will be; that way it pleases him when it's finished sooner than I said. It stops the situation arriving where he's getting impatient because you're there after you said you'd be gone.

When I've explained that, then I ask him how I can best fit my working time in with his routine so as to cause the least disturbance. Our working hours are daytime hours, not like theirs. You've got to remember at any time of the day more likely than not there'll be someone asleep. So if you've got any banging or hammering to do, you plan when's the best time to do it, like when they're all up together round about midday for their dinner. You've got to warn people beforehand if noise is unavoidable; then you save yourself a lot of trouble and the possibility of bad feeling.

Another good thing is to ask the keeper's advice about the best way of doing something. You've probably made your mind up how you're going to do it; but if you ask their opinion more often than not they'll leave it to you because you know best. You've got to be tactful: if you go there adopting a like it or lump it attitude they can make your life much more difficult for you than you can make theirs for them.

One thing that can cause a lot of trouble is food. You never know how long a job's going to take; I've always found it best to take more food that I'm going to need. If I think I'm going to be on a light for three weeks, I grub-up for six. That makes sure I don't run short and have to beg off the keepers, and then when I go ashore I leave what I haven't used behind for them. We get a good daily subsistence allowance: but there's some DLF who try to make themselves an extra week's wage out of their subsistence by cutting down on food they take off with them. The keepers know this; you can understand they're not sympathetic to a man who hasn't brought enough with him to allow for delay and starts to cadge off them.

My job's different to Ray's; his is all inside work, while mine tends to be mostly outside; repointing the stonework of a tower, concreting a landing stage, cutting out new steps, things of that sort. It can involve working up to my waist in water sometimes, clipped on with a safety line. I don't like that much, it's not pleasant in winter and I'm not a great admirer of the sea. There's too much of it from my point of view. It only takes six gallons of water to knock a man over, so it's not the easiest of places to work in.

I'm not a man who tends to disregard it or take it lightly, the sea. Some of the DLF, if they're anxious to get off from a place because they want to get home they'll send a message ashore to say it's fit for a boat to come out when it isn't. When the boatman gets there he may be dubious about trying to get them off and won't come in close: then they start calling him names and swearing at him. To me the boatman's the expert who knows his job; if he says it's not safe then it's not safe. I can't see why anyone should expect him to risk his life even if they're stupid enough to risk theirs for the sake of getting ashore a day sooner. If it means missing a day I'd sooner miss it and stay alive.

That's one of the reasons I prefer to go on jobs on my own. Sometimes it's too big for one man and there has to be several of you. If I'm there on my own then I'm the only one who can upset people: if anything goes wrong it's my fault. That way I don't get involved in trouble started by other DLF people. We talk of keepers as though they were all of one kind, and similarly a lot of keepers look on the DLF as though they were all the same; so if one causes trouble somewhere, we all get blamed for it.

I've met all sorts of keepers, you get a tremendous variety among them. There's not many now I could say I hadn't learned to get on with. Considering the life they have to lead it's remarkable how many make lighthouses places you enjoy working in and look forward to going back to.

I don't know if you've met a PK called Steve Collins, 'Big Steve' they call him. I always like going out on his tower. You spend most of the time laughing with Steve, the things he gets up to. He's got a cassette tape-recorder like the one you're using now; one time I was off there and a new young SAK came out. Steve got me and one of the AKs to do a bit of recording before this chap arrived; then he put the recorder in a cupboard under the stairs. When this SAK came out he'd been there a few hours and we were sitting round having a cup of tea and Steve pressed a switch that started the tape-recorder.

The voice came out from the cupboard as clear as a bell, 'Help! Help! Let me out!' We all kept our faces straight and ignored it. A couple of minutes later and this voice started shouting again. Steve shouted back at the cupboard 'Shut up, keep quiet!' and went on drinking his tea. This SAK was completely taken in by it, he fidgeted about and then he said 'Who's that, who is it?' Steve scowled at him absolutely dead serious; he said 'It's the SAK you've been sent to replace, he gave me a lot of trouble so I only let him out at mealtimes.' I think he could have kept it up longer if the AK and me had been able to stop ourselves bursting out laughing at this lad's face. He really believed it, he was looking at Steve in genuine horror.

He's a bit mad is Steve, you have to be if you're a keeper. Another time, this is some years back, we were sitting down to our dinner and he was up at the top of the tower on the gallery doing something or other. The man who was cook shouted to him the food was ready. The next thing we knew Steve appeared outside the kitchen window, waving to us to let him in. He'd come down the outside of the tower from the top on a rope. A real lunatic he is.

It's meeting people like him and other keepers of different types that keeps the job perpetully interesting for me. Some of them I've known over fifteen years right from when they first joined the service; you can see how they change. In most cases it's for the better; but there are a few, as the years go by you wouldn't believe they were the same people as when you first knew them.

There's one I know lives on the lighthouse so much in his mind he can't get away from it. One day he came ashore for his leave and caught the train to go to the town where he lived. He met a friend on the train and they went in the buffet and started drinking. Then he had to change trains somewhere; and he caught one going in the wrong direction, six hours later he was back trying to get on the relief boat to go off on the light again. It's sad a man should get to that state.

Some of them do seem to sink themselves into the job. There's some when they're ashore never go out anywhere without their uniform on; to the shops, to the pub, even out to see their friends. You'd think they were Admirals: they do in their own minds.

When it's got to that state I feel sorry for them. No job could be worth it to me that I'd want to remind myself and everyone else about it all the time. When I'm home I'm home; I like to forget about work, I don't need people to know it involves going on lighthouses. I don't think it's important, there's nothing special about them to me. They're not romantic places or exciting ones, they're only work places the same as anywhere else. Some of the younger men in the DLF think we ought to have Trinity House badges on our overalls. To me that's ridiculous, I think it's a form of snobbishness; I can't see any difference to it in working on the docks or in the coalmines or on the railways.

A job's a job; this one's a good one. I'm an ordinary workman paid to do a job and I get on with it. If I didn't like the people I worked for and the people I worked with, I wouldn't stay in it. I get satisfaction out of what I do, not out of fancy notions.

Susie Archer

The Other Half of
the Bed

11

The sky stayed overcast and sullen; the endlessly running white crested waves on the sea broke continuously against the rock and sent searching fingers of foam clawing up its sides. The wind dropped slightly but not much: it was whistling through the telephone wires outside the cottages. The relief was three days overdue.

The tall young woman, lanky and thin in frayed faded jeans and a red T-shirt grimaced irritatedly as she looked out of her window at the weather. Her long black hair was fastened with a green elastic band into a pony-tail that swished across her back when she moved. An oval pale face and deep blue eyes. She glanced into the carry-cot on the settee to make sure the baby was still asleep and flopped down dejectedly on the floor, crosslegged on a cushion by a big tray with a jigsaw puzzle on it. From time to time as she talked she fitted in another piece absentmindedly, without looking at what she was doing. She lit cigarettes one after another from stubs of finished ones before stabbing them out in an ashtray under a chair.

– They said on the television last night the weather was going to improve, I can't see much bloody sign of it. There's nothing gets me down more than overdues on the middle relief like this. If it was the end of Bobbie's turn off at least I'd have something to look forward to, I'd know he'd be coming ashore as soon as the sea went down. This is only the end of his first month, his second month doesn't start counting till the relief's been done. These days are just wasted time.

Once when he was SAK on a tower he had eleven days overdue in the middle, then another fifteen days overdue at the end. That meant he was off three months at a stretch, all but a few days. Someone told me the record so far as that any keeper's had to do is sixteen weeks and two days. I should think his wife must have gone round the twist.

I made up a tin for Bobbie this morning, with some meat pies and some tarts and some buns; I put a lettuce in and some fresh tomatoes and then I sealed it all up. If the overdue goes on much longer I'll have to undo it all again; they say you shouldn't fasten it until you know for certain the boat's going. When I got up this morning I was so fed up I thought if I sealed up his tin it might make the sea go down; but it hasn't worked.

This place is bad for reliefs, you wouldn't think it could be with it being so near the shore. Apparently the landing's round the other side, in a narrow bit between two rocks: there's one direction that if the wind's blowing from the sea starts running very heavy and it's not safe for a boat to go in. I've never been out to have a look at it; I'll wait till the summer when the weather's better. Everyone says it gets very rough and bumpy on the water in the winter.

Why I'm going on playing with this damn jigsaw I don't know. I've done it so many times I could do it with my eyes shut. I keep promising myself I'll buy myself another when I go down into the town. It's a nice picture when it's finished though. It's a scene of Venice, that's my favourite place, I'd love to go there one day if I ever got the chance. There's a lot of other places I want to go to as well, I've never even been to London yet. The Norfolk Broads, I saw a programme about them on television, it looked fabulous.

I don't know what it is but I like anywhere where's there's water. Not sea water, I don't like that; fresh water, rivers and lakes and ponds and things. Ever since I can remember as a kid water's always fascinated me; I like the feel of it and the noise it makes. I love the rain too; in the summer as soon as it starts to rain I go out for a walk in it. I like to take my shoes off and run about on wet grass, water always makes me feel somehow clean and nice.

When I was little we lived in a house that had a tap in the yard. That's all it did have, it didn't have a bathroom. We had one of those big old metal baths; I was always taking it out at the back and filling it up to the top, then I'd take my clothes off and jump up and down in it. If anyone came near me to try and make me stop I'd scream and splash water all over them. I used to drive mum spare with it; one of the earliest things I remember is her yelling at me and trying to get me out.

We were very poor, my mum must have had a hard time with us. There were three kids; I was the eldest, I've a younger brother and sister. Our dad died when I was four; the only thing I can remember about him is he used to come home drunk. I think he worked in the dockyard when he did work.

All mum had was a widow's pension or National Assistance or whatever it was in those days. I know it wasn't much; but she was very good, she always saw to it we were properly fed and clothed. There was never anything extra for pocket money or sweets: the biggest treat we had as kids was a bag of chips she used to buy between the three of us every Friday night from the fish-and-chip shop.

I never remember her going off in the evening and going out on her own, not once; she always used to read us stories at night until she was ready to go to bed herself. It must have been a hard life for her, she can't have been all that old. I'm twenty, I suppose she's forty-two or forty-three so she can only have been in her early twenties then at the most. She's still alive, she's living with my sister in Northampton. I haven't seen much of her in the last few years, not since I got married. We write to each other for Christmas and birthdays but that's about all.

Being the eldest I had to leave school when I was fifteen and go to work because we needed money. I had a job as a waitress in a coffee bar. That was how I came to meet Bobbie. He used to come in the coffee bar twice a week in the afternoons on his own; he always looked very lonely, he didn't seem to have any friends.

After a time we got to know each other and he started coming in every day then for a chat. I was young and green in those days; he told me he didn't know anyone because he'd been away at sea. I liked him, I really fell for him even though he was a lot older than I was; he's ten years older, nearly eleven. One day he asked me if he could meet me after I'd finished work and we went to another cafe for a cup of tea.

He said it was only fair, he'd put all his cards on the table: he told me he was married but it hadn't worked out, he was separated from his wife and going to get a divorce. I liked him because he was so honest about it: he could have spun me a tale if he'd wanted to and I'd probably have believed it. But he made it clear from the start what the position was.

I said it was all right with me and we started going steady. My mum wasn't a bit keen when I told her the situation, she wanted me to find someone my own age. That was one of the best things about him to me: compared with Bobbie all the boys I knew seemed like school kids. He'd had a lot of unhappy experiences, he'd never had a proper family life himself either. His life had been a mess up till then, he said all he wanted was a chance to properly settle down. Mum said he ought to prove himself first; but he said he couldn't do it without me. I wouldn't have given him up then no matter what anyone said. He was very tall and handsome; he still is, he looks a bit like Steve McQueen.

By the time his divorce came through I was expecting. It wasn't a case of us having to get married, you don't have to marry someone even if you are going to have a baby if you don't want to. If you don't love each other I think you shouldn't.

I told Bobbie he didn't have to marry me if he wasn't certain; I told him to go away and think about it, specially since he'd had one marriage a failure. He said all right he would: he went off and he was back half an hour later with a big grin all over his face saying he'd thought about it.

I was not quite seventeen when we got married. A few weeks after we did I lost the baby. Bobbie could have walked out and left me, but he said he wanted to settle down and have a family. I started another baby and we lost that one too. Bobbie was doing odd jobs and couldn't get steady work. Then one day he came home with an advert he'd seen in the paper about lighthouse keepers; he said he'd talked to people about it and they'd all told him it was a good steady job. He asked me if I thought I could put up with it and I said yes, all I wanted was to see him settled in something he liked; if he thought he could stand the life I was certain I could. We thought there might be difficulty about him getting references because his work record had been bad, but we managed to get round that and he was accepted as an SAK.

When I look back on it I think it was a good thing I didn't have a baby at that time. We'd no proper place of our own to live and no money. I stayed with his sister, for the first eighteen months it was hard because he was away a lot and the pay was very poor. I was used to that sort of thing because of my own childhood, so I got through it all right.

He was made up to AK six months ago and appointed to this station and we came to live here. It had the house and everything to go with it, since then we've never looked back. What's in the past is passed, it's over and done with and forgotten now. I think it proves Bobbie meant it when he said he wanted to settle down. He likes the job very much apart from the going away from home part, but that won't last for ever. We've got Mandy, the house, the job; I think we've been very lucky. It'd take something really drastic to make us want to give all this up when we've had such a struggle to get to it.

The worst thing is being separated; I do have to make a big effort to put up with that. It takes a big effort because with Mandy still being a baby Bobbie's all I've got. But there are a lot of compensations. Nothing makes up for him not being here but if it wasn't for that I wouldn't have all the things I've got. Compared with what I've had in life up to now it's paradise; from next to nothing a few years ago now I've got nearly everything.

The cottage is very nice and large, it's got two bedrooms and a lovely view. The kitchen's got a cooker, a fridge and a washing machine. The central heating's free, so's the use of the telephone; there's no rent to pay, and no repair bills. Nobody could say Trinity don't look after the people who work for them.

The only little grouse is there's only the one telephone between the four cottages. There's a plug in each cottage, so if the phone rings and it's not for you and it's in your house, you have to take it round to the person it's for. That's not much fun on a cold night when you've just got yourself ready for bed, having to go trailing round in the dark. Janet's friends are always ringing her up late in the evening; if we each had a phone of our own it'd save a lot of bad feeling. I don't use it a lot myself; sometimes I ring up my brother but that's about all. It never seems to fail if I have it in here that the next call is for her.

Apart from things like that the only other difficulty is being stuck up here such a long distance away from the town. It makes it awkward for shopping specially now I've got Mandy. Margaret'll always get me anything I want when she goes in, and she looks after Mandy if I want to go into town for a change myself. But you don't like to be asking someone all the time. I wouldn't leave her with Janet, she and I don't get on very well. She's going soon now: I hope someone nicer comes, someone nearer my own age.

Janet's very stuck up, she looks down her nose at me because I'm not educated. She thinks I make too much fuss if the relief's delayed and Bobbie can't get ashore. She told me once if I was going to be a proper keeper's wife I'd have to learn to.put up with that sort of thing.

I suppose I shall learn to in time, but up to now I'm not very good about it. I can't help it that I miss him as much as I do; I hate it if there's even so much as one day's overdue. When he's away all I do is count the days and nights. I sit and knit and I watch television and do jigsaw puzzles; then I do jigsaw puzzles and watch television and sit and knit; it goes on like that, I can't stir myself to do anything else. I flop round the house all day like this in old jeans, I never eat properly and I don't sleep.

When a boat goes out round the rock in good weather and brings back a letter from him, I read it once every hour after I've got it; and I go on reading it four or five times a day every day until I get the next one. I take it to bed with me at night and sleep with it under the pillow. I hate it when I'm on my own and he's not there where he should be in the other half of the bed.

For three or four days before the relief's due I get more and more worked up about it. I lie awake all night listening to the weather, hoping and praying if it's calm it's not going to change or if it's rough that it's going to go down in time. When I know the relief's definitely going to be done, I don't sleep a wink the night before. I wash my hair, then I usually get up about five o'clock in the morning and start cleaning through the house from top to bottom. I scrub all the floors, clean all the paintwork, polish everything in sight until it's spotless.

About an hour before he's due I go and have a bath, then I do my make-up and try to make myself look as nice as I can, perhaps put on a new dress I've bought that he hasn't seen before. I don't go down to the harbour to meet the boat: you can see it coming from the bedroom window, as soon as it comes in sight I rush and put the kettle on.

I don't think he ever notices the cleaning I've done, he comes rushing in throwing his bags down all over the place. If he feels like a cup of tea we have one, but if he doesn't we don't. The first few days he's home he hardly sticks his nose outside the door.

He's usually very tired when he gets ashore because of the hours he's been stopping up in the night on watch; he wants to make up a lot of sleep but I don't let him, he can sleep all he wants to when he goes back.

I'm very possessive when he's home, very jealous of him going out doing anything on his own; I want him all the time here with me. His hobby's fishing, he's very keen on it; sometimes if it's a decent evening he goes out fishing from the rocks down at the bottom of the cliff. We have terrific rows about it, I get really mad with him when he goes off and leaves me. We have rows about all sorts of other things too, like whose turn it is to get up and make the tea. We're both very quick-tempered; only the nice thing in quarrelling is the making up afterwards.

Sometimes we have a row during his last few days ashore: that's awful, it's usually my fault and I could kick myself afterwards. We've never had one yet on his last night but we've come near it once or twice: I couldn't bear it if we ever did and he went off before he got over it. I think if it happened I'd be down there at the harbour half an hour after he'd gone begging one of the boatmen to take me out to apologize to him no matter what the weather was.

Sometimes it happens there's an overdue when he's ashore and he's delayed going back. He hates it, he wants to get off again, but I'm glad when that happens, it's like being given extra days as a present. When it's getting towards the end of his leave I start hoping the weather'll turn bad and he won't be able to go. Some people say they'd sooner have the relief over and done with: I can't understand that.

The worst time of him being ashore is the last day of his leave. I can't help it, I'm saying to myself all the time 'This time tomorrow he'll be gone.' The night he's left I sit looking at the television but I can't bear to switch it on. I keep thinking the night before he was sitting next to me. It's horrible, it always takes me three or four days before I get over it. I keep bursting into tears because I'm so wretched and miserable. Margaret says it'll wear off and I'll get used to it, and I suppose I shall. The first few nights I go to sleep on the settee in here because I can't stand lying upstairs in bed without him. It seems so empty and cold, and I miss him and worry about him.

I get specially worried about him when he's out there and the weather's like this. I know he's miles up above the water and couldn't come to any harm; but I've made him promise me he'll never go down near the landing if it's the slightest bit rough. There was a keeper a few years ago who was drowned when he was fishing. When you've heard of something like that you can't help worrying, ever.

Margaret Vincent

Mrs PK

It was five days before the wind lessened and changed direction,
and the sea began noticeably at last to subside.

Five long and dispiriting days of waiting, watching and being
disappointed; five days of frustration, impatience and irritation,
reacting to weather as though it had human characteristics,
investing it with obstinacy, even vindictiveness; eventually almost
attributing personal animosity to it. As they succeeded one another each day seemed longer than the one before; waiting became
obsessive and impotent inactivity a full-time occupation.

Margaret Vincent, a Yorkshire woman of fifty-two, quietly
spoken with neatly cut grey hair and brown eyes. She was
motherly towards everyone. Each day she made midday dinner
for the DLF men, and kept them supplied with mugs of tea;
every day she called in at each of the cottages to see how their
occupants were, stopping for a minute or an hour depending on
their mood. If she went down into the town she always asked if
anyone wanted anything brought back; when she did any
baking of cakes or buns she alleged she'd made too many,
would be extremely grateful if someone could help her out by
taking the surplus off her hands. Her back door was always
unlocked and at any time anyone could walk into her kitchen
to borrow anything they needed; if they felt like having a cup
of tea or coffee with her while they were there she'd be very

glad of their company, she said. Without her presence the five days of waiting would have been more than dispiriting.

*

– It must be really rotten for you, love. No doubt about it now though, it's definitely bucking up a lot today. You'll be going off tomorrow certain, you take my word for it. The days mustn't half have dragged for you; never mind, you'll be there tomorrow all right. The store's got your food packed ready for you haven't they? I'll give them a ring first thing in the morning to make sure they don't forget to put your meat and fresh vegetables in. Leave that side of it to me, you'll have plenty to do getting yourself ready without things like that.

Don't forget what I told you, Jacko's been out there hundreds of times, he's a first-class boatman, knows exactly what he's doing and how it's done. He can be a bit coarse in his language but you'll not have to mind that. So long as you do what he says you'll come to no harm, he never takes risks. The moment he says jump for the steps of the landing, you just jump right away and then you'll be fine. Mind you've got your lifejacket fastened properly; don't rely on Alf to check it for you, ask one of the men who's helping Jacko to look at it and make sure it's done up right. Stanley or Bob'll be down on the landing when you get there, one or the other of them'll be waiting to give you a hand. They'll look after you, there'll be nothing to worry about.

It can be very cold and windy on the water once you've got out beyond the quay this time of year; you're sure you've got plenty of waterproof things to wear? I've got a tin with a few things in for Stanley, I'll give it you to take to him if you wouldn't mind. I'd ask Alf to take it if he was better organized, but he can't help being the way he is, poor man. Have you not met him yet? He's very nice, you'll like him much when you do.

Come in tonight for a last chat and a drink before you go won't you, like you promised? And see you get to bed early and have a good night.

Before that, her conversation was normally more concerned with other people than herself.

– I think of myself as a very lucky woman. Anyone with a husband like Stanley and a daughter like Catherine couldn't want for anything more. Life's been good to us: thirty years this year since he started to work with Trinity, they've looked after us wonderfully all through; they must be the best people to work for in the world.

There've been difficult times now and again, there's bound to have been in that length of time. But we've had as good or better than anyone else; and no matter what I had to put up with, Stanley had it harder for him. He always took what came for my sake and Catherine's and I'm not the one who'd have a right to complain. I've always told him if he ever wanted to do something different it would be all right with me, we'd make the best of it together. But he never has; all along he's done what he thought. All our lives we've put what was best for Catherine first, ever since she was born. It's paid off in the end, the way it's turned out; there can't be no doubt about that.

She's studying medicine at university now, she's going to be a doctor. Next year she's going to get married; she's engaged to a nice young man who's going in for civil engineering. Stanley was always determined she should have a decent chance in life since he never had one for himself. He's very proud of her, we both are; it's nice when everything comes out at the end the way you hoped it would. You can look back and feel you did right, and that's where you get your reward. There's only a few more years to go: then Stanley'll retire, so we've got that to look forward to now.

It's a long time to look back over, thirty years. Stanley wasn't in the lighthouse service when we first met; he was a clerk in an office on the railways. He wasn't settled at all, he wanted to do something better with his life than that. But he'd never had the opportunities: not enough schooling, no money in the family, the usual story for a lot of people in those days. When we first met he was thinking of going to sea; when we decided to get married he gave that idea up because it would have meant being away.

He was still interested in getting into something to do with the sea though: that's what first put the idea of the lighthouse service in his mind. One of his bosses had been in it himself when he was younger: Stanley asked him to tell him about it, then when he came home we talked it over together and I encouraged him to apply. Like it always is in the service the first year was the worst: once you've got through that all right you've security then for the rest of your life.

We moved around a lot at first when he was an AK; sometimes he was on land lights but mostly it seemed to be on rocks and towers. We never stopped in one place more than two years before he was moved on. Not many lights had cottages attached to them in those days, so we were living mainly in council accommodation. We were thinking about trying to save up our money and buy a house, so that wherever he went then we'd have a permanent home.

Sometimes I wonder whether we did the right thing or not when we decided all things considered we wouldn't. There's a theory in the service that if you buy yourself a house you're leaving yourself open to being permanently kept on sea lights. All land lights have got accommodation: if you have a house of your own, Trinity doesn't need to bother about finding somewhere for you to live and they put you where it suits them best and give the lights with houses to others who accommodation is a problem for. That's the theory; whether it's true or not I don't know.

What made up our minds for us not to was that we got a nice land light. Catherine had just come to the age when we were beginning to have to think about her schooling; and we were told in confidence we wouldn't be moved again from there for a good few years. We both felt it was very important for her to be settled in one place: she was obviously bright and it looked as though if she was given the chance to stay in one school she'd do well. Stanley went to the Trinity office and had a talk with the district Superintendent about it. He asked him his opinion what he thought would be the best thing to do about buying a house, and when he told him we could rely on not being moved for a fairly long while it was that which decided us.

That's one thing you always do feel: you can discuss your problems with Trinity even if they're to do with the family and not just the job. They're very helpful, we've always found. The Superintendent was as good as his word and we were at that same land light over twelve years, so Catherine was able to stay at the one school all the time. Your children's education is always a big problem, other people have had a lot of worries on that score. It's because of the way Trinity helped us then that we've accepted things since that we might have felt differently about.

They were a very happy time for us, those years. Catherine's said herself when she comes to look back on it she's very conscious she had a stable childhood. We'd have liked more children but it wasn't to be; apart from that things were pretty nearly ideal for her. It was one of the best land lights there is, not far from a town but on a beautiful piece of coast away from the crowds. There can't be many children who've had the chance to grow up in that sort of environment, in a place with what amounted to its own private beach. In the summer when she came home from school every day the first thing she did was change into her bathing costume and go down the cliff path at the end of the garden for a swim.

She wasn't a child who deliberately kept herself to herself, but the things she liked most were the sea and the countryside. She had them both on her doorstep. She used to spend hours on her own, walking along the shore collecting shells or watching the birds. Each Christmas and birthday it had to be either a telescope or a pair of binoculars, or a book about nature and wild life. By the time she was thirteen she'd got past the picture book stage, it had to be something really authoritative about whatever the subject was. As she got older she became more interested in birds and knowledgeable about them than ever; now she's grown up she's taken up ornithology seriously as her hobby. Her father always encouraged her to learn as much as she could. When he was on the early morning watch, if he saw something that'd interest her like a rare bird that was a migrant he'd wake her up and take her up the lighthouse tower so they could look at it together through the glasses. She made him promise he'd always wake her if he saw something interesting no matter what the time was.

It was a marvellous environment for her right up to the time she went on to grammar school. Then Stanley was offered being promoted to PK. We knew it'd mean he'd have to go back on sea lights and start at the bottom again as far as stations were concerned. But with Catherine obviously being all set for going on to university in another couple of years he took it because of the extra money it would mean. He's never been a great one for being ambitious to get to a position of authority; I think if there'd only been himself and me to be considered he probably wouldn't have taken it. It was mainly for Catherine's sake; even though students get good grants you feel you've got to help them financially as much as you can. Training to be a doctor's a long business; we wanted to be certain the money would always be there.

The first place he went to as a PK was a tower; that must have been far harder for him than here. At least on the rock he's not in any danger and he's got a bit of room to move around. If he's got to be away from home out at sea on a lighthouse, I'd much sooner it was a rock light than a tower. They've got nothing to protect them there against the sea.

You can see the rock from here and that makes me feel he's not too far away; I always try to think of it that he's still close at hand. It doesn't take all that long to get out there by boat in the summer: they run pleasure trips round it and I go on one every week so we can give each other a little wave.

This is a good station and a nice one to be at because of the other people here. It makes all the difference if you've got good

neighbours: we always seem to have been fortunate in that respect.
I've always found other people in the service easy to get on with;
you'll find most of the cottages are friendly communities, just
like the lighthouses where the men work. If there's a good
atmosphere ashore there'll be a good one out on the light.

I look at it that if you're the wife of the PK it's up to you to
play as much part in the job as you can. He's responsible for
things out there; I'm responsible ashore for looking after the
community attached to it. It'd be hopeless if the families didn't get
on; the wives' husbands have got to work together, it'd make it
difficult for them if there was unfriendliness between their families.

The wives are leading an unnatural sort of life with their
husbands not at home, so it's natural they get a bit upset now and
again. I think it helps them if they feel they're not on their own;
and however different we might be in our outlooks and character
we're all in the same situation.

For instance Janet and Susie are very different from each
other, but they're both fine girls. I've heard one or other of them
say from time to time that they don't really get on. Perhaps on
the surface they don't, because they come from different back-
grounds and their ways of looking at things aren't the same.
But I know if either of them was ever seriously ill or in trouble
the other'd be the first to step in and lend a hand.

All the way through Trinity, whatever people's moans and
groans about each other are, they all feel they're part of the same
family. As things are at the moment, I think Susie does feel a bit
on the outside because she hasn't been here long. But when Janet
and Paul go and somebody new comes then Susie won't be the
new girl and that'll help her.

Janet was saying about the SAK who'll be coming ashore when
Alf goes off on the relief that she was thinking of asking him to
have a meal with them in the evening. I said to her why not
suggest to Susie she's the one who invites him to have something
to eat, so she can have a chat with him on her own and ask him
about Bobbie. Janet said straight away she thought that was a

good idea. You've always got to think about things like that and try not to let situations that cause bad feeling arise. If I get a chance to have a word with him myself and ask him about Stanley I will, but it's more important for Susie to have as much time to talk to him as he can spare.

I don't know there's much more I can tell you about the shore side of lighthouse life that you won't have heard before. I shouldn't think I'm any different from any other keeper's wife; I've got the same feelings about when he's ashore and when he's away. A bit more experience in length of time at it, but otherwise not any different.

*

The last evening, late. In her burgundy velvet housecoat she sat on the settee with her feet up and her hands clasped lightly in her lap. Sometimes while she talked her fingers touching her wedding ring turned it gently round.

– The shock more than anything: when your husband's made up to PK and has to start going away all over again after so many years. No matter how much you've tried to prepare yourself for it mentally, it still does come as a shock to you how much it hurts. You think you're old and wise and experienced: you hadn't expected you'd find yourself crying as much as any young wife who's only been married for a few years every time he goes away.

I don't go down to the harbour to see him off: he says he prefers me not to, when he's down there he's busy loading his things in the boat. He's right, it's only dragging it out and makes it harder for both of us. After he's gone I go upstairs and watch the boat disappearing out beyond the end of the quay, then I go downstairs in the kitchen and make myself a pot of tea.

I get thoroughly ashamed of myself; I think whatever would Janet or Susie say if they came in and saw me. I'm the PKs wife, supposed to be experienced and used to it. I usually manage to pull myself together after an hour or so; but every time it still knocks me off balance that I feel it so much. I think it's because Catherine's not here now; before she went away I always had to put a brave face on it for her. Now no one's here and I don't seem to do half as well.

The thing that makes it hardest is I know how much Stanley hates going. At first he didn't seem to mind too much; but the few years since we've come here he's aged a lot, I think it's getting harder for him every time. To some of the younger men like Paul and Bob, it's still a bit of an adventure; but there's nothing of that in it for Stanley now. Through the whole of his last week he gets quieter each day that goes by. On his last night we'll be sitting watching the telly and I can see by the look on his face his mind's not on it. Sometimes I think he's almost going to be sick. I put my arms round him and give him a kiss, I say 'Never mind love, it'll soon pass, each day you're away is one day nearer to you coming back again.' It's no comfort to him, but it's all I can think of.

There've been times when he's been looking so ill I've almost said to him why doesn't he go down to see the doctor and get a note that he's not up to going back. It's a big temptation to do that, particularly when it's getting near Christmas, or it's his birthday say the following week. But I don't think he would ever do that, only if it was me that was ill. However bad he's feeling, he knows if he does someone else would have to be sent to take his place. It'd probably be an SAK somewhere that we'd never met and never heard of: but for all we know he might only have got back to his own home himself the day before. If Stanley reported sick that man would have to pack up his bags and rush off to get here so he could take his place.

I don't like it at the end of Stanley's shore leave if there's an overdue and he can stay at home a few more days. Every day he can't go back because of the weather there's some other woman going through misery because she's waiting for her husband who isn't there. It might be one of the girls here, it might be the wife of an SAK living somewhere else. But whoever it is, if you've got your husband someone else hasn't got hers. We'd both much sooner the relief was done on the day; we can't look on it we've got an extra bit of happiness because we know it's at someone else's expense.

While he's off, when I'm out shopping I keep my eyes open for any little thing I know he specially likes; say a jar of brandy butter or a tin of anchovies, anything I know he's particularly fond of. The night before he's due to go I wait till he's packed his clothes and then I'll slip it in among them so he'll find it when he comes to unpack. I know each time he eats some of it, it'll remind him I bought it for him; he'll know it means I was thinking of him when I did.

Him going away again, it's brought us even closer together than ever. We've always been very happy, but everyone takes each other a bit for granted; it's certainly stopped us doing that. I can see it particularly in Stanley; he behaves in ways now I'd never have thought he would. He seems to have become much tenderer and more affectionate; and he'll show it in front of other people which he'd never have dreamt of before. A little thing like putting his arm round my waist in front of other people; he would have been much too shy to do that when other people were present. It seems to have gone out of him, the embarrassment of letting other people see we love each other.

When he's home now, he seems to want to be somewhere near me every minute. I tell him after his meals to sit down and put his feet up and read the paper or have a bit of a nap; but he won't. After every meal he comes in the kitchen to help me do the washing-up. He says it's because he wants to be where he can see me. If I go upstairs to do some vacuuming, he'll be up in five minutes to see what I'm doing and asking me to come down again soon. Five minutes after that he'll be making a cup of tea and calling out to me to come and have it with him.

Another change is that he was always one for eating at home; he liked home cooking, we never had a meal out. Now he'll say 'Come on love, you've been on the go all the morning doing the washing; put your hat and coat on, we'll have lunch in the town and a look round the shops afterwards.' Once a week we go out for lunch when he's ashore, and every Saturday evening we have a meal at the Chinese restaurant. For a man who'd never go out if he could avoid it, something like that's a tremendous change.

The only time he still doesn't want to go out is in his last week: the days are very precious then. He doesn't like me to do any housework so I don't, I just let things go. All he wants is for us to be sitting quietly and watching the telly or reading. It mightn't sound a lot to someone else but it does to me. It's a wonderful thing to have it made plain to you that to be with you is all your husband wants.

The first day he comes home it's always the same. The moment he comes in the house he goes upstairs to have a bath, then he changes into his favourite trousers and puts his old cardigan and slippers on. While he's doing that I make a pot of tea. Until he's had his bath and got changed, he never really feels he's come home; that's when he can start to relax. I can see it starting to drop away from him, all the tension and worry and tiredness. For his lunch I make him exactly the same meal every time, his favourite one; he knows what it'll be. A pork chop with roast potatoes and onions and tomatoes, and treacle tart and cream. Then he puts his feet up for an hour: if the weather's nice we might go out for a stroll, then we come home and have scones and jam in front of the fire for tea.

We have a quiet evening, Catherine usually rings up on his first night to say hello and have a little chat. We'll look at the telly for a while, then we go to bed early, usually about half past nine after we've watched the news. It's then when he's back next to me in bed and his arm's round my shoulder and we've given each other our goodnight kiss; that's the moment I feel he's really home. There's nothing to compare with it; if anyone asked me what I meant by happiness, it's that: going to sleep together with your husband with your arms round each other after being married for thirty-two years.

Off

Low tide in the small harbour at the foot of the cliffs, half an hour after sunrise on a morning in early February. It was deserted, drab and gloomy; and wet and cold, a blustery breeze was blowing across it from the east. Thin grey-slatted curtains of rain drifted in from the sea; out in the bay the dark green waves were broken and crested with spray, and heavy black clouds hung over them, ponderous and threatening in the sky. Eight o'clock. The day was having to struggle to emerge from under the bedclothes of the night.

Clusters of gulls fluttered squawking round the dim silhouettes of deserted rowing boats, fighting and squabbling raucously with one another as they scavenged along the line of dirty brown seaweed and bits of rubbish left on the sand by the departed tide. They had the beach to themselves; no other activity or sound, apart from the low soughing of the wind.

Suddenly becoming more clearly visible standing out in contrast against the sombre background, a large glistening white cabin cruiser could be seen, tied-up fore and aft against the far end of the quay in the deep water. Freshly painted, it had a high and elegantly streamlined superstructure with radar equipment on the top of it, and pale blue handrails round its sides with life belts neatly lashed on at carefully measured out intervals every few feet along.

It was creaking quietly to itself as it rocked gently up and down, riding the waves with graceful disdain. Its prow pointed confidently out across the sea towards the rock, as though waiting to demonstrate the assurance with which it would soon be cleaving through the water, unerringly and effortlessly getting there.

The words *Sea Rider II* were neatly lettered in gold on a small board below the flagpole on its stern. The well-deck was covered over against the weather with a tightly fastened light green tarpaulin. There was nobody aboard and no one near it.

It belonged to the managing director of a marine engineering company in the town, who used it at weekends; and had nothing whatever to do with carrying out the relief.

– Heh you there, you silly sod! Never mind arsing about having a morning stroll on the quay looking at the scenery. Come down here and lend a hand with these bloody boxes.

An enormous man with long arms and massively broad shoulders, wearing rustling black oilskins and thigh-length sea boots; his face almost invisible under a black sou-wester. He was standing between two sand-dunes at the top of the beach, in a corner beneath where the quay joined the road. Behind him, sheltered by the dunes, was a weathered low wooden shed with a rusty corrugated-iron roof, its double doors propped open facing the sea. Outside it on a sloping and sanded-over concrete runway, a battered red diesel launch lay on its side.

– Well at least someone's turned-up on time for the relief, he said.

Three elderly men in torn yellow oilskins and wellingtons, two with bushy black beards and knitted woollen skullcaps and the third bare-headed and bald and fat with a long white scar down the side of his face, were struggling to get the launch upright and balance it in position by jamming empty oil drums and heavy blocks of timber under it.

When it was almost level the big man in the black oilskins

walked over towards it, stretched out a long sea-booted leg and kicked it violently so it stood straight. Two of the men propped it up with their backs: the third fetched more oil drums out of the shed and heaved them in place underneath it to support it.

The name of the launch was just discernible in crudely carved capitals in the flaking paint round the stern. It was called *Greyhound*.

Round the back of the shed two younger men in mackintoshes and gumboots were unloading cartons of groceries fastened with string from a small van which had backed on to the sand off the road, and putting them in a heap on the beach. When they had finished lifting them out one of them slammed the doors shut and banged on the side with his fist. The van's wheels spun in the sand before they got a grip; it lurched up on to the road, and drove away.

The pile of cardboard cartons lay in the drizzling rain. The man in the black oilskins put his hands on his hips and looked down at them.

– Jesus Christ, he said. One thing's bloody certain, Alf'll never take the risk of starving to death.

The young men in mackintoshes lit cigarettes and watched the van driving away in the distance. After it had disappeared from sight they stood looking along the road. The rain was soaking the cartons.

– Bugger the sod, said the big man. All right, don't just stand and count the bleeding things. Start getting them in the boat.

One of the young men grimaced: the other one sighed wearily. They began to carry the cartons down to the launch, picking them up one at a time and wrapping their arms round them and struggling with their weight as they stumbled over half-buried boulders in the sand. Upright, the sides of the launch were higher than their heads when they got to it; they had to hump the cartons with their shoulders up to the bald headed man standing in it waiting to take them. As he grappled with each one he staggered a few feet along inside the boat with it, then let it fall with a thud.

Every time they went to the pile to get another carton, the young men paused and looked along the road. The light was improving.

The big man bent down under the launch to inspect the propeller, and said something to one of the bearded men in yellow oilskins. After a muttered conversation he went into the shed, and came back with a heavy steel wrench and handed it to him, pointing. He watched for a few minutes as the bearded man hammered at the propeller shaft with the wrench. The clanging noise echoed round the harbour; startled, the seagulls flew up into the air squawking in protest.

The big man swung his arms vigorously across his chest, slapping his hands against the side of his oilskins. He looked at the noisily flapping gulls, then beyond them at the sky over the sea. He pursed his lips and walked up to the edge of the road and looked along it. Coming back past the heap of cartons he casually picked one up in each hand by its string and carried them over to the launch. When he reached it he held them up in the air until the bald headed man took them from him and dragged them in.

The men in mackintoshes panted determinedly up and down the beach with the cartons.

– For Christ's sake hang on a minute, the bald headed man in the launch shouted at them. I'm trying to arrange them where they won't be sliding about all over the place when we get on the water. Heh Jacko, we need some rope to tie these buggers down.

The big man peered into the boat over the stern.

– You stupid fat burke, Cyril, he said. You must be off your bleeding head. By the time all this lot's in there won't be room to fart.

As the number of cartons being piled in the launch increased, the bald-headed man stumbling around inside with them seemed to be getting taller: more and more of his body and legs could be seen. He was walking about on top of them.

– That's all she'll take, Jacko, he said, nearly overbalancing and falling out over the side.

– I'm not making two bleeding trips out of it, said Jacko. He turned and saw the other bearded man who was standing at the edge of the road, looking anxiously towards the far end of it.

– Ivan! Fetch the bleeding punt out.

The bearded man stepped back off the road and disappeared into the shed. There was a sound of falling metal and scraping wood; the roof rattled and shook. After a time he eventually reappeared struggling out backwards with a coil of thick rope over his shoulder, dragging a rowing boat up behind the launch.

Jacko took the rope off him and began to tie it through a metal ring bolted on the rowing boat's prow. Watching him, the bearded man fumbled inside his oilskins for a packet of cigarettes and tried to strike a match with his damp red fingers. The other bearded man stopped battering the propeller shaft with the wrench and stood up, lighting a cigarette himself with his lighter cupped in his hands. They stood side by side smoking and exchanging monosyllables, occasionally glancing unenthusiastically out at the sea.

– Would you mind looking at my lifejacket and checking I've tied it properly?

Jacko fastened the final knot in the rope through the ring, and jerked it tight. He looked over his shoulder.

– What, you a strong swimmer then?

– No.

– So what bleeding difference does it make whether it's done up right or not?

The last of the cartons had been put in the rowing boat. Nobody seemed to have anything left to do.

The bearded man went back to the propeller shaft and gave it three final resounding blows. Then he lit another cigarette and took the wrench back in the shed. When he came out again he brought two spades with him and gave one of them to the other bearded man. They began sporadically to dig a shallow trench down in an erratically unstraight line in the direction of the sea from the end of the concrete runway through the sloping wet sand.

The bald headed Cyril sat crosslegged on top of the cartons jammed in the launch, watching them disinterestedly; he hunched up in his yellow oilskins with the collar round his face against the intermittent squalls of rain. The young men in mackintoshes stamped their feet and blew on their hands. Jacko walked moodily up and down the beach behind the shed, pressing small rocks at random into the sand with his feet; his unfastened oilskins flapped noisily in the wind.

He turned up the brim of his sou-wester, put his hands on his hips, and peered intently along the road to where it disappeared at the end of the curve of the harbour and turned off up the hill out of sight towards the town. He scowled; the rain dripped down his hook-nosed face.

– Same as sodding usual, he said. Bloody waiting again for who we're supposed to be here for, the fucking lighthouse keeper.

Time passed.

A shining white Ford Cortina appeared at the bottom of the hill. It came rapidly along the road with the rain-spray spurting out from its tyres, and glided smoothly to a halt opposite the end of the shed.

The rear door swung open. Wheezing and coughing and with a series of grunts and gasps, the passenger in the back sea painfully wriggled and jerked himself out. He was carrying a large faded canvas gripbag in one hand, and a bulbous orange lifejacket, a navy gaberdine raincoat, a peaked white cap, a brown paper parcel and a roll of torn newspapers in the other.

Struggling, he slowly emerged into view. Nearing fifty, he was short and thick-set, with a circle of thinning grey hair above his ears round his bald head; a florid complexion and pale watery blue eyes behind steel-rimmed spectacles. He wore a creased and rumpled navy serge uniform with 'Trinity House' in gold on the shoulders of the jacket, a white shirt with the button missing at the collar, and a black tie with its knot almost out of sight somewhere round the back of his neck.

When he had prised himself and his encumbrances out of the car into the open, he shivered unhappily. He put the gripbag and lifejacket and parcel down: struggling into his raincoat he dropped his cap and it rolled off the road and on to the sand.

He buttoned his coat, stumbled over his lifejacket and retrieved his cap; he wiped it down on his sleeve before putting it on. It was too small for him, and he had to hold it on his head with one hand. He went round to the back of the car and took out of the boot a battered suitcase held together with rope, a heavy wooden box with metal handles, and a large cardboard carton tied-up with odd lengths of knotted string.

He slammed the lid of the boot shut, tapped on the car window and waved. The taxi-driver gave a tight-lipped nod and drove away: he had a relieved look on his face.

– A bloody good afternoon you lazy sod, said Jacko.

– Morning, Jacko, he said, apologetically patting him on the arm with an expression of regret. What's up, bit late am I? You know what them taxi people are though, you can never rely on them. Bloody hell, it doesn't look so good this morning. Are you sure you can do it? I mean I don't mind hanging on for a while if you –

– The bleeding tide, said Jacko. Jesus Christ you ought to know by now, it'll have turned in half an hour.

With a shrug of resignation, the man unbuttoned the strap round his cap and pulled it down and fastened it under his chin. He looked round at the others, nodding in greeting as he fumbled to get his arms through the armholes and hump his lifejacketon. He let it hang unfastened.

– Hello, lads. Sorry I've kept you. See you've put my boxes in the boat for me, you shouldn't have troubled you know, I'd have done it all right myself. Who are we still held up waiting for now then, is it the writer chap?

He walked over amiably, stretching out his hand.

– How do you do, pleased to meet you. Tawney, isn't it? My name's Alf. Right then Tawney, you stick near me; I'll look after you. Would you mind giving us a hand with these few bits into the boat? Never feel too good you know after a ride in a car.

Getting the loaded launch into the sea was simple.

Jacko paid-out a length of thick rope attached to its prow, lifted it on to his shoulder, and turned to face the sea. Three men stood at each side, ready to pull at short loops of rope fastened along it. Alf went round to the stern to push.

Jacko ground his heels into the sand to get a firm foothold; he bent his back and tightened the rope. He began to strain: then suddenly he gave a tremendous bellow.

– Now!

The men at the sides kicked out with their feet, knocking away the supports. The launch wobbled slightly and hesitated; the metal strip on its keel started to grate as it ground forward over the sanded concrete of the runway. Careering along the shallow trench through the sand it gathered so much momentum down the slope of the beach that the men at the sides were less concerned with pulling it than with trying to keep it upright.

Stumbling over a lump of rock halfway, Alf fell on his knees and was left behind.

Without pausing Jacko plunged into the water, turning aside when it was up to his waist. The launch hurtled past him in a cloud of spray and then stopped abruptly, swaying gently from side to side. It was afloat.

Jacko waded ashore to the others who were standing at the end of the water. Alf came hobbling down to join them.

– It isn't half a dangerous way of doing things that is, he said. I could've broken my bloody ankle back there you know, just for a minute I thought I had.

Following the groove cut through the sand by the launch, the young men in mackintoshes effortlessly dragged the rowing boat down the beach to the edge of the water. They held it steady in the shallows while the passengers clambered in. Taking the end of its towing-rope, Jacko got into the launch and tied it to the stern. The young men gave it a final push to float it on the water, then turned and walked away back up the beach. The bearded Ivan scrambled to the front of the rowing boat and pulled it against the launch so that he could climb up into it: the others stayed in the crowded rowing boat.

In the launch, Jacko yanked aside some of the cartons and removed a side panel from the wooden cover over the engine in the middle of the deck, and put his foot inside to press on the starter. It gave a low whining whirr, then stopped. Jacko pressed it again. It rattled with a short high-pitched metallic screech. Jacko stamped on it hard: the engine coughed, spluttered, then suddenly roared into life. A thick cloud of blue black smoke billowed out of the exhaust pipe just above the waterline in the stern.

Jacko bent down inside the cover to adjust something, looking at it closely, listening with his head slightly on one side until it was throbbing steadily. Satisfied, he nodded at Ivan and they put the panel back.

– Amazing old engine that is, said the bearded man in the rowing boat.

– Doesn't sound like it's running so good though Ernie, said Alf despondently.

Jacko cleared his throat, spat into the sea, wiped his mouth with the back of his hand, and turned to the wheel. He slowly pulled back a thick metal lever nearly as high as his chest, ignoring the grinding protest of the engaging gear. With a jerk the launch moved forward, dragging the rowing boat along low in the water, at the end of the towing-rope a few feet behind.

– Right then, said Ernie. That's it, we're away.

– The rain's left off anyhow, said Cyril. Mightn't be too bad you know, today.

– Aye, said Alf. It mightn't be.

He sank down on his haunches, wedging himself against the side of the rowing boat between the wooden box and his cardboard carton, and started to tie the strings of his lifejacket. Remembering something, he stopped and took a folded handkerchief from inside his jacket and held it under his chin. When he had pushed them out of his mouth with his tongue, he wrapped his false teeth in it carefully and pushed them deep into the pocket of his trousers. Then he finished tying his lifejacket and looked up.

– Can I try one of your shigars, Tawney? I don't know, it might just help; I'm not all that good on the she you she.

The launch chugged on through the water. The rain had stopped and the sky was clearing a little; the waves were small and placid, and the rowing boat packed with its passengers undulated gently over them. Apart from the cold breeze the journey was extremely pleasant from the beach across the harbour as far as the end of the quay.

The first wave hit the front of the launch there with the force of a battering ram, making it quiver from end to end. The second was stronger and struck it head-on, sending a towering cascade of spray up into the air. The third and fourth crashed into it almost simultaneously from opposite directions, and the fifth burrowed underneath the prow and lifted it vertical before letting it drop again with a jarring crash. As the launch plunged and rose again the rowing boat jerked after it like an aquatic dodgem-car, bucking and bouncing over the water and careering from side to side.

– Yes that's right, said Cyril. I thought it wouldn't be too bad.

Black and lumpy as iron, the waves rolled thicker and steeper. The launch and rowing boat wallowed and teetered over and through them in a succession of thumps and jolts, staggering and buffeting and boring through trough after trough of metallic sea in a confusion of foam and billowing spray. Progress seemed slight: only the growing size of the rock when it could occasionally be caught sight of from the top of a wave confirmed any was being made.

Lunging swaying and snorting, the launch juddered on. Clinging to one another cramped in the rowing boat ricochetting about on the end of the rope behind it, the passengers huddled together, sopping and chilled. In the noise of the wind and the sea and the launch's engine, conversation was fragmented and difficult.

– Sorry, I can't hear you. What did you say?

– I said why are you going, the bald-headed Cyril shouted. What do they want a bloody sign-writer out there for anyway?

Ivan was yelling something over the stern of the launch at Ernie; Ernie shouted it across the rowing boat to the bald-headed man.

– He's asking where you've put the waterproof sheets to cover the boxes with.

Cyril thought hard.

– Underneath out of the way, he said. I put the boxes on top of them.

As it came nearer, the rock seemed to be changing colour: from black to umber, umbre to ochre, ochre to fawn. Smooth in appearance from the land, now its soaring sides were jagged and deeply fissured, with great white smears down them on the droppings from its thousands of inhabitant gulls.

Alf was slumped in the stern of the rowing boat, his putty coloured face dripping with spray. He was not bothering to wipe his glasses dry. His head was tilted sideways flopping on his shoulder, his eyes were closed. The boat slapped and clumped up and down in the water, and heeled and rocked and swayed. It swayed and rocked and heeled and slapped and clumped up and down in the water; and it went on.

– I had a brother-in-law once, shouted Cyril. He was thinking of going in for being a lawyer.

– That's got bloody nothing to do with writing, you fat burke, bawled Ernie.

– I know that, Cyril shouted back. I'm just telling him because I thought he might be interested that's all.

Alf opened his eyes and slowly rose on his knees, twisting himself round and putting his head over the stern and vomiting repeatedly into the water.

Ernie put his hand on his shoulder to steady him. Cyril watched him expressionlessly.

– He's not all that good on the sea isn't Alf, he said, running his thumb thoughtfully down the long white scar on the side of his face.

– Used to be a fisherman myself, he said. On the trawlers. Deep-sea trawlers. Could get quite rough sometimes out at sea on those.

Alf folded his arms on the edge of the boat, resting his forehead on them. He leaned forward and retched over the side again, then pulled his head back, rolling it from side to side and wiping his mouth on his sleeve. Ernie patted him on the shoulder.

Rolling and rising and plunging in tandem, the boats struggled level with the curved end of the rock, keeping out in the water away from the turmoil of boiling foam thrashing round its serrated base as they passed. It loomed up over them in the sky, barren and huge.

Round the other side almost at water level a small platform of concrete with railings painted red came into view: from the back of it steps wound up the rock face behind it out of sight. Opposite protecting the platform from the main sea waves was a long bare rock twenty feet high. From a metal pulley on it a thick rope hung in a loop over the gully between the rocks and then disappeared up the face of the bigger rock into the sky. Dangling from the middle of the loop was a green nylon net with bags and packages in.

Some of the waves coming in from seaward threw up clouds of spray when they broke against the smaller rock. Between it and the platform the narrow stretch of water was turbulent with small ebbing and rising waves of white and green; compared with the sea already crossed it was calm. Because it was sheltered from the boisterous hustling of the wind the gully was eerily quiet.

Ernie shook Alf's shoulder.

– Come on, Alf, he said. Come on, Alf, you're all right now, we're there.

Alf groaned, and lifted his head.

– Thank Christ for that, he said. It seems to get further every bloody time.

Two men were standing on the platform waiting. One was tall and fair-haired, with a donkey-jacket over his overalls. The other wore a blue uniform and an orange lifejacket; his peaked white cap was at a rakish angle on his head. The SAK; he was small and looked fresh-faced and young. Both were holding poles with metal hooks on the end.

Jacko throttled back the engine of the launch, and stood on

his toes to have a critical look over the prow at the gully ahead. After he had considered it he spat on his hands, rubbed them together, and began slowly and carefully to steer the launch in. He took it past the platform so that the men with the boat-hooks could pull the rocking rowing boat in against the edge where there was a gap in the railings: it bobbed violently up and down, sometimes level with them and the next moment six feet below.

– There's a lot of bloody water in here, said Ernie. This is the bit I don't like.

Alf stood up, put his false teeth back in his mouth and pushed his way across the rowing boat towards the platform.

It's the only bit I do like, he said. At least it means I'm getting back on to bloody dry –

The boat dropped and lurched suddenly, and he lost his balance. He fell backwards and sat down squarely in the middle of the top of his cardboard carton. It caved in under him.

– Bloody hell, he said. I thought I was going to fall in the water then; thank Christ for that. Here someone, give us a hand.

Struggling he was hauled back to his feet. He stood impatiently by the side of the boat close to the platform.

Jacko was watching the water sluicing in between the rocks, measuring the rise and fall of the rowing boat caused by each wave.

– Wait for it, he called. Hang on Alf, wait . . . wait. Jump!

As the rowing boat rose level with it, Alf leapt for the platform. The two men caught his arms as he landed full length on his stomach, pulling him upright and steadying him. Alf shook hands with each of them. The seat of his gaberdine coat was streaked with wet yellow smears.

The SAK squeezed himself past Alf and stood at the edge of the platform between the gap in the railings.

Jacko was looking ahead, watching the approaching waves.

– Ready again, he shouted. No, not yet . . . wait for it. Wait . . . now . . . jump!

Nobody moved. Jacko turned round.

– You bleeding idiot, he yelled. For Christ's sake what's the matter with you, are you deaf?

– My fault, called the SAK politely. Sorry, I thought you meant me.

– You needn't bloody move till I've gone you needn't, Jacko roared. Then you can jump in the bleeding sea. Get back out of the way you brainless sod. All right, again now . . . wait . . . wait . . . and . . . Jump!

The rough surface of the concrete platform was wet and hard to be jerked on to face down.

– Morning, said the fair-haired man in the donkey-jacket, mildly. Thought perhaps you'd decided you didn't want to stop.

– Good lad, said Alf. Nothing to it, is there? Bob, this is Tawney: Tawney, this is Bob. Well we'll not hang about down here, we don't want to be in the way. First thing to do now is go up and help Stan.

He set off up the steeply winding narrow steps. After the first hundred had been climbed he stopped, panting.

– You get a good view from here, he said.

Down in the gully, the SAK had got aboard the rowing boat. The net with his baggage had been lowered into it and emptied; he and Ernie and Cyril were putting the first load of cardboard cartons in it. Looking down, Alf watched them critically. Jacko jerked on the rope as a signal: it tightened, then the net with the cartons began to rise in the air above the boat and start its journey up the rock.

– Lovely, said Alf. He's good on the rope, is Stan. We'd best not hang about though; come on, let's get up to the top and give him a hand.

Another hundred steps and he stopped again, gasping.

– Have a look yonder, he said, pointing to the horizon. You can't see much today, too muggy. When it's nice there's some little islands out there, sometimes they'll stand clear up out of the water. They look so near you'd think you could almost touch them. Ah well come on. Stan'll be waiting for us; we mustn't leave it all to him.

After the third hundred steps, Alf stopped and slumped down breathless and wheezing.

– There's three hundred and fifty two of these buggers, he said. Feels like you're climbing bloody Everest. No point in killing yourself Tawney, let's stop here for a bit of a rest. He's very good on the rope is Stan, he'll manage all right on his own.

He breathed in and out deeply, getting his breath back slowly and looking out over the sea. The clouds were going away and the sky was beginning to brighten and turn blue.

– When I was that SAK's age you know, I was up and down here three or four times a day. Used to do it for exercise. But that was a long time ago, Tawney, a long time ago. Feel it more when you get older; I reckon I've had it now, I've gone past my best. Nice, the view from up here. Specially on a good day, makes you feel like you're on top of the world. You can't see nothing or nobody when you sit here: when the sun's shining it's grand. Ah well, suppose we'd better get on.

The steps came up out on to a flat plateau of stony ground. In the middle of it the lighthouse and its square of surrounding buildings stood white and gleaming. A few yards away from the top of the steps was a small hut with the machinery for operating the winch inside it. There was a large pile of cartons by it, and the net was coming up into view with more. Waving acknowledgement to the man in the hut, Alf stepped forward to steady the load as it swung to the ground.

The net sagged loose, and he dragged out his canvas gripbag, the wooden box with the metal handles and the squashed cardboard carton. He took a penknife out of his pocket and cut its string. When he opened it, inside the lid on top of the other contents were six papier-mâché egg-containers crushed together into one glutinous dripping yellow pulp.

He took them out slowly, holding them at arm's length and dropping them one by one to the ground. He scratched the back of his neck and looked at them.

– Well I'm buggered, he said. Now how the bloody hell did that come about?

A tall grey-haired man in overalls came out of the hut and walked over and shook hands.

– Hello, he said. Morning, Alf; I've told you before, we get a bit bored with omelettes you know if we eat nothing else all the time.

(1st day Thursday, 11 p.m.)

Finally to have arrived, actually to be here at last; strangely, it doesn't feel strange. While they were happening the days spent hanging about ashore watching the weather and hoping it was going to improve seemed interminable; apart from the time spent tape-recording conversations, they felt like a kind of endurance test. But I wasn't aware of their value as an informative beginning; and more importantly as a useful mental preparation. I'd have been sick in the boat if I hadn't been preoccupied with satisfaction that at last I was on the way.

In the small community of the cottages, being at close quarters with people whose lives revolve almost entirely round the rock, the mental impression being created wasn't obvious. It only became apparent after arrival that it didn't seem alien; the place Paul regrets leaving, Bob looks forward to coming back to, and Stanley puts up with.

Paul had shown me plans of the buildings and photographs he had taken; they are roughly as I expected, but more spacious inside. Apart from the fact they're perched on top of a high rock in the sea, the first impression was of similarity in appearance to the land light in general arrangement but with less living accommodation. The main block is in the shape of a capital 'T' with the entrance at the foot of the upright. The lighthouse tower rises above the junction with the bar across the top; the corridor under it leads to the bedrooms and sitting room in one direction and to the kitchen in the other. Engines and generators are in outbuildings, the whole complex surrounded by a wall.

All more or less as I imagined, so no great feeling of unexpectedness then. More importantly the two keepers already here don't seem like complete strangers: an impression of them already from the people in the cottages ashore. Stanley is taller and thinner than imagined, and not a very close resemblance between Bob and Steve McQueen. Both quietly spoken: they move about very slowly, presumably the result of having been here already for a month.

I'd heard little about Alf apart from the few cryptic remarks: they obviously left a great deal unsaid. After the journey together in the boat he didn't seem a total stranger either. Someone who takes his false teeth out discards some conventional social barriers.

He was in great discomfort in the boat: not asking for sympathy or making any pretence that he was hardened. He accepted his lack of dignity with dignity. During the exhausting climb up the steps after we'd landed, it was strange how his spirits lifted and his personality seemed to expand; and somehow there was more to it than relief at being on land. During one of the halts for rest he said he'd gone past his best: but even as he was saying it, it seemed a contradiction of him mentally.

A jumble of impressions, many things happening, much said; awareness that things were going on even though something different appeared to be happening or being said.

Winched up, the cartons and luggage were loaded on to a trolley; it took several journeys to get them over to the main entrance. Bob appeared up the steps eventually and lent a hand. At no time did Stan display any interest in the arrival or departure of the boats, or go near the edge of the plateau to watch. A glimpse of them in the distance in the sea as they were heading back towards the shore. Neither Stan nor Bob gave them so much as a glance.

The cartons were stacked inside the door in the hallway. Most contained Alf's food and mine, some were extra provisions for Stan and Bob. The meaning of Stan's 'we' in the mild joke about the omelettes became clear; the eggs Alf had sat on were not only his own but what should have been a further supply for everyone.

No one unduly annoyed about it. Alf put the blame on his own clumsiness, making no reference to the way the rowing boat had been rocking about in the gully. Bob and Stan kept reassuring him it wasn't important: they referred jokingly to occasions they'd done something similar themselves. A sense of mutual comradeship being asserted.

No immediate unpacking of cartons to see if there'd been any other damage during the journey. Outer clothing taken off and hung up in the hall; Stan and Bob took off their gumboots and changed into slippers which were inside the entrance door. We went on down the corridor and turned left to the kitchen.

Its cream coloured walls bare and impersonal; it could be an ordinary kitchen anywhere. Spacious, light and airy, big windows in two of the walls. A stainless steel sink with a double draining board, a big electric cooker, massive refrigerator, small anthracite boiler, red formica topped table in the middle with kitchen chairs. Low cupboards, all formica topped, round the walls. Floor white and green plastic tiles. It looks like what it is: a plain modernly equipped labour-saving kitchen.

Cups, teaspoons, milk jug on the table ready, sugar in a bag and a packet of biscuits. Kettle simmering on the cooker: Bob brewed the tea, Stan poured it out. No saucers, no sugar bowl, no plates. Tea hot and strong, with the flat taste of reconstituted powdered milk. After the cold wet uncomfortable boat journey, it was reviving.

The only thing brought in immediately from the luggage was a small waterproof bag. Stan opened it and took out an assortment of envelopes. Most of them official-looking ones addressed to the Principal Keeper. He put them aside to be looked at later. He and Bob tore open and read in silence the thick long letters their wives had sent. Alf gulped down three cups of tea in quick succession saying 'That feels much better now' after each one.

Desultory conversation, Stan and Bob exchanging details of domestic news. Alf making joking remarks about the boat trip, saying the extra weight of me and my luggage had made Jacko go round the rock twice before he could find a channel deep enough to bring us in. He asked who was cook for the day. Bob said he was and Alf looked anxious.

– You've not cooked dinner for me have you?

– No of course I haven't.

– No, good. Can't eat anything the first few days after I come you see, Tawney. It's the journey, upsets my tummy. Who's on the middle watch tonight?

– You are, said Stan. I've switched the turns round.

– Oh ta, thanks. Don't go to bed the first couple of nights either, Tawney. Takes me a while to get over it, I stop up all night and make myself useful round the place instead.

– What he's saying is when he gets here we might just as well take a holiday, said Bob.

– That's right, said Alf. It is, it's quite right is that.

Stan was immersed in reading his letter. Bob folded his up carefully, tucked it in the pocket of his overalls, and rolled himself a thin cigarette between his fingers. When he had lit it he tilted his chair, rocking slowly backwards and forwards on its back legs. A small tattoo on his left forearm; 'The Saint' symbol, a matchstick figure with a halo. He blew out a stream of smoke, tapping his fingers, whistling tunelessly. Stan finished his letter and turned back to the beginning of it; suddenly aware of Bob's behaviour he glanced up, gave a slight smile and shrug, and put the letter away.

– Sorry. Right well, yes.

– Tell us something about it then, said Bob. You know, like put us in the picture and tell us what you're up to.

Explained what I was trying to do, how it came about I was there and why, how I liked to work. Stan nodded his head from time to time, occasionally asked a question. Alf said 'Yes, I see, I've got it now' at one point and 'Sounds a rum sort of idea' at another. Bob said nothing: he looked over the top of my head all the time out of the window, tilting his chair up and down. When I said I hoped they might be willing to tape-record conversations, he lowered his gaze sudddenly and gave me a sharp look.

Very conscious as somebody at the cottages said that this was their home. I was there not at their invitation but because Trinity House had said I could be. Trinity House, however, would not influence whether they chose to talk to me or not. This was a matter for them personally, I said. If in the meantime they wanted to see the sort of thing I'd done previously, I'd brought two of my books and would leave them lying around. One was about a psychiatric prison, the other interviews with some unmarried mothers. Bob grinned.

– Bags me first for that one, he said.

When it had been talked about and anything in the nature of a decision by anyone had been avoided, I asked Stan what to do about cooking my food.

– Good Lord, he said. What makes you ask that? We'll do the cooking for you: one more doesn't make much of a difference. Table's got four sides to it. Only thing we want to know is which you're better at, drying or washing-up?

The cartons were unpacked. Tinned food and packets put

in the pantry cupboard in the corner of the kitchen. Not much effort to separate one person's from another's. Vegetables and fresh fruit in a wire rack, meat in the fridge. A long discussion about which of it would keep longest and what order it should be eaten in on different days. Alf made another pot of tea and sat drinking it; Bob began to peel potatoes in preparation for lunch.

Got my luggage and Stan took me along the other corridor. The first door off it was to the sitting-room; small and cramped because most of the space was taken up by a table against the wall, with a radio transmitter above it. A television set in the corner, three wooden-armed easy chairs in front of it in a row.

At the end of the corridor the bathroom and a separate toilet; other doors off it to individual bedrooms, all presumably basically the same as mine in size and shape. It has a window at one end, bare wooden floor, a central-heating radiator, cupboards for clothing, a mattress on a low divan along one wall. If I wanted extra blankets to put on top of my sleeping bag, said Stan, there's no shortage of them. This room had previously been occupied by the SAK. 'He didn't do a very good job of sweeping it out before he went' Stan said disapprovingly, seeing a cigarette-end on the floor.

As he was going out of the door he stopped.

– Margaret says she's well in her letter. You saw her often while you were ashore waiting. How is she, I mean really? What was your impression? Does she seem to be managing all right?

Dinner at half past twelve: pork chops, mountains of carrots, tinned peas, tinned tomatoes and mashed potato, gravy. Afterwards tinned treacle pudding and custard. Alf ate nothing; he sat continuously drinking tea. He turned his chair away from the table so he didn't have to look at the food.

When the washing-up was done, he said he felt rotten and was going to bed, and disappeared. Stan and Bob settled down to several games of cribbage; Bob won them all with evident relish. Stan looked as though he was struggling to concentrate, shrugging his shoulders each time he lost.

– You play this? We'll have to teach you, it'll make a change for Bob to have someone else to beat.

In the afternoon went outside for some fresh air; looked round the sheds at the engines and generators. A huge red fog horn on a concrete dais behind the buildings, pointing out to sea above the surrounding wall. The wind cold and blowing hard: the sky blue and clear with large cumulonimbus clouds out over the sea. Darker towards the land. Looking towards it, hard to grasp I'd been there only a few hours earlier. It seemed remote and unreal, completely detached by distance and time. If that feeling comes so quickly at the beginning it's understandable why to Stan the arrival and departure of the boat in the middle of the two-month turn-off is not of much interest and its return to the shore better ignored.

At about half past four went back in the kitchen: Stan was on his own. Bob had been up since four in the morning and had gone to have a sleep. Stan made a pot of tea; at the sound of the rattling of teacups Alf appeared, saying he felt worse lying down than he did walking about, and anyway he could do with another cup of tea. After we'd drunk it Stan asked me if I'd like to go up the tower with him and see how the light worked.

The tower is fifty feet high: being on top of the rock this makes the light about a hundred and fifty feet above the sea. Like the land light, everything inside is spotlessly clean; the stairs, the brass handrails, the cogwheels and shafts of the machinery. The illuminant is two banks of what look like motor-car head-lamps back to back; sixteen of them on each side arranged in rows of four. A switch is pressed to light them, another to make them turn: as simple as that. From inside the light is seen as it really is: a straight beam of light revolving. From the distance it's only visible while it points straight at you, therefore it looks as though it's flashing. The glass of the lantern is plain plate glass.

Stan explained in detail how it worked. I nodded and made understanding noises at what I hoped were the right times. He shone a flashlamp round, read the thermometer on the gallery outside the glass, took the inside temperature from one inside, looked at the barometer. When we came down into the sitting-room he entered the figures in the log book, turning back for a quick look in the front of it first.

– Any questions you want to ask anytime you're here, don't hesitate if there's anything at all you want to know.

– A couple of things about what you've just been doing. As you didn't go outside on the gallery, how do you know the wind direction and force?

– The direction, there's a weather-vane dial in the roof of the tower; you probably didn't see me shine the torch at it. The force you can tell by the noise against the glass; it was humming when we were up there, so that's Force 5. When it gets up to 6, 7 and 8 each one's got a different pitch, you notice it automatically.

– The other thing is that in the column headed 'Light Exhibited' you've written 16.52. How can you be specific about the exact time?

He laughed.

– That's sunset time, the official time for lighting it.

– I didn't see you looking at a watch and timing it to the minute.

– Trinity House is famous throughout the world for its reliability and accuracy. We've got the sunrise and sunset times on a newspaper cutting: we keep it in the front of the log-book and enter them up from that.

The only set mealtime is dinnertime, at twelve-thirty. Who-ever's cook for the day prepares it for everyone. Otherwise you eat what you like when you feel like it. About once every two hours someone brews a pot of tea; in between people make themselves cups of coffee. A sort of general teatime about half past five or six. Stan says he always has something to eat then, a snack like beans on toast. 'Or an egg when we've got any.' He explained this while eating; also that it's taken for granted that you wash and dry-up and put away everything you use as soon as you've finished.

The boiler heats the water. There's always plenty: for the central heating, washing-up, and for four people to have a bath a day if they want one. In the bathroom there are no toothbrushes, face flannels, razors, towels or pieces of soap; each man keeps his own things in his own room. You wash your own clothes. In short each man looks after himself.

Bob got up at seven o'clock and spent most of the evening watching a war film on television. Noticed he'd been looking at the book about the psychiatric prison; it was on the floor by his chair.

As he'd been on the middle watch last night and will get up at four tomorrow morning, Stan went to bed about nine o'clock. Alf wandered around unable to settle: he kept 'going to have a lie down', and reappearing half an hour later to make more tea. Have the feeling he hasn't got much in common with either Stan or Bob; not that they're on bad terms, but when he's ashore he's not at the cottages and part of that community.

Tired after an eventful day; got into my sleeping bag on the lumpy mattress at about half past ten. The room is warm because of the radiator, but garish because of the unshaded light-bulb hanging in the middle of the ceiling. The wind sounds brisk outside; the noise of the sea breaking against the rock sounds far away below.

Will take the subject of tape-recording conversations as and when it comes up with each person: no hurry about it. To make a guess I'd say Bob is least likely to agree, Stan most likely. As for Alf I couldn't guess at all: know nothing whatever about him and he may prefer to keep it like that.

*

(2nd day Friday, 9 p.m.)

Stan cook for the day. Told him I hoped as far as possible he'd try to ignore my presence and carry on with usual activities so I could watch the routine of an ordinary day. 'I'm afraid you'll find it dull and uninteresting,' he said. 'Every day's an ordinary day, there's not much difference between one and the next.' An impossible request for him to comply with: but he said he'd do his best.

Throughout what struck me most was the slow pace at which everything's done. Nobody's short of time; things are deliberately spun out to make them last. Everyone speaks slowly, moves slowly, eats and drinks slowly; markedly, with deliberate effort.

Very noticeable is the absent minded obsessive concern with the minute trivia of domesticity. Seeing a teaspoon lying on the table after a cup of tea has been stirred with it, someone will automatically pick it up, rinse it under the tap, get a tea towel and dry it, and put it back in the drawer. If there's a tiny smear of butter on the table, he'll wipe the surface clean, wash and wring out the cloth and polish off the table top. While carrying on a conversation and not with any suggestion it's a chore; simply to occupy himself.

An apotheosis of it after dinner. When the washing-up was done Stan dismantled the cooker and washed every detachable part of it thoroughly in soapy water: dried them, reassembled the cooker, wiped it down, and gave it a final careful polish with a duster. What he'd been cooking had not boiled-over or dirtied it. Merely to do something to occupy himself with. Asked him how often he did it; 'Every third day when I'm cook. But the other others aren't so particular.' He wasn't criticising them: he said it with a self-mocking smile.

The day centres round the kitchen so whoever's cook becomes the central figure of the day. Stan was a great help in conveying the slowness of pace. No forced conversation; exchanged remarks now and again, but long periods of silence accepted without embarrassment. Bob was occupied most of the morning out in one of the engine sheds. He came in occasionally, Alf appeared from time to time but what he was doing in between wasn't apparent. Presence beginning to be taken for granted. The first few times they gave me a word of greeting, but soon stopped bothering.

Stan said ask questions about anything I wanted to know. I did through the day. He answered them in detail, on occasions going to fetch papers or notebooks rather than relying on his memory.

He wanted to make sure what he was saying was right, he said; a man who likes to be correct. He became amusedly interested in checking his memory about things he took for granted.

What food in what amounts he brought off with him for a two-month stay. He recited the list and I recorded it to get him accustomed to the tape-recorder and to speaking in an ordinary voice while it was running.

When he'd finished he got out the copy of the written order he put in at the grocery store each time, and asked me to play back the recording so he could check if he'd forgotten anything. He hadn't. He'd itemized the list in identically the same order it was written out; that pleased him.

Supplies for 56 days. 2 lbs. tea; 1 box (72) tea-bags; 2 jars (18 oz. each) instant coffee; 6 large tins powdered milk; 16 lbs. sugar; 4 lbs. butter; 2 lbs. margarine; 1½ lbs. cooking fat; 2 uncut loaves; 6 lbs. plain flour; 4 lbs. self-raising flour; 56 lbs. potatoes; 26 lbs. carrots; 2 large cabbage; 2½ lbs. fresh tomatoes; 4 lbs. cheddar cheese; 24 Oxo cubes; 2 lbs. rice; 8 lbs. jam; 4 lbs. marmalade; 8 pkts. cracker biscuits, 4 lbs. bacon; 24 eggs; 3 pkts. soap powder (large); 4 tablets toilet soap; 8 toilet rolls; 4 tubes toothpaste; 8 pkts. sweet biscuits; 1 tube mustard; 2 jars pickle; 4 pkts. cereal; 2 boxes (12 assorted) cheese spread; 4 lbs. onions; 24 tins peas; 24 tins broad beans; 24 tins baked beans; 24 tins carrots; 2 lbs. fresh sausages; 12 tins sausages; 36 asst. small tins spaghetti, macaroni, snacks etc; 6 tins corned beef; 12 tins minced beef; 24 tins stewing steak; 6 tins plums; 6 tins pineapple; 6 tins strawberries; 6 tins fruit salad; 5 lbs. cooking apples; 5 lbs. eating apples; 2 tins syrup (2 lbs.); 6 tins luncheon meat; 12 small bars chocolate; 18 boxes matches; 1,000 cigarettes; 12 asst. tins soup; 12 tins tomatoes; 12 oranges; 6 unripe grape-fruit; 1 drum salt; 1 drum pepper; 2 bottles sauce; 2 lbs. fresh steak; 4 lamb chops.

Fresh meat vegetables and fruit in small quantities because they won't keep long. For the first week eating is 'nearly normal'; after that it's almost entirely out of tins. They bake their own bread. Towards the end of the first month if he is beginning to get short of something he sends a radio message asking the keeper coming out on relief to bring further supplies. Margaret baked two large fruit cakes for him to bring.

He said yes, rather a monotonous diet. 'Years ago' as ideas occurred to him he added later items to the list like chocolate and grapefruit. Now he was bothering less about it.

What clothing he brought out each time, would I be interested in that? 'I don't need it written down on a list, I could pack my kit with my eyes shut. If I've forgotten anything, even something light like a pair of slippers, as soon as I pick the bag up I can tell by the weight.'

Clothing and personal gear. 4 pairs of underpants, 4 vests,

2 pairs of pyjamas, 6 pairs of socks, 4 working shirts, 2 nice shirts, 2 pullovers, 1 pair of working trousers, 2 pairs of comfortable casual trousers, 12 handkerchiefs, 1 light jacket, 1 pair of slippers, 2 towels, 1 facecloth, 1 hairbrush, 1 comb, 1 razor, shaving-soap, 1 bottle of hair shampoo, 3 packets of razor blades, a tin of lighter fuel, a packet of throat pastilles, a nail file, a pair of toenail cutters, a sponge bag.

Aspirin, sticking-plaster, indigestion powder, laxative? 'No, those come in the category of "First Aid", they're in the station kit issued by Trinity.'

I mentioned that when we'd been recording the grocery list washing-up liquid hadn't been included; and wasn't used. Incongruous in that well equipped kitchen to see them swishing round an old tin with nail holes and bits of soap inside in the washing-up water. 'A very grave matter that is,' Stan said. 'All cleaning equipment is provided by Trinity House. We say it should include washing-up liquid; they say it's for the personal benefit of the keepers so if they want it they must buy their own. The argument's raging throughout the service; there's even talk the Elder Brethren are going to appoint a special committee to look into it. A decision's expected any time within the next few years. Outsiders like yourself have got no idea of the problems we face.'

Bob's afternoon watch began at four o'clock. Knowing the call round to test the receivers and transmitters in the group was at half past four, asked him if I could record it. Bob sat at the table in the sitting-room in front of the transmitter; Stan explained what was going to happen.

The test centres on the coastguard radio at End Point: the six rock and tower lighthouses in the area take part, not shore stations. They identify by their call signs: Victor, Delta, Charlie, Alfa, Oscar, Tango.

A minute before half past four, Bob switched on the transmitter. The test began with a three-minute listening-in period of silence. All receivers were tuned to the same longwave band used for distress signals by shipping. The waiting was to make sure it was clear for the test. Exactly three minutes after half past four the voice of the operator at the coastguard station came crackling through the receiver, followed in rapid succession by the replies.

Telegraph, Coastguard, End Point calling the group, Coastguard End Point calling the group, how do you read please, over.

– End Point, Victor, going down.

– End point, Delta, going down.

– End Point, Charlie, going down.

Bob pressed the transmitting switch.

– End Point, Alfa, going down.

He released it again.

– End Point, Oscar, going down.

– End Point, Tango, going down.

'Going down' meant having established the distress call wavelength was functioning, the operators were then going to tune to a known different wavelength for all further conversation. Bob turned the dial on the transmitter, waiting for his turn to speak; the order was prearranged and always the same. Again the coastguard went round them in turn.

– Good afternoon, the group. Victor Victor Victor, from End Point, how do you receive me please, over?

– End Point, End Point coastguard, Victor replying, good afternoon to you, you're coming in loud and clear, how do you read me?

– Loud and clear Victor thank you. Delta, Delta, good afternoon, End Point here, are you receiving me, over?

– End Point, Delta, replying, yes, good afternoon. Well not a very good afternoon out here at the moment, sea's breaking over the top of us but nothing else to report, over.

– Cheers Delta, coming through loud and clear all the same thank you. End Point to Charlie, End Point to Charlie, how do you hear me, over?

– End Point, End Point, Charlie here, getting you loud and clear, good luck Delta, over.

– Thank you Charlie. End Point to Alfa, End Point to Alfa, good afternoon Alfa, are you receiving me, over?

Bob flicked the transmitter switch again.

– Alfa replying, good afternoon Brian, yes receiving you well, over.

– Thank you Bob. Oscar, Oscar, Oscar, End Point to Oscar, come in please.

– End Point this is Oscar, Oscar here. Bit of a sea with us today too, grin and bear it Delta, over.

– End Point to Tango, how are you receiving please Tango, over?

– Tango, Tango to End Point, you're loud and clear on both wavelengths, are you receiving me on this one, over?

– End Point, yes Tango, thank you, reception good on both. Cheerio the group, best wishes Delta and Oscar, End Point over and out.

Some of the voices were indistinct and almost inaudible, others very clear. Nothing to do with the weather conditions round the different lighthouses, Stan explained; it depends on their geographical situation in relation to where we were and on local atmospherics.

He and Bob listened intently to the recording when it was replayed.

– Christ, said Bob. I'd no idea my voice sounded like that. Does it really sound like that to you?

– Exactly like that, Stan said. That's nothing, you want to hear mine.

Bob said he did. Played back Stan's list of his provisions and clothing, and continued to the end of the recording of the radio test. They were as intrigued by the recordings as I'd been at hearing voices from lighthouses in an area of over a thousand square miles.

Alf's absence is as noticeable as his presence. Have hardly seen him all day; he's spent most of it in his room. He's come in the kitchen and made himself tea, then taken it back into his room. His period of watch today was between four this afternoon and eight this evening; during it he should have done the radio test and lit the light. Bob did both; no mention of the fact they were not his responsibility.

The wind rising steadily. Went up inside the gallery of the tower about six o'clock; the difference in the sound of it against the glass obvious, though it wouldn't have been if I hadn't listened because of what Stan said. Last night it was humming, tonight it was higher pitched and making the glass shake.

Seeing the recorder when I went back in the kitchen Bob asked what I'd been doing: when I said I'd been recording the noise of the wind he said he'd like to hear it. He wanted to know how to operate the recorder. 'I like learning how to use things,' he said. After I'd shown him he clowned about doing interviews with me and Stan and playing them back. By the time they'd finished both were much more at ease with the recorder.

Stan brought a Trinity House pamphlet into the kitchen while Bob and he were drinking tea, with details of victualling money and rock money which are in addition to basic salary, and rent allowances.

– Victualling money is paid to keepers on rock lights but not land lights, 'rocks' being a generic term which includes towers, towards the cost of the food they buy to take off with them. 60p a day for each day they are actually on the rock or tower. If a relief is overdue and they can't get ashore, it's paid for the extra days; and if they're ashore and can't get off it's paid from the day the relief is actually due.

Rock money is an additional daily allowance but with a division between the different types. 60p a day for towers, 48p a day for less spacious island rocks such as this, and 36p a day for large islands which have their own population and are not greatly different from the mainland. One or two land lights are so isolated they are classified as 'rocks' and keepers on them receive an allowance.

Assistant and Principal Keepers have a house provided if one is attached to the station they're at; free local council accommodation if not; or 89p a day rent allowance. Towards rent, SAK's receive 39p a day if single, 50p a day if married, but only when they are not actually on a lighthouse.

Asked Bob to read it out and record it all. When it was played back he said 'Well I suppose if that's what I sound like, that's what I sound like, but you could have bloody fooled me.'

As well as an impression of an ordinary day, I've been given a lot of information. Both Stan and Bob have got completely used to a tape-recorder: they've handled it and made recordings.

I've picked up some of their attitude; a lessening anxiety to get on with doing things. The fact nobody shows impatience to be interviewed is as important as that they haven't said they won't be. No one bothers about trying to impress their personality.

Seeing the light on in my room, Bob tapped on the door a few minutes ago. 'Have you brought any more books like that prison one with you?' No, only the one with interviews with unmarried mothers. 'Alf's still got that, he hasn't finished it yet. I enjoyed that prison one by the way,' he said.

*

(3rd day Saturday, 8 p.m.)
Bob's day in more senses than one, and not over yet. He was up late. There's a board on the wall near the kitchen door; before you go to bed at night you chalk on it what time you want to be woken up by whoever's on morning watch. He'd been on

the middle watch, and had put that he wanted to be called at 10.0 a.m. Alf ('Feeling much more like my old self this morning, Tawney') was morning watch man and knocked on his door: Bob had a bath, cooked himself breakfast of tinned sausage, tinned tomatoes and baked beans, then said 'The rest of today's easy for me, what would you like to do?' Whatever he liked. 'All right then, show you a few things, talk to you about a few things, O.K.?'

He took me on a tour of the engine sheds and generators. As technical in his explanations as Stan had been about the light; miasmically responsive and struggling to understand, the puzzle was not how they worked but what they were for. Mostly to generate electricity for the light, for the machinery which makes it revolve, domestic purposes, for the power for a radio beacon used as a directional aid for shipping. And for the fog-horn. How did that work? He'd demonstrate. 'If you like, let's try and make some recordings of it.'

One of the engines produces compressed air: this goes into metal tanks in a building under the fog horn. Bob scampered about opening and closing valves, then started the timing mechanism. Every thirty seconds the horn emitted a shattering bellow: the fact it was during broad daylight with not a wisp of fog anywhere to be seen didn't bother him. 'It doesn't matter: it's supposed to be tested once a week.'

Trying to record it proved a failure; the volume of noise was too great. Bob made several attempts himself and also failed.

He takes pride in his knowledge of the machinery of the engines and explained them with something approaching affection. That he's mastered the technicalities gives him great satisfaction. Stan's explanation of how the light worked had been dispassionate, as though he was taking a technical college class: Bob's of the engines was more personal, like someone demonstrating his new car.

Alf was cook. Dinner was the usual meat and masses of vegetables and tinned steamed pudding; today he ate for the first time himself since his arrival.

Bob was looking through a magazine Alf had brought. He read out a joke about a yachtsman who sent out a radio distress signal. The coastguard receiving it radioed 'What is your position?' The yachtsman radioed back 'Company Director'. Bob said: 'I bet it could be true, I can imagine that type of person.'

'Show you some other things this afternoon.' He went into the sitting-room; thought I was in for a demonstration of the radio transmitter perhaps, but wasn't. Instead he showed me the 'State of Weather' descriptions issued by Trinity House, used in the weather log when it's entered every three hours. Eighteen different categories. Fine distinctions to a landsman: the difference between 'Cloudy' and 'Overcast' is that a cloudy sky is one in which blueness or greyness can be seen between clouds, whereas if it's overcast the clouds are not detached from one another.

This was another personally satisfying demonstration: he said 'Give me a test, ask me some questions to see how many I get right.' What does 'Z' stand for? 'Haze.' What's the letter used to denote squally conditions? 'Q.' He knew it by heart.

This led to general talk about weather and weather conditions, and the meaning of the jargon of shipping forecasts. He described it simply and recorded it on tape.

– In the weather forecasts a wind that's 'backing' is one starting to turn in an anti-clockwise direction and means poorer weather's on the way. 'Veering' is when the wind's moving clockwise, and in general is going to bring better conditions. An 'anticyclone' or 'high' is made up of subsiding air and means clearing skies; a 'depression' or 'low' is ascending air and it's a bad weather system.

Very interesting, weather. The more you study it, the more there is to learn. I've got two or three books about it; got quite interested in it since I joined the Service. Morse code, that's another thing I've learned. And how lights are described by navigators: lighthouses, buoys and things.

A 'fixed light' is continuous and steady. 'Flashing' means the periods of light are less than the dark intervals between. 'Occulting' that the light periods are longer than the dark intervals. An 'Isophase' is one which has light and dark periods that are equal. 'Alternating' means different-coloured flashes.

Later in the afternoon he asked if I'd like to go with him and see if he could catch 'a couple of nice pollack for our teas'. We went down the steps to the concrete landing platform. 'Come on'; he climbed under the safety railings and went along the rock just above the water to the far end of it. Out of the shelter of the gully round there, the waves were crashing unhindered against the rock from the sea. A protracted wetting climb until we reached a narrow fissure with a small hollow. Sixty feet deep the water below, he said: the best place for fishing from on the whole rock. We stood in a space about two square feet, the waves breaking behind, their force carrying the spray whirling clear high in the air.

He cast with a powerful jerk of his arms on his long rod, standing with his feet planted apart a foot from the edge of the drop into the water. He used a lead weight and feathers on the line and lost four feathers and two weights in the first ten minutes. 'Sea's running a bit too strong.' A red rubber imitation eel on the hook instead; flicking out the line, reeling in when the sea dragged it out too far. Repeated casting; no results. Once when a particularly heavy wave crashed into the rock behind and a huge cascade of spray went flying over, he glanced up with a smile. 'Good, eh?' On another occasion laughing: 'Nothing to beat it you know, this is the life.'

In an hour he caught nothing. 'That's it then, no luck today.'

We came back up the steps. The sense of a man occupying himself intently with intense enjoyment. Not catching anything was unimportant. Back up the steps without pause or effort on his part.

In the kitchen making tea and toast he said: 'Doing nothing after my watch finishes at eight o'clock, go and have a chat in my room after that then, shall we?'

*

(4th day Sunday, 10 p.m.)

Up late. Bob's day as cook, joking about roast beef and Yorkshire pudding he was going to make for dinner. It was stewed steak: and Yorkshire pudding most of which Alf ate.

Bob did a lot of cleaning today: mopping the floors of the corridors and rooms, taking up rugs, piling chairs on tables, dusting. Nothing ever has the chance to get dirty: this was another time passing occupation, not a vital necessity.

All the newspapers Alf brought with him were at least a week old, and some considerably more. Each carefully read page by page by Stan and Bob. Alf's interest in them is the crossword puzzles. 'I save them up while I'm ashore and bring them off when I come. Till I've finished one, I don't start on the next; that way it spaces them out you see, Tawney.'

Sunday is a working day, the same as any other. Stan and Alf spent most of it on radio beacon maintenance, doing something to or with the batteries, and oiling and cleaning the generators.

Wind very strong. Went out this afternoon and climbed down from the top of the rock to what looked as though it might be a sheltered place to sit and look out over the sea, and found Alf there doing just that. 'Hours I spend here' he said, 'you know, just sitting and looking. Either here or round the other side of the steps, but it's too windy that side today.' Did he read, snooze, or merely sit? 'Oh no, just sit and look and enjoy it; I wouldn't want to spoil it with reading or going to sleep. Mind you, I like a good read, I'm a big reader. But not outside, I can't concentrate.'

Nobody spends much time in the sitting-room and there's little television watching. The communal room is the kitchen; if you want conversation that's where you go. If you want to be on your own, you go into your bedroom; nobody disturbs you, it's strictly private territory. A constant series of withdrawals for brief periods by all, at some time or another throughout the day. Not meant or regarded as being unsociable.

In the particular direction it's in, the wind is blowing straight into the end of the toilet outlet pipe down at the bottom of the rock near the sea. Have never seen a toilet with a swell on the water in it before. Mentioned it at teatime. Bob said 'You want to try sitting on it with a Force 10 blowing; you have to wear your lifejacket when you go and have a shit.'

Refuse disposal. Empty tin cans, packets, vegetable peelings, everything: all go into a plastic dustbin in the corridor. Today it was full. Bob spread sheets of newspaper on the kitchen floor and divided it into five heaps. Then he went outside and came back with five large lumps of rock. These were wrapped in with the rubbish, one to each parcel. Outside at the edge of the rock facing seawards, he hurled them down towards the water. The rocks weren't to make the parcels sink, they disintegrated before they reached the sea. They were to make the parcels throwable against the wind: otherwise the rubbish would have blown back into the lighthouse yard.

A discussion round the kitchen table in the afternoon about lighthouse keepers' hours of work in comparison with other jobs. 'When you tell people you get a month's leave every third month their first reaction is "Four months' holiday a year, bloody hell that sounds cushy",' said Bob.

'They don't know what they're talking about then,' Alf said: 'We spend eight months solid on duty, which is more working time in a year if it's added up than people who do a five-day week.'

Stan said 'We do a seven-day week for eight weeks in succession, but we're not on duty all the time so I reckon it about evens out.'

We got a piece of paper to work it out.

In other jobs time off is 52 weekends per year (104 days), plus 6 public holidays, plus 14 days' annual holiday; total 124 days. Subtracted from 365, that leaves 241 eight-hour working days; total 1928 hours work per year.

For keepers, watches duty over each period of three days and nights is 24 hours total on duty. This means a 56 hour week for 36 weeks of the year, and totals 2016 working hours. So it's 88 working hours more per year than a five-day-a-week man, not including extra working time during overdue reliefs or time spent on domestic duties on the day you're cook.

'And the other thing is you've got to be here all the time, you can't go home when you're not on duty' Bob said. They were interested in the arithmetic.

The subject of pay followed; Stan got another Trinity House leaflet with the figures.

An SAK gets about £20 a week. An AK starts at £21 a week plus a rent free house, rising to just over £23 a week; then remains at that until he becomes a PK. A PK starts at £25.50 per week, rising to about £30 a week, plus a house. Adding on the daily victualling and rock money while on duty, Stan said he got a total of about £45 a week while he was away, but paid for his own food out of it.

'Not a lot really when you come to look at it,' Bob said. 'No but not a little either,' Stan said. 'And no one could say it was hard work.'

Alf is on the middle watch tonight: he said 'That'll be as good a time as any for us to have our chat Tawney, eh?'

*

(6th day Tuesday, 6 p.m.)
Since the day after I arrived the wind increased steadily: by yesterday it was roaring across the plateau so fiercely you could lean on it. But it began to drop at last, last night. Little chance of getting ashore tomorrow as intended; 'too much sea' in the gully for a boat to get in. Went down to look this morning: like a cauldron, and with the water breaking over the landing platform.

Didn't make any notes yesterday, due to being up until four in the morning with Alf. Have done little today except chat inconsequentially. Stan asked if I'd like to have 'a talk' with him this evening.

*

(7th day Wednesday, 11 p.m.)
Cleaned out my room, but the boat couldn't get out today so I didn't go ashore. 'Overdue yourself now,' said Bob. 'Give you an impression what it feels like.'
Not really. The wind has dropped completely tonight and Stan says I'll be ashore tomorrow 'for certain'. Remember Margaret used the same expression when I was waiting to get here. One day's 'overdue' after a week's stay is not like it must feel after eight weeks.

Cook for today, Stan spent most of the morning defrosting the fridge. The same meticulous attention as he gave to cleaning the cooker: washing out the inside, drying it off carefully. He does it once a week he says.
Tired. Sitting in bed listening to the sea and wondering whether the boat will come tomorrow or whether it won't.

Writing on a Blackboard 15

A dozen books and a leather framed enlargement of a colour snapshot of Susie on a shelf over the bed; a half complete model of a tiny sailing ship near an empty whisky dimple bottle on a table under the window. He drew the curtains and switched on the bedside lamp in his room, and shut the door. The low easy chair was too small for him, but he lay nearly prone in it with his legs stretched out in front of him across the floor. Fair-haired and thin-faced; sometimes while he talked there was a faraway look in his pale blue eyes, and sometimes he nibbled thoughtfully at his fingernails. He held his tobacco tin on his lap and smoked roll-ups one after another.

– The wind's getting up now all right, looks like we're in for a blow. Force 8 when I did the log at six o'clock and it's gone higher since then. I had a bit of a struggle deciding whether to talk, you know. Must be some sort of measure how much the job's done for me, built up my self-confidence; six months ago I don't think I would have. Somehow this last year's proved something: to me I mean, inside myself. It might be asking for trouble to say it but I think I've turned the corner now.

It shook me at first when you came, I thought I'd have to make up a fairy-tale. But then I thought hell why should I, the past's over and done with. I saw you look at the tattoo, I read the book: so you know I've been in the nick.

The usual story, you must have heard it hundreds of times. Father and mother divorced; lived with my aunt, started getting into trouble when I was about eight, from then on she didn't want to know. In a children's home when I was twelve: remand homes, approved school, borstal, prison, I've done the lot. Always the same thing, thieving. Starting with little things, working my way up, learning like everyone else does the main thing is not to get caught. I wasn't very good at it: not good at thieving and no good at not getting caught.

Up till when I was eighteen I never put my mind to it seriously. It was a case of if I saw something lying around, I'd nick it. I hadn't thought of crime as a way of life, you might say. That only started after I'd been to borstal. Till then I thought the only thing wrong was I'd been unlucky getting caught. I met people there who helped start me thinking if you were serious about crime you had to put as much thought into it as you would any other career.

Most important of all was you had to begin at the other end. First you find out who wants what, and what price he'll give you for it. It's only when you've arranged that you go out and look around for what's required. You make your plans as to how you're going to get it: and if you do get it the stuff's not in your hands more than a few hours. I wasn't big time: mostly steady work breaking into stores and factories. And no violence, I never touched that; just thieving plain. I got nicked now and again, like anyone else. If you worked with a regular gang there was always the chance the Law'd hear a whisper. I did two short prison sentences; the longest was two years.

It's a bit of an effort for me: I mean to remember that person I'm talking about is me. That was the way of life, it was the only one there was; it never crossed my mind to try and do anything else. Mostly I was living in London around the East End; everyone I knew was involved in that sort of life.

Birds, girls, there was a succession of those. All same kind, criminals' girls: they looked after you, kept house for you, slept

with you, lived on the proceeds you earned. Then when you got
nicked they always said the same thing, they'd wait for you until
you came out. But they always did the same thing, which was
that they didn't.

Like other mugs, there was one I met who I thought was
different and I married her. At that time I was working with a
well-organized gang that never did any jobs in London, only
in the provinces. We were in, out, back in London and the stuff
passed on to whoever was handling it all inside a few hours.

I was married to this girl about four years: she wasn't what
you might call a faithful type, but I was potty about her. That's
not a good thing to be about any woman when you're in that
game. We split up, it was inevitable she went off with another
man. When I got my last sentence, when I came out I still hadn't
got over her. I'd got a bit of money but not much, and I started
wandering round the country on my own. Not thieving, just
trying to think about my situation and what I was going to do.
I'd got a feeling I had to stay away from London: if I'd gone
back I knew I'd be propositioned about another job. So I started
wandering round the coast from one town to the next.

One day I happened to go into a coffee bar; it was an afternoon
I'd nothing better to do. That was how I met Susie, she was a
waitress there. On the face of it it was ridiculous: I was a small-
time thief from London, wandering aimlessly about and she was
just a very pretty young innocent girl. She'd never even been
to London. I don't know to this day what it was about her; if
I sat here until relief day was the first Sunday after the twenty-
ninth of February, I still couldn't tell you what did it. I just
looked at her and knew she was the girl for me. Plain bloody
ridiculous: for a start I was ten years older than she was, let
alone everything else. And what could she know about someone
who'd led my kind of life that wouldn't make her run a mile
if I mentioned it?

It was like being in a kind of dream, I couldn't believe it was
me hanging round there, going back to the coffee bar to see if I

could get to know her. I thought about it, and I thought it was ridiculous. But I thought it was so ridiculous there was nothing to be lost if it didn't work; so the only thing to do was to put it to her straight, tell her what I was like, everything. I took it for granted a girl like her would tell me to push off.

I met her after work and took her out for a cup of tea, and I told her absolutely straight. That was the first time I'd ever been completely honest with anyone. I found myself saying things which up till then hadn't even crossed my mind, like wanting a chance to settle down and go straight. All the crap that criminals give straight people; but I really meant it.

She didn't bat an eyelid. She just said 'Yes I see' and 'Thank you for telling me' and 'Yes I'll go out with you', and that was it. Well there was one other thing she said as well. She said 'But if you ever so much as nick a teaspoon that's the finish. I shan't listen to any arguments and I shan't give you a chance: once more and that's the end.'

I've never lifted anything from anyone from that day to this, and I never would. It's just she asked that one thing of me: no thieving. I've never had money to throw around as I did in the days I was thieving, but what I have got is more important; I suppose I'd have to call it self respect. I stayed round to be there near Susie, I wrote to solicitors about a divorce, I got odd jobs driving vans, but mostly I was living on my savings and they were slowly disappearing.

By the time the divorce was through she was pregnant; that made no difference to either of us, we'd have got married anyway. I'm not sure she believed it then, but I think she does now. She lost the baby, then another one; Mandy when she came, obviously she's very special to us.

I got into the lighthouse service by a fluke, I happened to see an advert for it in the paper. What to a lot of people might have been the off-putting thing, being away from home, being on your own and not able to see anybody; well to somebody who's been in prison that's nothing. It doesn't worry me one bit: I miss

Susie and I miss being at home, but it's not like prison. You're proud of what you are. There aren't all that many lighthouse keepers around; you feel you're a bit special. I mean like authors, well they're ten a penny aren't they compared with lighthouse keepers? I think there's fewer of us even than there are members of the Royal Family, if you take all their relatives into account.

It was a bit dodgy about references when I put in for the job. We had to scrape round a bit, find a couple of people who'd got fixed addresses, but we managed it. The SAK training was hard and it went on a long time; longer than average compared with others I've talked to. Sometimes it's crossed my mind perhaps Trinity know a bit more than they've let on, and that's why they put me through the hoop, to see if I'd got it in me to last. When they made me up to AK, it seemed like they were saying I'd proved myself.

What they were giving me a chance to do was build a completely new life for myself; it was like someone had wiped off the writing on a blackboard and said 'Go on then, all that's forgotten; now start from the beginning again and let's see what you can put on that board.' Education: nil. Occupation: nil. Abilities: nil. You have to weigh up yourself and think what you can do: cut out fancy ideas you've had about yourself and start back from the beginning. You need to have something inside you that makes you able to live on your own.

If you have that sort of ability to start with, then whatever else comes has got to be something you put into it. If you want to make a lot of money then this isn't the job for you. But if you want something unusual and a bit exciting, that's one of the best things about lighthouse keeping: not exciting in the sense it's dangerous but it has got lots of things special about it. Like when I'm fishing off the end of the rock like we were this afternoon; it's not dangerous but it's that little bit unconventional. One of those big landowners, he'll have his own private lake to fish in; when I'm down there I've got my own private ocean for fishing, and how many people can say that?

And there's a lot of other things that go with the job. I can do all sorts of things that seven or eight years ago it wouldn't even have crossed my mind they existed. I know how generators work, I can look after them and keep them going. I could go on to a technical college if I ever wanted and learn how to be a proper engineer.

Or there's things like weather; if you are a keeper the weather's going to play a big part in your life so you study it a bit, it makes you feel you know what's going on around you. Morse code, that's something else: you don't need to know it but my view is if you've got the chance to learn you should take it, and the same with anything else. It makes the job more interesting, and you can't tell when these odd bits of things you know mightn't come in useful. It's like being offered a free education.

Then there's the domestic side. That's something else to me that's important, I don't think it's lowering yourself for a man to do it, I think it's great. Sometimes I wake up in the night and say to myself 'My God, I can bake bread!' It makes me feel terrific.

I keep coming back to this prison thing because of the contrast all the time. In prison you don't do anything: you get up when the bell rings, you do boring work all day, you eat your meals when the bell rings, you go to bed when the bell rings. You don't think, it's not allowed by the rules. Being a lighthouse keeper away from home is like being in prison only instead of it being bad it's good: and on top of all that you get paid for it. I like it all, I think it's great. All that 'A' Alfa, 'V' Victor, 'C' Charlie stuff on the test, it's like playing at Z cars, I enjoy it like anything.

Those books there on the shelf, they say it all for me really. If you'd met me in the nick, in my peter, I'd have had half a dozen westerns there, that's all. What I've got now is two books on weather, a book about sea birds, a cookery book, one about sea fishing and another about fishes of the world, one about different rocks and stones; only a couple of adventure stories, all the rest are about proper subjects, things you can go into and learn about.

Sometimes people ashore who don't know anything about me say 'I don't know how you can stick it, it must be just like being in prison.' It's all I can do to keep my mouth shut. I want to say 'It's absolutely nothing like being in prison at all; it's more like the exact opposite as it happens, and I know what I'm talking about.'

Whatever it is to do with the life, whether it's out here or at home with Susie, I enjoy it. I couldn't say there was any particular time that I didn't like, apart from leaving Susie when I have to go. It doesn't sort of tear me apart though like I know it does her; I think this is because I'm older, and I'm used to being on my own. I'm not at my happiest when I am, but I don't mind it. Susie says I'm happiest when I'm fishing. She's said it to me in so many words, 'You're happier out bloody fishing than you are in bed making love with me.' It's true, I am happy when I'm fishing, very content. But if she ever said that same thing to me, 'If you ever go fishing again that's the finish, that's the end': if she ever did say that, then I'd get my fishing rod and take it with me and walk out of the door. And I'd go round the back yard and break it up in pieces and throw it in the dustbin.

Assistant Keeper Alf Black

The Candle

Quarter to one in the morning, and the wind angrily howling in the night outside. In the brightly lit kitchen Alf cheerily fried up bacon, eggs, tomatoes, sausages and fried bread, set the table with plates and knives and forks and salt and pepper and the sauce bottle, and with bread and butter and biscuits and shop-cake and a pot of tea and the milk bottle and sugar bag, and rubbed his thick fingered hands together and sat down. An amiable Lancastrian, loud-voiced and talkative, eating and laughing and lively and animate; the crack glazed patina of a pretendingly thoughtless lonely man.

 – Sit yourself down, Tawney, we'll feel better when we've got this inside us eh? Have a good tuck in on my second middle watch, that's what I always do. First two or three days I don't eat nothing or do nothing because of that boat trip; then after that I'm as right as rain. Funny how it takes you like, but you learn from experience: when I first come here I used to think I couldn't stick it, I'd have to give it up. Only now I know how it goes with me and I don't worry no more about it.
  Settled in yourself now have you? Good; it's a rum life at first though isn't it till you get used to it? A lot of people wouldn't understand it would they, that you'd look forward to coming every time to a ruddy great lump of rock like this stuck in the sea. I'd much sooner be on a nice place of this sort though than

on one of those bloody horrible towers. Do you not like the
sausages, have I overdone them? I'd have done a few chips
for us if I'd only thought; never mind we can fill up on bread
and butter, eh? You pour us out the tea then and tell us what
to talk about.

I don't mind talking about myself if you want; it's a bit hard
to think what to say though that anyone could put in a book
that'd be interesting. I've not had an interesting life you see,
Tawney, there's not a lot to tell.

What sort of a man I am, well that's a difficult one for a
start, I must say. An ordinary sort of man, forty-nine, coming
up to fifty: getting on now, there can't be no argument about
that. Not married, a bachelor: never wanted to get married, don't
know why, never seemed to crop up somehow, never met the
right sort of woman I suppose. There was a lady once, but that
was a heck of a long time ago now, when I was a young man.
But she upped and married somebody else so there's never been
no one since.

I was born in Manchester; my dad was in a cotton mill, I
didn't know him very well. I was only little when he died, four
I'd have been, somewhere around there. There was eight children
and I was the youngest: four boys and four girls. Where they
all are now I couldn't tell you, it's something like twenty years
I've heard of anyone in the family. We split up after our mum
died, that'd be when I was twelve. My eldest sister was married
with her own family so I went to live with her. I finished my
schooling when I was about fourteen and I think the first job
I had was in a bakery or something like that. It didn't last long,
then I did a few other things, factory work and that sort. My
first what you might call proper job was just after I was eighteen,
I went into a second-hand furniture shop. I was in that it must
have been something like five years all together I think; and a
right boring job it was and all.

What happened was I met this man and he told me he was in
the antique business, he said he was looking for a bright lad to

start at the beginning and learn the trade. He was in the antique business: he had a chain of shops all over the place. Some of them were posh and others no more than junk shops. The way he told it me I was going to start at the bottom in one of the poorer shops and then work my way up from there.

All it was in the way it turned out, I was either sat in a shop in a back street all day waiting in case any customers came in; or now and again when he was going to a sale he'd take me to act as a porter for loading things into his van. It wasn't no kind of a proper sort of job at all. If an assistant at one of his second-hand shops didn't turn up for work, I'd be sent to that one for the day. But if all his assistants turned up at once, like, then there was no shop I belonged to so I got put in his warehouse sweeping up. I wasn't very bright and I hadn't had much education; I think if he'd told me at the start what the job was I'd not have done it. Only there was always these promises, you see; so I hung on because he was for ever telling me he was going to move me up the tree.

The bad thing was I never got no Saturday afternoons. That was very bad because the one thing I was interested in those days was sport. I'd always been keen on football, I used to play for one of the local clubs. I was a big lad for my age, once I'd got the ball it was difficult to knock me off it; I'm not saying I was Bobby Charlton or anything but people used to tell me I ought to think on about the idea of trying to take it up professional.

It was that time when I ought to have been playing every Saturday that I got this job where I couldn't. Another bad thing about it was I never met other lads of my own age. Where I lived with my sister was right out in a village in the country; there was nothing there, it was a place where the only entertainment for anyone was to go down the pub.

Perhaps it would have happened anyway, but that was the long and short of it; I took to spending my spare time drinking in pubs instead of going out mixing with people or playing football. At first this man didn't mind much; you know, that I didn't turn up to work when I should. Only all the time you see I was getting lazier, flabby and out of condition and not like a young man should be.

I still think if he'd moved me on a bit and given me more to think about I might have made something of myself. Or if he'd given me the sack sooner then I might have turned my mind to something different. Anyway none of that happened, it went on till he threw me out because I was drunk one day and fell over something: I think it was a piece of china that he'd just bought.

I wasn't doing anything with my life then except drink: all my wages every week went on that. My sister kept on at me, and in the end she said if I couldn't keep off it I'd have to leave her house. It's not a good story to tell whichever way you come to look at it. She said I'd got an opportunity with this man, but when you're young five years is a long time when you don't feel you're getting anywhere. It was partly the football as well, I perhaps ought to have tried to get with one of the clubs and put my mind to that. I didn't so it's no use wondering now what might have been.

I joined the Lighthouse Service when I was coming up to thirty; but what did I do for the other five years before? I think mostly just sort of wandered around job to job, casual work, labouring. I worked at a garage a bit on the petrol pumps on the forecourt, in a bakery again for a while on the night shift. None of them lasted that long. The main thing was the drink, that was what my money went on. It went on like that till I come into this.

You could say if you liked it was the drinking got me into it. That's how I first heard about it, from a chap in a pub I just started having a chat with. He was a keeper himself, he told me about it and I thought it sounded worth going into a bit further. When I applied the tests they give you're nothing very difficult, I got references from two brothers-in-law, so that was it. They must have been short of lighthouse keepers at the time, that probably had something to do with it.

It'd got nothing to do with the sea or anything of that sort, the main attraction to it was it'd take me away from towns and the land. No pubs, nowhere to go where I'd have too much and not turn up at work. When I put in I said I never wanted to go on a land light. They were good about that, they kept putting me on rocks and towers: and they have ever since. I've never once been on a land light, not all the time I've been in. Being a bachelor you see, that helps: it's the married men want land lights and get given them. If somebody tells them that's what he doesn't want they never have to bother about him no more.

I've not been in the service twenty years; I've been in it fifteen. There was a time ten years ago wher I left it, I thought I'd conquered the drink thing: every tour of duty I'd spent two months on a light without a drop. I thought if I could do without it so often so regular, then it wouldn't give me no problems any more. There was a man I met in Leeds, he wanted us to go in a little business together, a newsagent's shop. He was going to put up the capital and I was going to be the manager. I thought I'd give it a try, so I gave Trinity my notice. Six months and I was back as bad as I was before, drinking and wandering round. It got very bad that time, I was living rough. You couldn't say I was anything else than a down and out tramp. It got to the point of Salvation Army hostels; I thought I'd had it then, I did.

But one day I happened to be lucky, I ran into a keeper who'd known me, we'd been together a lot. He gave me a real good talking to, he said I was going to end in the gutter if I didn't watch out. I was well in the gutter by then anyhow, he could see that. He said write to Trinity and say I wanted to come back, see if they would. I didn't think there was much hope but they wrote back saying I could. It must have been they were short of keepers again, and I was experienced, I don't think they'd have looked at me otherwise. Coming back in like that I'd lost all my time, my service time you know for seniority. That didn't worry me, I'm not bothered about getting up to PK; so there it was, they took me back. I've learned my lesson and I've stopped in ever since.

So that's about all there is to it, Tawney. I told you it'd not be very interesting. Oh aye, I'll go on if you want; tell you what, how'd it be if we did the washing-up then if you like we can go in my room and settle down in there?

Everywhere in his room on shelves and round the ledges and in cupboards there were books. On top of the lid of the wooden box in the corner was a dismantled antique carriage clock. He sat propped up comfortably with pillows, his feet up on the bed.

– Two different men, I've been two men so long now. When I'm ashore I live in digs in Manchester. My landlady's a good old soul, she knows what I'm like; I've been with her nearly all the last ten years. When my pay comes through the first thing we do is take the rent out, the money that pays for my keep the four weeks I'm there, plus a bit for her to keep the room for me while I'm away. Then the rest of it's mine: and over the four weeks I spend every penny there is of it on drink. If I want any food she'll make me something to eat, but often I'll go days and not touch a bite. Go out and have a good drink, then back home and sleep it off. I don't go far, there's four or five pubs in the neighbourhood and I'll always be in one of those. Nothing else, that's all, just drink. Don't talk much, you know what it's like in pubs; you might get into conversation with someone for an hour or so then you'll never see them again.

I don't feel the need of company, it's not the companionship I go in for, only the drink. I don't drink in my digs, that's an agreement we have. I think that's good, people who are drinkers on their own are what's called alcoholics and I'm not one of those. I can't be because when I come off here there's no liquor on lighthouses so I do without. Anyone who can do eight weeks at a stretch once every three months regular can't be an alcoholic, no one could say that. Where it gets difficult is like this time, where there's an overdue and I can't get off. All I do while I'm waiting then is stay in the town and drink.

It puts me in rotten shape for the boat journey, what with being a bad sailor and that. But once I've had two or three days with nothing to eat then I'm on my feet again right as rain. I'll be fine now till the end of my turn; then when I go ashore the first drink I'll have will be on the station where I catch my train. If there's an overdue going ashore I'll not be panting to get ashore and have a drink, it doesn't take me like that. That's another reason why nobody could say I was alcoholic; it's not I can't do without it, I can. But only so long as I'm in a place where I can't get it. I accept it then and it doesn't worry me.

When I'm out here I'm a different man. I'm never lonely and I don't need company; I talk to the other two when they talk to me, but it wouldn't bother me if neither of them never said a word. I think sometimes how would it be if they weren't here and I was here completely on my own? It's crossed my mind from time to time; and I think I'd manage, it'd suit me fine.

It couldn't ever happen but if it did there'd be no problems my end. If Trinity sent a message through one day they needed two keepers urgently, so they were going to take them off and leave me on my own I'd say yes, that's all right with me. I'd see the lamp was lit, I'd potter round cleaning the place and keeping it tidy, I'd see to the engines and do the weather; then the rest of the time I'd be sitting out there on the rock looking out at the sea or in here reading or doing my clocks.

My clocks are like that one; I've got three in the box, I do them up for a little antique shop in Manchester. Take them to pieces and clean and oil them, then put them together again. There's a name for it isn't there, 'horology'; that's what it is, that's what I do. I'm not pretending I know anything about them simply because of having them pass through my hands. I don't think I've ever read a book about clocks, I think it's a knack you pick up. The man I do them for's never had no complaints from his customers, so I suppose I must've got a certain amount of skill.

I do a lot of reading when I'm out here, I'm a very big reader. What you might call travel books mostly, I don't like stories; anything that's made up, I don't like that. I like to learn about places, different countries in the world. I've never been to any of them, but there's a lot I feel I've been to, in my mind you might say. My favourite one is Russia, I don't know why. Any part of Russia, that's what I like to read about best. The way people live there, the different cities from the frozen ones up north to the hot ones in the south, the different tribes and customs and their way of life.

If I ever see anything on the television that's to do with Russia, I can't take my eyes off it. Sometimes they'll show a bit of one of those celebrations they have, say a victory parade in Moscow. You'll see those big crowds yelling and cheering; when I see something like that I imagine myself being one of them, jumping up and down cheering. Not the ones up there taking the salutes, I don't see myself one of them: I'm one of the ordinary ones, one of the great big crowd, that'd be me.

It's got nothing to do with politics, I'm not interested in them. I don't understand Communism, I couldn't tell you the difference between that and anything else. I think it must be the sort of family feeling they seem to have in a country like Russia. They say in Russia everybody's part of a family, all part of one big state. That's the bit appeals to me, perhaps it's coming from a big family myself. Funny when you come to think of it why; I hadn't thought of it like that before.

All those over there are books about Russia. Then those up there are history books, and those are about different favourite people I've got. Sort of historical people like Julius Caesar and Napoleon and Leonardo da Vinci and people like that. He was a great man Leonardo da Vinci, I think he must have been one of the best there ever was; he knew pretty near everything there was to be known did old Leonardo.

The other thing I'm fond of is the old Greek legends and stories, the myths like and things. I like them all, anything of that sort. Words all together you know, I think they're very nice. Most of all in my life I'd like to have been sufficiently educated to write a book. To me that must be really wonderful to have written a book. But I've never tried it, you've got to have education for that and I haven't.

I know things, all sorts of things; but they're bits and pieces with no rhyme or reason to them. I bring a lot of newspapers with me when I come to do the crosswords in. There'll be some word and I'll know it straight off because I'll have read it somewhere. The other two look at me, they know I haven't got an education and I speak rough: yet I know that word or a bit out of a quotation. It really puzzles them how I could. Shakespeare, I know nearly all the characters' names and quotations and things; operas too, I wouldn't know one from the other as far as the music goes but I've read the stories of them in a book. Once I've read a thing somehow or other it seems to stick in my mind. I couldn't always tell you who'd written it though.

That's a big question isn't it, what's the thing I've read seemed the nearest to the way I look at things myself? I suppose it'd be something that I read once years ago now, I couldn't tell you who wrote it though or what it was in. It seemed to come close to how I saw things. It was something to the effect of sort of summing up of two ways of looking at life, but I can't put it in the exact words.

It was to the effect that to some people life is like darkness with a box of matches and to other people it was like darkness with a candle. Everybody's in the darkness, the man who wrote it was saying. Some people have a box of matches and every so often they strike one; it gives them a glimpse for a minute what life's like, then it goes out. The other sort, to them life's darkness but there's a candle burning in it they can look at when everything's dark. Sometimes something will get in the way so they can't see the candle; but that's only temporary like, the candle's still there.

If the thing in the way moves or you move yourself a bit to one side, then you can still see the light.

I think he must have been a religious writer, but I don't remember it being what you might call a religious book. I've got the idea it wasn't in nothing of that sort. That's why I remember it so clear, because I wasn't expecting to come across it. But I'd say that was how I saw things, and I incline more to the second one I suppose. I hadn't really thought.

You could compare it to a lighthouse, that's very funny when you come to think about it. The lighthouse is a sort of fixed point isn't it, that helps with navigation? And what I'm doing is to keep the light going for people to make their way.

But it's the fixed point in my life too isn't it you know, yes. Like that chap said to me if I hadn't come back in the service I'd have been in the gutter for good, I'd have been dead. Four times a year I come out here and this is where my proper life is; this is where it's clean and fresh and all things like that. Out here's the sort of light and ashore it's the sort of dark. So long as I keep coming the candle's still glowing for me; I think that's it, I think it is that, it's right.

Crikey, Tawney, I haven't half got into deep water you know, who'd have thought? It's really funny is all that. It's surprising what you come out with sometimes. I'd never sort of pieced it together before like that. I like thinking about things though; it'll go on in my head a bit now, will that.

Principal Keeper Stanley Vincent

A Kind of
Clockwork Man 17

He made tea and we sat and drank it, talking quietly in his room.
A gentle-mannered man in an open-necked shirt and overalls
and slippers, thin and tired. His face was pallid and his lips were
pale; the light from the table lamp showed up the lines of strain
on his cheeks and threw dark shadows over the weariness in his
deep set eyes.

— You'll not get ashore today I'm afraid, I hope you won't
mind. But if the wind stays down like it seems to be doing, you
shouldn't have to wait too long. It'll give you the chance to
catch up on some sleep; you should do that, they're not good
for people broken nights aren't.

I hope you've found your stay useful, I hope we've been some
help. It's been company for us: something different, it's made a
welcome change. The monotony of these places more than anything else, that's what gets you down. Like I said, one day's like
the next; they go on one after the other, they're all ordinary and
plain. You've had chance to see it yourself, the sameness all the
time of the routine.

That's something should be got over to outsiders, there's
nothing exciting about it. I don't think they want to believe it,
they'd sooner hear romantic things. When I meet people ashore
and they find out I'm a keeper they're for ever asking questions
about it. I never know what to truthfully say. I think this must

be the dullest job in the world: but if you were to say that to people that wouldn't be what they wanted to hear.

I didn't used to feel like this, but as time goes on I'm feeling it more and more. It might be the job or it may be to do with my age. I don't get the satisfaction out of it I used to. I only stay in it now for the pension at the end. But even for that I'm not certain whether it's worth going on.

It's a dead man's shoes job. You can't get to PK unless the man in front of you falls down and dies. So you have this feeling all the time there's a man behind you waiting to step up and fill your place. Somewhere a man's waiting for me to die; you don't like that thought in your mind; you'd sooner go voluntarily and retire to get out of the way.

– I suppose everyone does this, looks back and asks himself whether he'd do the same thing if he could have his time over again. With no hesitation at all I'd say I made a bad mistake when I joined the service; it was the wrong sort of job for me.

I was like a lot of other people when I was young: you'll meet a lot who came into it as a last resort because they couldn't think of anything else. The happy ones are those who found it suited them; the unhappy ones, most of them saw soon enough it wasn't for them so they got out and left.

In my case I was a young man and I'd got this notion in my head I wanted a job that had something to do with the sea. I'd never properly thought it out. I wanted to get married, and this seemed the nearest I could get without having to go away on voyages all the time. But I never sat down and asked myself what I did best and tried to think along those lines.

Security and the sea; I thought no further than that. All the years I spent on the land light, I think I was being cowardly about life, not looking further than the end of my nose. It was too easy: we lived in a nice place, Cathy was settled at school, she was growing up to a fine girl. Time was going by and I was contented with the way things were. But life doesn't stand still, you don't notice it's slipping by. I should have had the sense to see that.

What I mean is I should have seen the day would come that Cathy would grow up and go away. Making something the object of your life, you ought never to forget if you've only got one child there's going to be still a good part of your life left over when she's moved on. You've only your job to fall back on then; so it ought to be work you feel is worthwhile. One with some result to it, some end product; that was what I needed.

The only end product in this job is people; other people and how you get on with them. That could give you satisfaction if you were the sort who enjoyed other's company. I don't; not to the extent it's sufficient for me to live two months at a time with two other men alone on a rock. This is nothing against Alf and Bob; it's entirely down to me. I don't find any satisfaction at all in this kind of a life. My only friend is my wife. I could do without everyone else there is.

I think I ought to have had the sense to see it. I'm not the sort who can live on his own, I need my wife. If he's that sort, a man shouldn't be in a job that takes him from his wife and puts him into contact with other people; not if contact with other people isn't his strong point.

I was reading a book some time back, it made me think not all the old ways of doing things were wrong. It was about Grace Darling. It only came about, all that business about her being a heroine, because in those days light keepers and their families all lived together on a light. Her and her mother and father, the lighthouse was run by them as a family, they lived out at sea on it for twelve years. I think that was a good idea; it's a much more normal way of life for a keeper than the system we have now that if it's a rock or a tower light the man has to keep going away.

I can see how as far as it went it looked right, life in the service for me. But I should have known better than that; I should have seen I got into a job that wasn't dealing with people and pushing me on top of them. I'm happier with things.

The only day I like here is when I'm cook, cooking and pottering about and taking the cooker to bits or cleaning the sink. I'm better when I'm occupying myself with things. You don't have to worry what sort of terms you're on with a cooker; you can't hurt its feelings. That's not a lot to say for your life that you and a cooker are on good terms.

I should have done something more in the nature of an occupation where there was something to show at the end of it. Like ships in bottles, but more serious than that. I'm talking about craftsmanship. All these years I've had this skill in my hands, but all I've ever used it for is a hobby. When I think about it, it makes me think there's no escaping from it that I've been wasting my time and wasting my life.

I'd like to have put myself to better use; to have made things, proper things, not curiosities people have on their mantelpieces for ornaments. I wouldn't want to have been a top man in whatever trade, but I would have liked to have spent my life in carpentry or something of that sort. Anything that I could have stood back from when I'd finished and known I'd made something of value to someone and they were going to use. I'd not have minded even if it had been something like shoes that were going to wear out and be thrown away. That wouldn't have worried me, I still have could felt what I was doing was of practical use.

Some people would say lighthouses are of practical use, to ships and so on. But in its own words, it's the Lighthouse Service: and I can't see a lighthouse keeper provides more useful service than say a 'bus conductor or someone like that. It's not in providing a service I ought to have been; not a man like me. It's not proved enough for me to sit back and be content with it, I'd like to have done something with my hands. To have been a skilled man, made something I could feel proud about. Some men feel proud to be keepers: for them that's all right, only for me it was the wrong job, it's not made me into a real person.

One of the big problems here in this place is I can't give my

mind to it, I can't get my head down and get on with it. It might
be better if I was somewhere else. Loneliness here is harder to
put up with because it's so near the shore. If I've got to be away
then I'd sooner be right away. Here you're in a half world all the
time and I find that a strain. Margaret likes it, feeling I'm only
just offshore; but to me it'd be easier if I was somewhere else.

When I first came I used to go out on the end of the rock with
a telescope and look at the shore; you can see the cottages quite
clearly. But I don't do that now, it makes it that much harder.
In the summer Margaret sometimes comes out on one of the trip-
per boats so she can wave. I haven't the heart to tell her I wish
she wouldn't because it upsets me afterwards for days. It means
a lot to her, it gives her a comfortable feeling I'm near. But to
me it's like purgatory. There's times the weather's so calm and the
sea's so flat I have to stop myself going down and doing something stupid like trying to swim to the shore.

The other way round, when I'm ashore then this place is
always right outside the window. I can't forget it, it's in sight; no
matter how much I avoid looking at it it won't go away. It's the
constant reminding: of home when I'm here, here when I'm
home. It isn't something I've talked to Margaret about, she's
always said she likes it as it is. Being separated's as hard for her
as it is for me; so if something like that helps I think that should
come first.

Every time I go ashore now, I'm more and more tempted not
to come back. I do, but only because it's the habit. If you've
spent your life doing your duty it seems to leave you without
any power in yourself to do anything different. You get to feel
like a machine; you act like a piece of clockwork, someone turns
the key to wind you up and off you go like a kind of clockwork
man.

The only thing that gives me pleasure when I'm out here is
my ships; doing them helps pass the time, and I'm doing something with my hands. I learned how to do them years ago from
an old PK. A thing that pleases me is that now Bob wants to

learn. I get more enjoyment trying to teach him than I do doing them by myself. I wouldn't like to think the art of them was dying out, so it pleases me Bob's carrying it on. He's a sticker is Bob, he's got patience: and eventually he'll get the knack of it, because he's shaping well. You don't find many younger men these days with the patience for that sort of thing.

It's a fiddly job, very painstaking. If you're not prepared to take pains you shouldn't attempt to begin. The most you can produce is one every two-month turn of duty, so you can't approach it as though it was going to be like a production line. One slip due to one bit of impatience, and that's it then you've ruined the whole thing.

You take a piece of fuse wire and dip it in glue to get a blob of glue on the end you can hardly see. Then you've got to place that spot of glue exactly where it should be, then be prepared to leave it two days to set. A lot of people couldn't be bothered with things as finicky as that, they'd want to get on faster. But if you won't do it on that sort of time scale it's better not to start.

A loop of wire, a whole series of them, each one perhaps three millimetres across. They're what make it possible, the way you fix them on the hull you've carved. If one single one of them isn't set and glued properly, three or four weeks later when you come to pull the rigging up with your cotton after it's inside the bottle the whole thing will give way and that's the end of your three weeks' work. I've seen men explode when that happens, pick the bottle up and smash it against the wall. You've got to have a lot of patience if you're going to succeed; patience to have done every thing right, then checked it's right before you go on to the next.

– Ships in bottles. And that's not much at the end of your life either to say you can do. Other men look back and know they've got more. My daughter Cathy, I get satisfaction from doing the right thing by her. But I don't think it's enough you can pat

yourself on the back that you've given your child a good start.
Putting your child first, it's nothing to take a lot of credit for.
You brought that child into the world, so you've got the duty
to do the best you can. But I don't think the child owes gratitude.
I couldn't accept we could be turning to Cathy for help; she's
got her own life.

I've never found the job a satisfying one, I keep coming back
to that; at the end of thirty years I look back and they've been
thirty wasted years. It's not made me a better person, it's made
me worse, put me into a rut until I've forgotten how to look
over the sides.

I've noticed this much more since I've come up to PK, I've
watched it happening. I've not wanted it to, but it has. I've
shocked myself in the last year with some of the things I've done,
such as the way I am now with the SAKs. I'm doing the very
sort of things all my life I always told myself I'd never do. The
SAK today is the PK tomorrow and if you give them a rough
time, years later when he's a PK he'll take it out of someone else.
This last SAK we had, I gave him a dog's life; I knew I was
doing it but I just hadn't got it in me to stop myself.

The sort of trivial things you look back at after and wonder
what sort of a mind you must have: a spanner left on a ledge in
one of the sheds for the engines, one time he forgot to flush the
toilet, even once when he was whistling I was swearing at him
for forgetting Bob was asleep. There's a right way and a wrong
way to point out something to someone, he must have thought
he was living with a maniac. A few years back I'd have done
no more than said an odd word.

The relief you came off on with Alf, I'd have given anything
to have been the one going ashore. I could have talked to Margaret about it, and I know what she'd have said: she'd have told
me it was strain, I wasn't really like that. She wouldn't have left
it there; she'd have had him in for a meal so I could have chatted
to him normally and got him to see I wasn't like he thought.
I'll tell her when I go back exactly what I was like with that SAK,

that'll be a help. But it won't take out of my mind the thought that next time one's here I'm likely to be just as bad.

– Which way to go now, what to do; I suppose all I can do is hang on. There's only a few more years before I'll be due for retirement; we're saving up every penny we can so we'll perhaps be able to get ourselves a house. When I was younger I used to say I couldn't see myself stopping in the service till I'd got a beard; but that's what I have, my mind's got a beard.

I get these kind of feelings particularly in the night. During the day I'm putting on a front for the others, having to keep them in mind so the station'll go on ticking over and everything stay calm. You can't tell them how you're feeling; they've got their own worries, they don't want to be hearing about yours. This is a bad station in that respect, the three of us get on on the surface all right but we never really talk. What Bob and Alf have said to you I don't know, but I have the feeling with them that they're both glad to be here. It seems to mean something to them more than it does to me. They seem to enjoy being here, but it's not like that for me: I feel trapped.

A few more years now, that's all. Well, I expect I'll survive.

The Tower

Different People,
Different Things

i. *Mary B.*

– Yes the tower does have particular connotations as far as I'm concerned, not very pleasant ones either. Simon spent three years there as an AK, I'll always think that particular period did it. If he'd been somewhere else, say on a land light for instance, I still think it's possible our marriage might have had a chance to work out and we wouldn't have been divorced.

We got married while he was an SAK; we'd known each other quite a time beforehand, we were prepared for separations and ready to accept them so I don't think either of us didn't know what we were in for. And we got through the year while he was an SAK without any trouble. His first appointment was to a rock light; it was a station with a group of cottages, we lived there for nearly four years. The other keepers' wives were a bit clannish, I never really felt I fitted in; and I found the PK's wife particularly difficult. She seemed to think her job was to run everybody's personal lives; she treated all the wives as though they were children who had to be fussed over all the time. Her attitude was that you hadn't married a keeper, you'd married the Lighthouse Service. She kept saying we were all part of one big family; that used to irritate me a lot. I'd got my own family, parents and brothers and sisters, so I didn't need another one. I could never get interested in the perpetual gossip and tittle-tattle about who was being promoted and where to, which was all they ever seemed to talk about.

All the same I survived that period too. We had our first child and I think I made a good adjustment to Simon going away and coming back all the time although it was a difficult sort of existence when he wasn't there.

I hoped when he got posted to his new station which is the tower you're talking about, that things would be better. It didn't have cottages of its own for the keepers' wives. I thought living in a council house in a town as we would be, that'd be better because when he was home we wouldn't still be wrapped in the lighthouse atmosphere as we had been at the cottages. By then I'd got our second child, I was really looking forward to the new life I thought we were going to have.

For about the first year it seemed to work all right, then I did definitely start to notice a change in Simon. Before when there'd been an overdue he hadn't seemed to mind. But it started getting obvious after a while he was obsessed with the place and couldn't wait to go back. I was spending two months thinking about him coming home; then when he did come he spent his entire month ashore thinking about nothing else but going back. I couldn't understand how anyone could be like that, particularly someone who'd been as fond of his home and of me.

I never did find out what it was about the place he thought was so marvellous. Time and again I tried to ask him and discuss it, but all he ever said was he felt happy there on a tower in the middle of the sea. It was almost as though he'd got another woman out there; or the lighthouse was another woman he loved more than he did me.

I was jealous: I felt I was in competition with it for his affections. What really put the lid on it was after about two years he'd been there, he was home for his month and he heard one of the other keepers had been taken ill and had to be brought ashore. Simon was on the phone straight away volunteering to go back when he'd only been home just under a fortnight. I could hardly believe my ears when I heard him ringing up. I told him if he was serious, if he did go back then that was the end. I'd pack up and take the children and bring them back here to my parents.

He went, and I'm not the sort of person who says something and doesn't mean it, so I did pack up and come back here. I thought that would shock him; I thought when he came ashore and found he hadn't a home or family to go to he'd realize what being in the tower was doing to him. If he did he didn't care, because he made no move to even try to come and see me.

I wrote him a letter saying I was prepared to have one more try for the sake of the children. I said if he'd put in for a transfer I'd go to any other station and start again, even it if meant living in Trinity House cottages. From all I've heard about Trinity they're good about that sort of thing; if a man said he wanted to move because he was having domestic difficulties I think they'd move heaven and earth to give it him. But he just wrote back and said he thought the best thing we could do was get divorced. It seemed to me if a man had got into that state, when he was prepared to write off his wife and children for the sake of a job, then it must be a terrible sort of job. Six months later he got transferred from the tower but he still didn't approach me. He's probably going to be on rocks and towers now for the rest of his life, because to all events and purposes he's a single man again.

This was two years ago, no nearly three now. I feel very bitter about it. Whether I shall ever get married again or not I don't know: if I do it'll certainly not be to another lighthouse keeper. Some people seem able to manage the life. And I still think if it came to it I could. I think I proved that, because I did it during the time he was SAK and for the years he was on the rock light. So I can't look on it any other way than it was the life on tower which changed him.

Occasionally you see a mention of the place in the newspapers or hear its name; whenever I do I can't help it, just to hear it makes me shudder. To me it's like some horrible ogre, the place I lost Simon to and my children lost their father to. It's almost as if he'd gone there and had an accident and been washed off into the sea or something, and never came back. After he went there he never did come back, I don't know why. I don't like thinking about it, I wouldn't have talked to you if Janet Bailey hadn't asked me if I would.

*

ii. *Eric G.*

– I spent two years on the tower, it was the last station I was at before I resigned from the service. I don't know I could say it was entirely due to that place, but certainly it had a lot to do with it. Being isolated there and having so much time to think probably had quite a bit to do with it. In a way I ought to be grateful to it on that score. At least it made me think; two years on a place like that does bring you up against things, it brings you up against yourself and helps you to take stock.

I went in the service straight after leaving grammar school. My father had been in it all his life; he didn't talk me into following in his footsteps, I took it for granted that's what I would do. About ninety per cent of people in it are like that; there for want of being able to think of anything better. To be frank you wonder whether there's anything else some of them could do, you can't see them fitting in with any normal ordinary job.

I was in it ten years. I had all the usual business of being shoved around here there and everywhere as an SAK. Their system of starting people off in that way is a bad one, very inefficient. I can't think any modern company would spend time and money on training people without finding out whether they've any aptitude. The first thing you ought to find out is whether someone's temperamentally suited: if you send him out on different lighthouses to see if he likes the life, and after a year he leaves, you've been wasting time and money.

All the time I was in the service from eighteen until I was twenty-eight, I was a single man. I wasn't staying in it for the security and being single they didn't give me a house. I was only staying in for one reason, which was that I wasn't thinking about what I was doing. It's a very insidious process; what happens to you doesn't encourage you to think, and before you know where you are you find you're too old to think any more. Being a lighthouse keeper is particularly bad in that respect: you work such a long stretch at a time you have less opportunity than most people to step outside the job and see what it's doing to you.

The ordinary person is a nine to five man who goes home every night and has weekends off as well: he's having breaks all the time mixing with other people and coming into contact with outsiders, and this lets him keep some kind of perspective. But a lighthouse keeper's nine to five working day lasts for two months; that's fifty-six days and nights at a stretch during which he's no contact with the outside world. He doesn't meet anyone apart from the two others with him. It's as though he's in a monastery or a prison, he's totally shut off from the world.

I began to notice it in time: that when I got ashore I didn't belong in the ordinary everyday world. I'd be talking about things which were real to me, which were what had happened when I was ashore previously. That was eight weeks before, they were gone and forgotten in the minds of everyone else. Or people would be talking to me about something that was going to happen 'next week'; and I'd realize it was meaningless, it had no relevance because 'next week' I was going to be back on the lighthouse.

You got very conscious of this. If you went into a pub for a drink you'd deliberately cut yourself off from other people; you'd sit in a corner on your own and wouldn't get into conversation because of letting your ignorance show. People would start to chat with you; they'd mention something that happened the week before, it might only be something trivial like a film at the local cinema, and you wouldn't even know it had been showing. It was inevitable they'd ask you if you were a stranger or where you'd been; then when you said you'd been on duty on a light-house, they'd start plying you with questions. So no matter which way you turned, you couldn't join in ordinary conversation.

Another way it used to affect me was in the streets with traffic. It could get frightening because you weren't used to the noise and movement and there were so many people. I was scared crossing the road or going into a large shop. I found it confusing and frightening, and all I wanted to do was get back where I felt safe; get even further away from the world and back to the lighthouse.

I think that was an appalling state for anyone to be in, let alone a young man as I was then. The existence was totally unreal; it wasn't so much a way of life, it was an escape from life. It's a harmful experience and one people could do well without. I think it very necessary to warn people about it, so they don't drift into it unthinkingly as I did. If you're not prepared to give up your personality to it then I wouldn't recommend it to anybody.

Being on the tower for two years could have settled things for me: the place was so isolated I'm not exaggerating when I say it could really have been the end of me as a person with a mind of his own. What jolted me out of the rut was a combination of circumstances: a new PK was appointed there and an SAK came out who hadn't wanted to go. The PK was one of the old guard; he insisted on everything being done the way he thought and he used to have terrible rows with the SAK.

It came to a head in my own mind because they both said the same thing to me, only from opposite viewpoints. The PK took me aside one day and said I ought to guard against ever letting myself become 'sloppy' like the SAK. Then the next day the SAK said something to me about the PK, to the effect he wouldn't like to turn out like that himself. Their two remarks and the contrast between them as individuals was what made me think hard about myself for the remaining couple of weeks while I was out there on the tower.

I gave my notice in when I got ashore; I got a job in the bank where I am now. I occasionally tell people I was in the lighthouse service twelve years ago, and that I spent two years out on the tower. Some of them look at me wonderingly and ask me don't I find being in a bank boring in comparison, don't I regret giving it up? All I usually say is 'No' and leave it at that.

*

iii. *Revd. Rowland W.*
– Some years ago before I came to this village I was for a number of years an Honorary Chaplain to Trinity House. This came about because my church was in a small town on the coast where there was an offshore rock light which had Trinity Cottages attached to it. Later I moved to a church in a port: and the offshore waters were part of my parish so to speak. The tower was in them so I regarded it as part of my duty to visit it in conjunction with the rest of my pastoral work. I always tried to go there certainly at Christmas time and Eastertide, and on other occasions as and when the opportunity arose. Additionally at one period there were two of the keepers' wives and families living in the port. So I would say that all in all over the years my work frequently brought me into contact with people connected with the service, as well as giving me chance to visit several actual lights.

Prior to that I'd had no connection whatsoever with the sea; in point of fact I'd been an Army Chaplain for twenty-five years. In that respect I was used to service life and service families and their problems; so there was a slight similarity, in that one was working with basically the same sort of person in the same sort of occupation. But the differences were more apparent than the similarities, particularly as far as the wives of the men were concerned.

In the Army you tended to find most of the servicemen's wives were much of the same type; they nearly all reacted in the same way to such a thing as separation for instance. On the whole they were very phlegmatic about it and took it in their stride. I think this could possibly be because service separations were frequently for long periods, six months was by no means uncommon, it could often be much longer than that. It was very hard for them to bear, but at least over that length of time they had opportunity to resign themselves to it, to accept their husband wasn't there and wasn't likely to be in the immediate future. I think in this respect, though not perhaps in any other, the wife of a soldier who was serving abroad had an easier adjustment to make than the lighthouse keeper's wife.

When I first began to meet lighthouse keepers' wives, I'd taken it for granted up till then that they would probably be the same as soldiers' wives: that is, women who were accustomed to separation from their husbands and accepted it as an unavoidable part of the job. But in fact this wasn't so at all, it was almost the opposite. I soon found myself wondering why it was that whereas soldiers seemed on the whole to marry very stable-charactered women, lighthouse keepers on the contrary appeared to have chosen to marry women who were if not actually unstable, then certainly very highly strung; with some of them it seemed they were inclined to be even slightly neurotic. Far from accepting their situation, some of them seemed positively to resent it that their husbands had to keep going away, and got very miserable during their absence.

This puzzled me for a long time because it wasn't at all what I'd been prepared for, rather the reverse. If Army wives, or for that matter the wives of merchant seamen or men in the Navy, could stoically accept long periods of separation how was it so many lighthouse keepers' wives appeared unable to do it without a great deal of strain and unhappiness? Could it really be true they were fundamentally different in type? And if so, how was it so many of what appeared to be exactly the wrong type appealed to keepers, or were in their turn attracted to keepers themselves? It was all most puzzling.

I came to realize that my expectations were wrong because they were based on a mistaken premise. It had nothing to do with such a generalization as a type of person: it was much more that the job itself was the cause of the situation. It was neither one thing nor the other, the separation I mean. It existed, and it was repeated; but when it happened it wasn't really long enough for a woman to rearrange her life to cope with it. From the women's point of view it was a constant changing backwards and forwards of her domestic situation that gave her little chance to make satisfactory adjustment.

No sooner had she and her children got used to living without a man in the house, and she herself to being the head of the household, than the husband came back again. For four weeks she then had to step into the background; then again after that short period the man would be away once more and she would have to take over. Whichever it was, the time when the husband was away or the time when he was home, was really only very temporary. I think it was this that so many of them found so difficult, and I don't think it's surprising they did; the perpetual temporariness of it must be an exceptional strain.

I think one therefore has to say not that it's surprising one should have found so many keepers' wives who appeared to be highly strung; what is surprising is how many of them seemed somehow or other to be able to cope with what must be a very unsatisfactory existence for a woman. She has all the responsibility for the day to day upbringing of the children, and yet has to remember her husband will be home again in a few weeks so she can't supersede his position in any way. It must be extraordinarily difficult to maintain that kind of situation for years on end as most of them have to.

The first time I actually went on to the tower I was fifty-seven, I believe. I'd watched the relief being effected on a number of occasions and I'd never greatly fancied the idea of being hauled thirty or forty feet up in the air on a rope from a small boat bobbing around in the sea. Of course there's a harness on the rope and you pull that up under your armpits, so even if you let go of the rope you're not likely to fall into the sea. Unless of course the harness has come loose and slipped down. However when I came to do it I found it was really nothing like so frightening as I'd imagined it would be; it's all over so very quickly you hardly have much time to think about it.

Also you're attached to the rope at an angle of somewhere around forty-five degrees: this means that once the men on the winch have started to pull you out of the boat, you can't see anything if you look down, nor can you tilt your head back to see where you're going. I found the most helpful thing to do was try to regard oneself as a parcel: there was nothing one could do about the situation. You're dependent entirely on the men who are hauling you up as far as the speed of the ascent's concerned, so one has to leave it to them.

Personally I always found coming off the tower and back into the boat much more disconcerting, because then you can look down and see where it is you're supposed to be going. From up on the tower, on the set-off as they call it, which is the kind of concrete ring down below the entrance door, the boat below in the sea looks very small. The boatman has the other end of the rope made fast inside his boat, but all the same one can't help worrying if it might be too slack for instance, in which case one would go into the sea. I have seen that happen occasionally to an unfortunate keeper; but it's rare, the boatman and the men on the winch know their job. They seem able to judge the right moment to let the rope slacken so you'll drop into the boat and not into the water. One can get a little wet at times if the sea's rough and the waves are breaking heavily, but on the whole I myself have been very fortunate and not had a particularly unpleasant experience.

The part of it which I thoroughly disliked is not strictly speaking anything to do with the going up or down the rope. It was when you're going up into the tower after you've been winched up out of the boat and have landed on the set-off. You get out of the harness and free of the rope; but you're then faced with having to climb up a narrow iron ladder to the actual entrance door of the tower. I'm told it's only about thirty feet up those what they call 'dog steps', but I must say I always found that part very hard. You've had a three-quarter-hour journey in the boat through rough sea out to the tower: then you've been hauled up in the air on a rope, spinning round and round as you go. Then you have to take the harness off, which as I say is a thing for your safety to ensure you won't fall from the rope, and make this steep climb up the cold wet rungs of the ladder to the entrance door. If you fell off then there'd be no protection for you since you're no longer in the harness. It always seemed to me a long and arduous climb at the end of what had naturally been a rather strenuous and tiring experience. For an elderly man it really was quite an effort: and always caused me a certain amount of trepidation.

It was all part of my pastoral work; slightly unusual for the majority of clergymen, but always enoyable, not least because of the hospitable welcome of the keepers when I went. It's an experience I'm glad to have had, and one that stays vividly in my mind. It's a very proud sort of place, the tower I think, standing there on its own out in the sea.

*

iv. *Amos D.*

– I'm the local boatman who does the relief of the keepers on the tower. I hold the Trinity House contract for it. I put the keepers on or bring them ashore, and now and again in between I go out with mechanics or anyone of that sort as required. So far I've done it just over twenty years, but I don't know there's a lot I can tell you about it. Anyone could do it, it's just a job that's all; there's nothing particularly special.

I shall be retiring before long, letting one of the younger men take over; one of the other local boatmen, there's several could do it just as well as me. Though I could be the last one: I've heard talk that in a few years the relief won't be done by boat no more. They say they've got plans for building a landing-pad on top of the tower and doing it by helicopter. You hear these stories, they've been saying that's what they're going to do for years, but nothing's actually happened yet. I'd like to see my quarter of a century out, then that'll be the lot. After I've done it twenty-five years it won't make no difference to me if they put a younger man on to it or change to using a helicopter.

I'm not a big talker, so all I can say is I do it because I like doing it. It's not all that difficult so long as you use your common-sense and don't take risks. You've got men's lives at stake, you have to keep that in your mind, you can't take chances over things like that. You've got to remember what's under the water, the rocks that you can't see. You know where they are from experience, so you keep your boat clear of them: that's about all there is to it, anyone who knows the area round here is as safe as you'd be yourself if you were showing someone round your own house at home.

The experience of it in my case comes from the fact I've lived round here all my life. When I was a youth and a young man I used to go out in a boat on my own down there round where the tower is, fishing and lobster-potting in the summer evenings on the low tides. That way you get to know where all the rocks are, more or less every one of them; you've been round them or over them, you've looked down at them in the water from your boat, you've actually touched some of them with your hands. So when it's the winter like now and a big sea running, you know exactly what there is underneath you: how large or small a rock is, what it's shaped like, how near the surface it'll be depending on the tide at that time. To anyone else the sea looks like a stretch of water with big waves on it, it looks like a blanket covering everything over. But you know what's under the blanket and where it is and whether it's safe to go near it or over it as the case may be.

From the quay the journey out to the tower in the boat takes perhaps three quarters of an hour or an hour depending on the conditions. There's not a lot you have to look out for on the way once you're clear of the harbour until you get down near the tower. There's an area there round it of about ten square miles with all the rocks underneath I've been telling you about. There's two or three channels you can choose from as to which one will be the safest to follow in. When you get there you stand off about fifty yards from the tower and decide whether you're going to tie up to the buoy that's anchored in the sea there, or whether you're going to let the boat ride free. On the whole when there's a big sea on I prefer to stay free, because it gives you more room to manoeuvre the boat and take account of the currents and the waves.

The sea is coming at you round both sides of the tower and you're riding on a cross current. There'll be a swell of maybe twenty or thirty feet rise and fall going on at the same time; so you have to take these factors into account as to where you let the boat go, whether you're going to put her ahead or astern, how far you're going to let the sea carry you in towards the tower or push you away from it and so on. In your boat you've got the keeper who's going on to the tower and his gear and supplies, and maybe two other men who've come along to help you.

One of the keepers on the tower throws a float down into the water with a length of line attached to it. You fish that out of the sea into your boat. Sometimes it can take a bit of finding after they've thrown it down, you keep seeing it and then losing sight of it again because it's not very big and you're going up and down on the waves. When you've got it, you pull on the line and drag the main rope into your boat; this is the one the men and their gear travel up and down on, the other end of it's attached to the winding gear, the winch on the set-off of the tower that's wound up or let out by the two keepers.

You have to work together like a team with them. When the

keeper in the boat has got into the harness on the rope, they start winding him up and you have to keep the boat the right distance away from the tower. The right distance is when the rope is tight but not taut, so you have to be all the time keeping your eye on it and on where your boat is. If you were to let the sea push you too far away from the tower, the rope could snap and the man would fall in the sea; on the other hand if you're carried too close in, the rope gets loose and the man would swing in against the tower and hit it and perhaps break his back.

You don't have to get excited about it. You just keep your boat as steady as you can and try and keep the right distance between you and the tower. You've got to keep your eye open for any big water coming at you round the tower, and make sure you're head-on towards it. If you were broadside on when if hit you, it's something like a thousand tons of water so if you took that over you, you'd either capsize or you'd be full and you'd sink to the bottom in a matter of seconds like a stone.

As he gets higher up the rope you have to move closer in towards the tower so the keeper can be caught hold of and pulled on by the others. Then for the one who's coming down off the tower into the boat, it's the same thing in reverse: you start off close in and gradually start to move out until you can get him into your boat. That's about all there is to it, it's straightforward apart from occasionally if the sea's heavy: you'll find he's only a couple of feet from you one instant then the next he's thirty feet up in the air because of a wave. It can't be nice for him when that happens but sometimes it can't be avoided; better that way round than if you misjudge it the other way so you're on top of the wave and he's gone down past you into the sea.

I'm the one who decides whether we go out and do the relief or not. If I say not, we don't go. You try not to take risks: you've got to make up your mind before you set off whether it's worth going out there or not. I don't like to think of keeping men waiting to come ashore when they've already been there two months, but I don't see any sense in risking lives for the sake of an extra day or two. If there's not more than a good fifty-fifty chance of being able to do it when I get there, I don't go because they'd be disappointed if they saw the boat coming and then they couldn't get off.

The only way you can judge is by going down to the harbour and having a look at what it's like down there, and estimating what it's going to be like when you get out round the tower. As a rough guide if the waves are a foot high at the end of the quay in the harbour, they'll be ten feet high at the tower. So if they're three feet in the harbour, they'll be thirty feet out there and that's too much to attempt it in, it wouldn't be safe. Another way you can tell if it's a fairly clear day is to look through your binoculars at the horizon. If the horizon isn't a straight line but is moving up and down in what looks like waves, that means there's a big swell on the open water out at sea and it's not safe to go. You've got to have a look at the sky too, sometimes the weather can turn quickly: it might be calm and bright in the harbour but by the time you've got out there it can have gone right round and be starting to get up rough. Feathery clouds are a bad sign: if you see those you know there's a change on the way, so you've got to take that into account.

I think the weather's a funny thing. It can be in the winter months specially, because it can turn the other way too. It can be bad for weeks, then suddenly it'll drop down to nothing almost, then go straight back up again. So there might be only one day you can do the relief on, one day in the middle of a whole period of weeks. Or it might be just one time on one particular day; if you get it right you can do it, then you won't have another chance for perhaps two or three weeks after that. If the relief's due or overdue you stand by; if you miss it then you've another long wait, so you've got to be ready for it if it does.

The total time it takes is up to an hour to get there, about half an hour to put a keeper and his supplies on and get the other one off, and then about an hour back again. Though of course it will be quicker coming home if you've had the wind and the tide against you on the way out. All together, two, two and a half hours, something of that sort. I don't find it a long time to be on the open sea in a thirty-foot boat myself, but that's because I'm used to it. Some of the keepers are not very good sailors, they start being sick as soon as we've left the harbour: that can't be all that nice for them to start off in that condition. I remember an SAK once, it was the first time he'd ever been out there, he was sick pretty near all the way. When we got to the tower he said to me 'Now I know why it's called a relief.'

The sea fascinates me, it always has since I was a boy. It's got such a power to it; when I go away on holiday I always like to go somewhere near the sea, I like to be near where I can go and look at it. I don't think of the relief as putting my own strength or the strength of my boat against it; I think that would be a foolish way of looking at it. Someone with that attitude would be the wrong person to be doing it to my mind. You can't pit yourself against the sea and win; you haven't a hope, the sea's too strong, it would be bound to win every time. I think you've got to accept that before you start; the sea's the master, not you. Any other way of looking at it could only come from someone who didn't know it.

The tower itself, I don't think I've got any particular feelings about. It's a place in the sea, what else can you say about it, nothing really. It's the place I go back and forwards to that's all. I've got my job to do with it, carrying out the relief, and it just happens I'm the person that does it. I like to do it on the right day if I possibly can; I don't like it if there's an overdue. But if there is there is, there's nothing can be done about it. I said earlier on I was the one who decided if the relief would be done or not, but that's not right: it's the sea that decides.

*

v. *Nigel E.*

- I'm eight and a half years old and my daddy's a lighthouse keeper on the tower. It's called a tower because it's like a tower, it sticks straight up out of the sea like that, it hasn't got any rock round it or anything, once you're inside it you can't get out again until the boat comes to take you home.

I know what it looks like because I've seen pictures of it in a book once. One time Daddy showed me some pictures of it that had been taken from an aeroplane, from a helicopter that was flying round it to take pictures of it. I don't know why they were doing it, I suppose it was just because they wanted to take pictures of it. It didn't look very nice in the pictures because you could see the sea was very rough all round it. It looked all right but it didn't look very nice, I don't think I'd like to go there. I might like to go there for about two days to have a look at it in the summer when the sea was very calm, but I wouldn't like to go and stay there for a long time like my daddy does.

He stays there for a very long time, I think he stays there about six months but sometimes he comes home to see us, but then he has to go back again. When he comes home he can't stay with us very long because he has to go back to look after the lighthouse, if he didn't look after it the light would go out. He made a joke once, he said he was a lighthouse keeper but if he didn't go back the light would go out and then everyone would call him a lightout keeper. He said it was a joke; he told it to me once just before he was going back there, he said I should tell it to my friends at school. I did and none of them laughed because they didn't think it was very funny.

When he goes to the lighthouse he wears a uniform and a cap with a badge on it and it's got a sort of stiff peak that sticks out at the front like that. Sometimes he lets me try it on but it keeps falling off. It's got a sort of strap on it that you can fasten under your chin when it's windy so it won't blow away, and it's got a white top but I don't know what that's for. I think it might be to stop people treading on his head. You see on the lighthouse everything's on top of everything, all the rooms are on top of the other, it's not like a house where everything is flat. The rooms are on top of each other, and if you want to go out of one room into another, you don't go out of the door, you climb down to it down some steps through the floor. If you were underneath and it was dark and someone else was going to climb down into the room, he might not be able to see you were there. I think that's why they wear caps which have white tops so people won't put their feet down through the floor on your head.

What a lighthouse keeper does is to make sure that ships are all right. They come past in the sea from all over the world, there are a lot of ships and they have to be careful not to bang into each other. When they get to where the lighthouse is they have to be careful they don't crash into the rocks. That's why the lighthouse is there, it's on the rock to warn the ships that the rocks are there and they must be careful not to crash into them; they have to keep out of one another's way and out of the way of the rocks as well. Sometimes it doesn't always work but it does most times. When it doesn't work you read about it in the papers or see it on the television, and then the police come and ask all the people on the ships what happened and whose fault it was and why it didn't work. It's like when you see a crash that there's been on the road with motor cars and somebody gets into trouble about it afterwards.

The only person who could never get into trouble for it at sea is my daddy. It's not his fault if there's a crash, his lighthouse always stays where it is. That's what it's there for, it's put there so people can see it and keep away from the rocks. They ought to make jolly sure they don't go anywhere near it. I think it's their own fault if they have a crash then when somebody's put a lighthouse there.

That's in the daytime. At night the lighthouse has a light in it and it keeps flashing on and off so the people in the ships can see it and keep out of the way. I'm not sure how it works. I think there's this big light and there's a switch like that one over there by the side of the door, and Daddy stands by the side of it and he keeps flashing it on and off with the switch. He does that all the time while it's dark, and then in the daytime people can see the lighthouse so he doesn't need to keep on flashing the light.

He does it all night; and then in the daytime he goes to bed and goes to sleep so he'll be ready to get up again when it's dark and start flashing the light again for people to see. I don't think he does it every night, I'm not sure. No, he doesn't to it every night because there's someone else to help him, I think they take it in turns. Daddy does it one night and this other man does it the next night.

I suppose it must be very boring standing up all night and switching the light on and off. I expect he reads a book or listens to the radio or something while he's doing it. He doesn't ever go to sleep though while he's doing it because it's his job to make the light flash; if he didn't and there was a crash he'd get into trouble about it, I expect they wouldn't let him be a lighthouse keeper any more after that.

He does other things too while he's there. I'm trying to remember some of the things he told me he does. I know he cooks things for himself to eat, he makes his dinner and looks after himself and does his washing and ironing and things like that, because he hasn't got Mummy there to look after him. If you're a lighthouse keeper you're not allowed to take your mummy, I mean your wife with you, you've got to do everything for yourself because there isn't much room on lighthouses because of all the rooms being on top of one another like I told you.

They're all curved. All the rooms are curved, they're not like these rooms they're like big circles. Not very big circles, not as big as this room, only as big as from there to there. Daddy told me once you could only take four steps and then you'd be up against the wall at the other side. Everything has to be curved because you can't get anything square inside a lighthouse unless it's something small like a chair. But everything else is curved, the tables are curved and the beds are curved: you can't stretch out in bed, you have to sleep with your back bent round in a curve like that.

I know he told me about some other things that they do as well, only I can't remember them. He said they do a lot of running about up and down the stairs all day long. I don't know what they do that for, just to see that everything's all right I suppose. One thing he told me once was that sometimes when the sea's rough it comes right up to the windows, and if somebody's left a window open all the sea comes in and they have to go and get a lot of buckets and cloths and things to wipe it up with. He said they had to keep all the buckets ready in case the sea started coming through the windows.

I should think it isn't very nice to be a lighthouse keeper, I wouldn't like to be one. I should think the worst things about it are that you get very lonely being there all by yourself in the night when it's your turn to make the light work. And you have to be very brave when the sea's rough and it's all coming in through the windows. I should think that you must miss being at home very much, and you can't do things like other people do like going to the shops. And there aren't any doors you can go out of, you can't go anywhere for a walk. It's not like here: I could go out of that door if I wanted to, or out of the front door or out of the back door: I could go round the front of the house or round the back into the garden or I could go out of the gate, and if I wanted to I could go and catch a bus or train and go anywhere I liked. Daddy can't do that, he has to stay where he is all the time on the lighthouse with nobody to talk to. I should think he wants to come home a lot sometimes but he can't, and I shouldn't think that would be very nice.

When he comes home he likes playing football with me, but he can't play football on the lighthouse so that's another reason why I wouldn't like it. Or cricket either in the summer, that's something else that we do, I wouldn't like that either. I think he gets lots of money for doing it though: when you're grown up you have to have a lot of money to buy things with so I should think that's why he does it really. I don't know how much money he gets but I think it's probably about a hundred pounds.

When he comes home is the best time, he takes me out and we go shopping and we buy clothes for me and sweets and ice-cream. When he goes away is the worst time because I don't know when he's coming back. Sometimes Mummy cries when he goes away, I've seen her. You can tell when she's been crying because her eyes get all red. Daddy said it wasn't nice for her when he went away and I should try to be good and to look after her for him, so I do. My sister Jennifer she's only four and a bit so I don't think she misses Daddy all that much. Mummy and Daddy say one day we'll all go to live on another kind of lighthouse where Daddy will be home all the time. I think that'll be very nice because I'd like to live on a lighthouse, I think it would be very exciting.

There's no one else in my class at school whose daddy's a lighthouse keeper. In my whole school there's no one else whose daddy's a lighthouse keeper, so that does make you feel a bit special really when you're at school. The other children are always asking me about it, once Daddy brought me some photographs home that he'd taken of the lighthouse and let me take them to school with me and show them to the teacher. She put them all up on the wall for everyone to see.

That was a long time ago. You don't really feel very special really, I mean not afterwards. The only way you feel special afterwards is not very nice. You're not sure when you're going to see your daddy again, and that's not very nice. I don't think it's really very exciting having a daddy who's a lighthouse keeper. Everybody thinks it's exciting at first but it isn't, not really. If I had to choose about it between one and the other, I think I'd sooner he wasn't a lighthouse keeper.

*

vi. *Jean E.*

– He's a real chatterbox is Nigel, I hope you got some sense out of him. It's difficult for a child to imagine what his daddy does, particularly as he's never seen the place where he works, only pictures of it. But I know how he feels, I feel like that myself sometimes, living here in the Midlands so far away from it. I've never seen the tower either. I don't suppose I ever shall; I did think of going down to that part of the world for our summer holidays one year so we could at least go out on a tripper-boat once to have a look at it. But I don't think Barry's very keen, he likes to spend his leave here at home; we've never been away together for a seaside holiday, he likes to go to the Lake District or somewhere like that. He's not a great one for the seaside, he says he gets enough of that in his job.

We've bought a house here because it's near my parents and because we both feel it's bad for children if they're perpetually moving about. A lot of people joined Trinity for the security, and I think that's true, it does give you security as far as work and the job side of it: once you're in you're in, unless something really drastic happens your husband'll never be unemployed. But unless you've got your own house you've got no real security in your home life: Trinity move you on from one station to the next every few years and you're always dependent on them for where you're going to live. Barry and I decided we weren't going to make that mistake, we'd have a permanent home which wouldn't change no matter where he went because it would be better for the children. There are problems enough in the life as it is, without adding that one as well.

I think the main one without a doubt is this question of who has the authority with the children. It's a perpetual difficulty which we recognize and talk about and try to solve: we don't quarrel about it or anything like that. Jennifer's too young yet for it to affect her, but I'm sure it will do as she gets older, just as it affects Nigel.

With Barry being away, gone completely out of our lives for

two months at a time, it's only natural Nigel looks to me for absolutely everything. I'm the person who tells him what he can do and what he can't do, what time he has to go to bed and all the rest of it. I notice all the time now when Barry's home that Nigel's getting very uncertain about their relationship and where exactly he stands. He'll come to me and ask me if it's all right for him to ask his Daddy something, like will he play football with him or cricket. This isn't Barry's fault, he does everything he can when he comes home to try and get on good terms. I feel sorry for him sometimes; Barry I mean, when I see him struggling to try and get his own son to talk to him. Even minor little details, if we're having tea and Nigel asks if he can get down from table, Barry'll say it's all right: but before he'll move Nigel looks at me first just to check, I have to nod. It's all very awkward and unnatural and partly my fault.

When Barry goes I feel a bit lonely for the first day or two, but after that I pull myself together and get into my household routine. It's not just a household thing, it's a whole way of life, it has to be. I like singing, I'm a member of the local choral society, I go out to choir practice one night a week. Another night, usually a Friday, a friend and her husband come round for a meal. On Sundays I go with the children to my parents' for tea. I do a lot of things like that, regular things, I have a routine for living. But then at the end of eight weeks it has to stop for a month while Barry's home, or most of it does. We'll go one Sunday out of the four to my parents, but on the others he likes to go somewhere else; he doesn't want to be tied to my routine and I wouldn't want him to be either.

Every time he's due home I get a slight feeling of apprehension about him coming. Eight weeks seems a long time to be without someone. I always wonder if he'll have changed in some way. I suppose it's stupid but I can't rid myself of it, even over food and trivial things. I find myself asking him does he still like cod or whatever it is. I even get to the state when I'm asking him how many sugars he takes in tea or coffee. This is what I mean when I say I think it's partly my fault Nigel's uncertain about his daddy; the fact is that I'm anxious about how I stand with him too, and I think children pick these sort of feelings up from you. There's no reason at all why I should be like that and it worries me that I am. We've been married for ten years; nothing has changed between us, we love each other very much, there's never been any question of anyone else for either of us or anything like that. But it's there, the feeling's in me and it'd be silly to pretend it wasn't.

I think it might have something to do with the fact that out of those ten years, Barry's been away on rocks and towers for over six of them, so we've only really had about a third of our life actually together. It seems to have got much more difficult somehow in the last three years that he's been on the tower. Since Jennifer was a baby, when you come to work it out he's hardly seen much of her at all; she's four now, and out of that four years he's spent less than half of it at home, so he hardly knows her. He wasn't here when she first started to walk, he wasn't here when she began to talk; each time he comes back she's grown so much and changed so much he hardly recognizes her he says. I know it's true, I can appreciate how he feels.

Another problem that doesn't concern just Barry and me, but much more Nigel, is the other children at school. I think this applies to the teachers as well. I get the impression that because his daddy's a lighthouse keeper. they all look on him as though he was some kind of animal in a zoo, they treat him as though there was something peculiar about him. If anything about lighthouses crops up they always make a point of emphasizing it in relation to him. I remember at the school carol service last year, I forget which one it was they were singing but I know it had some reference in it somewhere to a shining light: and everybody started turning round and looking at him, smiling and winking as much as to say they knew it had a special meaning to him.

I get the feeling that the teachers look on him in some way as being a deprived child; they go out of their way to be specially understanding and kind, and they're always emphasizing they know his daddy's away and it must be hard for him. I suppose this sounds ungrateful: I know they mean it for the best, but I can't help wishing they wouldn't do it, I'd prefer them to treat it as something ordinary and normal. I wish it could be got over to people that it wasn't something freakish, that being a lighthouse keeper is really not all that much different from any other kind of job. I suppose that's too much to expect. You wouldn't take it as a subject for a book if you didn't think of it in the same way, an occupation that was slightly odd and a matter for curiosity.

It's an isolated world out there, I've long since accepted it's got nothing to do with me. I know very little about it and I never could. Barry's made odd remarks from time to time about it; one time he brought some photographs home with him, but we don't really talk about it much. It's his world and one I can't share, I have to put up with that. I wouldn't like to become what they call 'Trinity minded', where all your life revolves round the service. I couldn't face the prospect for instance of living in a cottage attached to a station; that would have no appeal to me at all, to be spending all my time in the company of other people whose husbands were in the same job. I've heard it said Trinity's one great big family and everybody in it helps everybody else; but all I can say is I feel sorry for anybody who's got themselves in it up to their necks like that, it must mean a very limited outlook on life. I don't think they ought to bring their children up in that sort of atmosphere.

Barry's chosen this as his way of life. He's every right to do that, and the fact that he likes his job and is happy in it is very important. If he's happy with his work, that makes me happy; I'd hate to think of him doing something he didn't like just for the sake of me and the children. Whatever a man does it ought to be something that gives him pleasure and satisfies him. I'd rather he was doing what he wanted than spending his life on an assembly line in a factory or anything else that he didn't enjoy.

As long as he wants to go on doing it, I wouldn't dream of trying to persuade him to do something else just for my sake, because it was making me unhappy.

But when it begins to affect your children as they start growing up, like I see it affecting Nigel: I think then you do have to start looking at it again and wondering if it's the right thing. How a husband and wife lead their individual lives is up to them; if they can put up with separation that's their own affair for them to sort out themselves. But a child's a third person; the older he gets the more thought you have to start giving to how it's affecting him. I'm not at all clear in my mind yet about it, but I think in another year or two Barry and I'll have to think hard about this.

I think about it constantly because I'm here at home, I'm with Nigel all the time so I can't help think about it. I wonder if Barry thinks about it when he's away though; I'm not at all certain that he does. When he goes off to that tower I know in some respects it's a relief to him; he's leaving all the problems of daily life behind. But sometimes I've felt that just for once I'd like to go off there myself instead of him and leave him here at home with the children. Not in a vindictive sense but so he'd get a chance to know what it was like with them with one parent away. I've never said it to him; but I suspect sometimes what he goes off to shouldn't be called just a tower; it's an ivory tower.

*

vii.

The old man living by himself in his house on the island, built where he could still see it on the horizon; a place he'd been happy on and frightened on, a place where he'd felt lonely and a place where he'd been at home. A proper lighthouse, one of the great sea towers.

Four years ago now, nearly five. Knowing him fostered imagination; but I can't go back and see him and talk to him, he died last year . . .

Alex, swarthy-faced Cornishman sitting in a pub; that's right my handsome, but how to tell you what it's like, it's a different world out there, you'd have to come and see. Yes of course we'd have you it'd make a change instead of only talking to ourselves all the time . . .

The fair-haired giant, Steve; I reckon we could squeeze you in somewhere if you wanted to come, but Christ those cigars stink I'd worry more about dying from suffocation from them than about being smashed to buggery by the sea . . .

He's not mentioned the subject so he must have got used to them since I've been on his tower lee with him and Alex and Barry so far for nearly four weeks, in the middle of winter, and longer than expected or intended but it hasn't seemed to have mattered; time's passing has been unnoticed and unnoted until today which is Monday or Tuesday. It's all been enjoyable, and even the resulting disorientation and complete loss of sense of time has been an interesting experience.

A continuous spiral staircase goes up round the inside walls of the tower from the entrance floor to the upper lens. The three living rooms – kitchen, bedroom and sitting-room – are in an inner section, the staircase passing outside them.

The spine down the middle is the weight-tube. Until a few years ago the lenses revolved by a mechanism working on the grandfather clock principle, with descending weights on chains.

That mechanism is now driven by electricity, and the weights have been removed; but the tube still remains in position passing down through the centre of each room.

*

Steve is 47 'or thereabouts'. Married, four daughters, a Liverpudlian now living in Yorkshire. 'I've been in the Service since I was born.' More precisely, twenty-five years. PK for seven years, four of them on this tower. A thick bristle of fair hair, bright blue eyes, the build of a rugby front row forward. Big hands, nose, feet, ears, jaw; an ebulliently large personality as well, always talking, laughing and joking. Keeps up an uninterrupted flow of swear words, like everyone else.

Alex is 26, also tall, but thin. Six years in the service, two here. He is married, has a 2-year-old daughter, his wife is expecting another child in the near future. Very talkative, too.

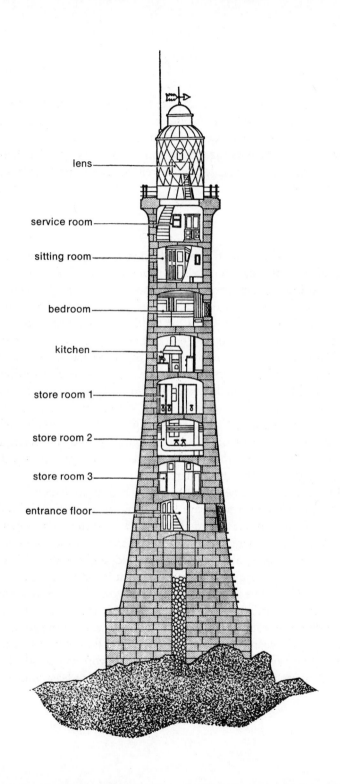

lens

service room

sitting room

bedroom

kitchen

store room 1

store room 2

store room 3

entrance floor

Barry is smaller and shorter; 32, brown-eyed, with fair curly hair. Stockily built, wears glasses; talkative but quieter in manner than Steve and Alex. Just as much to say but says it more quietly. He came into the service about ten years ago; has been here three. Met his wife Jean, children Nigel and Jennifer while I was ashore.

*

– Belt up the pair of you, as Principal Keeper it's me who should make the speech of welcome and it's me who's going to: so sit still and keep your flaming mouths shut. Right then, a short address by me, Principal Keeper Stephen St John Emlyn Hughes Liverpool For The Cup Collins, to our visitor on the evening of his arrival on our tower. It is being made under great difficulty in the kitchen owing to the presence of Assistant Keeper Alexander Aloysius Merton and Assistant Keeper Barrington Cheese Biscuit Pennington, who are both making a lot of noise because they're jealous and think they ought to be allowed to speak first. They're not going to though, there's going to be a bit of order and discipline around the place. If there isn't they'll get their teeth smashed in like they always do when they don't obey my orders.

Order Number One. We have now had arrived here in our humble abode a man who says he's going to try to write a book what will contain our recorded words. He will then muck about with them, alter them, turn them round and twist their meaning into the exact opposite of what we've said, and eventually issue the whole lot in print and make himself a fortune out of it. He says he will use our words and only our words: so this is going to cause grave difficulties. I happen to know for a fact that you two other see you next Tuesdays only know an entire total of one word between the two of you, or if you do know any other words I've never heard you use them. The word is one which I myself never use, spelt Pee Aitch You Kay; or at least you two think it is, because you're the biggest pair of ignorant layabouts in the lighthouse service.

So Order Number One is that this word mustn't ever be used in the presence of our guest. Otherwise his book will convey to the British public that all lighthouse keepers are a lot of foulmouthed yobs who go around swearing morning noon and night and can't speak proper. Which is true but we don't want it spread around. So I don't want to hear no fucking this and fucking that and fucking the other all the time, right?

Order Number Two is that from now on neither of you will even so much as open your bleeding mouths when this taperecorder is running without getting my permission first, and then getting me to translate what you say into decent fucking English what's fit to print.

Order Number Three is that while he's here with us, you will take the opportunity not only to use clean language but also smarten up your whole general appearance and behaviour. If you don't you'll end up being portrayed as the deplorable yobs you are, and it'll serve you both fucking right, got it? This is the end of what I want to say, except to repeat I insist you obey my orders and try to imitate me and speak decent. End of message and over and out.

*

– Good evening to the world, this is Assistant Keeper Sir Alexander Andrew Merton speaking. I would just like to say a few words to add to those our esteemed Principal Keeper has been saying to you. In the first place he is absolutely and indubitably wrong in attempting to convey the impression that myself and my noble comrade Mr Barrington Cheese Biscuit have a combined vocabulary which is so inordinately constricted that it consists in its entirety of one rude word. This is a load of balls and what's more is untrue. I myself for instance am familiar with such words as antidisestablishmentarianism and pusillaminous, both of which I use in natural ordinary everyday conversation as the occasion arises, which it does frequently on this station when the PK is out of the room. The only reason we don't use such words in front of him is because he's an ignorant sod who wouldn't understand them, and we don't want to make him feel embarrassed at being in the presence of people of greater fucking culture and sensitivity than himself, which includes just about everyone else there is.

The other thing I would like to make clear is any impression he might convey that as PK he is in charge of this station, or has any say whatever in the running of it, is absolutely and utterly false. He's of no use for anything except peeling potatoes and emptying the Elsan bucket. Which incidentally is an occupation we're trying to cure him of, since neither of us is keen on eating potatoes that have been peeled in an Elsan bucket. As for actually running the station, the only thing he could run would be a cold water tap. I might add, in fact I'm going to add, that if it weren't for the long and arduous not to say Herculean labours of myself and my friend Mr Cheese Biscuit Pennington, this light we tend here would almost certainly go out, and navigators and mariners would live in fear of taking even a single step on these waters because they would undoubtedly sink. Which isn't surprising when you come to think about it because anyone who tried to walk on water needs his head examining.

And lastly I'd like to add while I have the opportunity that in time you'll find there's only one person really worth listening to here, and that's me. Quite apart from the fact that I'm the only one who can speak real nice, I'm also the only one with any degree of perspicacity, sagacity, insight or sensitivity, and in addition to which my most outstanding characteristic is modesty. For this reason I beg anyone who might happen eventually to come across all this crap when it's been transcribed from the oral into the calligraphic or whatever it's going to be, to pay no attention at all to anyone else's contribution. So to put it all in one word, you other two can get stuffed and piss off, because you've nothing of value to contribute.

*

– God be with this lighthouse and all who sail on her. This is the electronically reproduced voice of Assistant Keeper Barrington Edwards-Smith-Pennington, otherwise known as Cheese Biscuit though don't ask me why, I've forgot. I will rephrase that. I dunno why the name arose, I must have forgotten, that I knows. Yes, it is quite true that many lighthouses are inhabited by poets; I would say it is not a generally known fact that poetical lighthouse keepers are on the increase nowadays. This may be because we're now getting a better type of man coming into the Service, not like the two previous ignorant gits you've just heard from and who are now trying to interrupt me and prevent me saying what I want to, and who'll get themselves battered into a pulp if there's any more of it.

Since you ask me, which you haven't but I don't intend to fuck about waiting until you get round to it, I'd also say yes it's true, the problem of violence is a very common one on lighthouses. Only last week for instance on this very tower on which we are actually at this moment sitting or lying, only last week none other than the Principal Keeper himself was seen slashing at his teeth with a razor while trying at the same time to shave himself with a toothbrush. My trusty colleague and master-pedestrian Alexander The Great Merton has been known on occasions to step on flies and crush them under foot. Which believe me takes some doing, particularly when they're his own and he's still got his trousers on. I admit it is a rare sight for him to wear trousers but it does occur.

However, to return to the problem of whatever it was you forgot to ask me about. I would say, speaking from my own fifty-five years as a Supernumerary Acting Assistant Acting Principal Keeper, which is the position I at present hold, with all the terrible burden of responsibility it entails, that unless and until this type of man you have previously heard from is thrown out of the Service lock stock and barrel the noble traditions of lighthouse men will no longer be upheld but will be downheld.

Seriously though, since neither of these other two ignoramuses has had sufficient education to think about it, I would like to extend the hand of greeting to you and welcome you aboard our humble tower. Thank you: could I have my hand back now please? Thank you. I hope to have the pleasure of speaking to you again shortly. It's not for me to boast, but it must be perfectly obvious from what you've heard so far that only one person here has anything worthwhile to say – so I leave you to draw your own conclusions. The others will go rabbiting on' and on; I'm a man of few words myself, but they're always very well chosen ones. So I suggest with all due modesty that for the sake of general interest you concentrate on the only person here who isn't crackers; namely me, Cheese Biscuit.

*

– Christ, I'm only the bleeding PK, I thought you were supposed to be the fucking writer, not me. How do you mean – all the way up from the bottom right to the top, me trying to describe it? Oh Jesus all right come on then, I'll have a go.

– Right, well we start here then, outside on what we call the set-off. Can you hear me with this racket going on, the sea battering away round the foot of the tower just below us? I'm not staying outside long, not in a Force 8 and all this bloody water shooting up at us all the time.

My God, you are going to be difficult aren't you? Why is it called the set-off, I haven't the faintest idea bloody why it's called the set-off. Because it's a bleeding great circle of concrete base, going down into the sea with the tower set off in the middle of it I suppose. Anyway here we've got this kind of circular concrete catwalk, about three feet wide and thirty feet up above the water.

This is what you landed on when you came up out of the boat. A rope goes from the top of the tower down to the boat, and it has another rope attached to it from a winch on here. The winch lifts you up and pulls you in towards the set-off. The winch hasn't got any brakes on, you have to rely on the strength in the arms of the two men turning the handles. If they were to slip or let you fall, you'd have had it.

We don't leave the winding-gear set up on here in winter because the sea's too high; it'd be breaking over it every day and making it rusty. We only set it up when somebody's coming aboard or going ashore. It takes about an hour to bolt the winch into the concrete and fix the ropes, and then the same amount of time to take it down again afterwards. All right in the summer but wet and freezing cold down here working on it in the winter. Fuck all else to see, so we'll go up the dog-steps now to the entrance door.

Exercising considerable restraint, I have to say no I don't know why they're called the dog-steps except to say I'm bloody certain it's got nothing to do with bleeding dogs. You show me a dog that could get up those and I'll introduce you to our tortoise that plays the violin. All right, can we go up now? Thank you, after you.

We've now ascended about thirty feet of metal dog-steps which are bolted to the outside of the tower and come up from the set-off to the entrance door. They stick out only about six inches from the wall, so you can't get your foot in the rungs properly, only your toes. Before you ask me I'll tell you I don't know, I presume they were designed by a man with either exceptionally small feet or an exceptionally small brain.

So here we are, having come in through the heavy gun-metal doors which weigh several hundredweight each. We keep them open when we can, so we get a bit of fresh air in through the tower. But most of the time in winter we close and bolt them against the sea. Here we're sixty feet up from the water, so that gives you some idea of the sort of seas we get. This is just a plain circular concrete floored room, about twelve feet in diameter and with a bloody great metal tube two feet in diameter in the middle of it. That's the weight-tube. Before they put the machinery in up at the top of the tower to make the lenses revolve, there were heavy weights on chains in it; they were wound up to the top inside this tube and then dropped down to make the lenses turn. I believe I'm right in saying they had to be wound up about once every forty minutes by whichever keeper was on duty.

The weight-tube was put in when the place was built nearly a hundred years ago. There's discussions going on at the moment about what would happen if it was taken out now it's no longer needed. Does it help to hold the tower up or doesn't it: could it be taken out to give more space inside or would that affect the structure? My own feeling is it wouldn't make the slightest bleeding difference. As I understand it the granite blocks the tower's built of were dovetailed into each other in such a way that it'll still be rigid enough to stand on its own, even with the metal tube down the middle taken out.

Nothing much else to see on this entrance floor except spare coils of rope and a lifebelt, and an inflatable rubber dinghy packed up there on the ceiling. Presumably that's for us if we want to leave in a hurry; which might not be possible depending on the circumstances. The only other thing of interest is that manhole cover in the floor. Underneath there is our freshwater storage tank; it holds about a thousand gallons, and one of the Trinity House tenders comes round from time to time to top it up. It's pumped by hand with this pump up to the kitchen. Now we go up an open metal stairway curving round the wall up to the next level through a hole in the floor.

Now then, this is another plain granite-walled room with wooden cupboards all round it, where we store the detonators and charges for the explosive fog-gun which we'll come to when we eventually get to the gallery at the top of the tower. There's nothing else on this floor except a door over there to the place where we keep the coke for our cooker in the kitchen.

Up another open metal staircase round the wall, and now we're on the next floor which is the lower of the two oil-storage floors. Seven big oil tanks full of the paraffin for the light.

Fascinating, you could stand here for hours contemplating them, couldn't you? You might, but I couldn't. All right then, up we go again to the next floor; another stairway curving up and round the wall and we come to another lot of oil tanks round the wall, painted yellow like the ones below. No prizes will be given for working out this is called the upper oil-storage floor, in contrast to the one beneath which is called the lower oil-storage floor. Fucking marvellous thing, the English language is.

Everything's dark and gloomy, yes. When I first came here this was what surprised me, I think it does everyone else too. When you see it from outside, the tower's white granite so you take it for granted it's going to be light and airy inside. The reason it isn't is that the walls are very thick; there's an outer wall and an inner wall, with a space of about three or four feet in between. The windows are one to each level, small, and double too of course, outer and inner. So you don't get a lot of light in through them. We use the space between the windows of this floor to keep our fresh vegetables in; it's cool and away from the heat of the kitchen, and anyway we haven't got room up there for them.

Before we go any further I'll try and explain something else. Up to now, the three stairways we've come up have been a continuous spiral, anti-clockwise round the inside of the walls, and opening directly on to each level. The next three rooms have got doors to them because the staircase goes round the outside of them.

So to the next floor, up concrete steps now, we open the door and here we are in the kitchen. A circular room about twelve feet in diameter. This will be about eighty or eighty-five feet above the sea. We get lots of spray up here, waves breaking just below the window sometimes. Right, now what's first? The weight-tube running down the middle of course; a small curved formica topped table fitted round one side of it. Behind it up against the wall, just room to squeeze in on it, an old bench seat with brown leather cloth cushions on. One small wooden

chair which only the PK is allowed to sit in, but he can only sit
in it if one of the other two layabouts hasn't already collared it.

If you take the cushions off the bench you'll find cupboards
underneath where we keep our store of pornographic books and
magazines, and spare tins of food. Above it on the wall are three
more cupboards, one for each of us for our main lot of tinned
food. Going round the wall to the right of the bench is the
window; underneath slightly to one side of it, the sink. Two
taps, one with a silver painted pipe and the other with a red
pipe. They're not hot and cold; the silver one's fresh water and
the red one's rain water which we use for washing-up or washing
ourselves with. We only use the fresh water for drinking. In
the sink a plastic washing-up bowl, which is also used as our
bath. If you want an all-over wash, you put it on the floor and
stand in it. You could sit in it if you wanted to; at least some
people could.

Over the sink a small bathroom wall cabinet with a mirror
in its door. Open it and four sections inside, one for each man's
toothbrush, brush and comb, after-shave lotion, razor and so on.
One of these days I'm going to make a strict rule about people
keeping to their own section; at the moment bloody well near
every fucking inch of it's taken up with things of Alex's. It'll
probably stay in that sort of shambles till I go off my head and
tip the whole lot out of the window into the sea. It might be
simpler to throw Alex into the sea, but it's a subject I'm giving
considerable thought to before reaching a decision.

Further along round the wall, next to the sink is the cooker.
It's a Rayburn, it runs on coke: the coke store is the cupboard
down on the oil-storage floor, I pointed that out to you. On top
of the Rayburn is a copper boiler which we keep full to the brim
all the time, to give us a constant supply of hot water for washing
and washing-up. Every time you use any out of it, you're expected to refill it to the top again, except in the case of Barry: if he
ever remembered to top it up after he'd used it it'd worry us
because we'd take it as a sign of abnormality.

In what space is left between the cooker and the door is the dresser where we keep our crockery and cutlery. Not much of it because we haven't got room. Five cups on hooks, no saucers, four or five dinner plates, a few dishes and odds and ends, and the salt and pepper. Butter and bread and things like that which we're using all the time, we keep outside in the space between the windows on the staircase opposite. On the wall above the dresser is the r/t set; that's our only link with the mainland.

Most of the daily life of the lighthouse takes place in this room; the three of us in a space twelve feet across with the weight-tube down the centre. Two paces from the door to the tube, two paces from the tube to the window. Fortunately most of us are small. Nothing much else in here: a piece of old string strung across with our towels and the drying-up cloths on, a calendar on the wall, a tattered old pin-up fastened inside Alex's food cupboard door so he can see her every time he opens it. And that's about the lot.

Well now, our only inflexible rule is that every time you're in the kitchen you sit down and make a cup of tea and have a smoke. It's exhausting work trying to describe a place you've taken for granted so long, particularly when you know some-body's tape-recording what you say. If we were to go down to the bottom and start again and you were to play it back as we went, I'd notice half a dozen things I'd forgotten to mention even though they were right in front of my eyes.

Let's have a listen to it while we're having our tea. Give the other two a shout so they can come and hear it as well; it'll prove to them my language is nothing like as terrible as they're always saying it is. They say I can't talk without saying effing this and effing that in every sentence. I don't think I did once, did I? I think I did very well, to be honestly modest about it. Anyway, wind it back and switch on and we'll see.

*

– In view of that deplorable effort by the Principal Keeper who's now exhausted because he's senile, it has been decided that from here on upwards the description should be done by me, Assistant Keeper Sir Alexander Merton. He may be all right for oil tanks and coke bunkers, but the really interesting part which is to come now needs someone with a sharper eye and a better command of language to do justice to it. Onwards and upwards to the bedroom.

Just about room to turn round in here, but not much more. It's another inner room with a door, and the staircase going up outside it. It's got three bunks curved round the wall in a row. They're shaped like bananas, otherwise they wouldn't fit in. About five foot ten inches long each, so you can never stretch out your full length. Correction, ordinary sized people can't: midgets like Barry are all right. Blankets, sheets, pillows: foam-rubber mattresses with boards underneath, not springs.

Weight-tube down the middle as usual, and a cupboard under each bunk with fitted drawers and shelves inside it for personal gear. In the small space under the staircase a curtained off section for hanging things up. Only one of the bunks has got a window to it, that's mine, I like a view of the sea. A curtain to each one; when you get inside you pull the curtain to, and you have an electric light bulb and switch over your head. The curtains serve two purposes: one to keep the light out while anyone sleeps in the daytime, the other so you can read in bed with your light on without disturbing someone who might be sleeping. And we usually keep the door shut as well, so this room's nearly always completely dark.

Up on top over the three bunks there are two smaller ones that have to be reached with a movable ladder. They're the same length but only two feet six inches in height. One of them we use for stowing spare gear in, the other we use for stowing our visitor in; he knows bloody well what it looks like so he can describe it himself if he wants to.

Outside the bedroom door, opposite it on the stairs is a

double window; and on the ledge inside it is an old half-pint pewter beer mug. This is our urinal: when you've used it you open the outer windows and tip the contents out. As a matter of great scientific interest, if when you turn it upside down you can see the piss fall out and blow away, the wind's Force 7 or less. If you can't see it come out and it just goes whoosh and disappears, the wind's Force 8 or more.

Up the stairs again and now we come to the sitting-room. A kidney-shaped table round the weight-tube, three old Parker-Knoll chairs; near the window three small fridges along the wall, one for each of us, and a small portable television set on the top. A bookcase on the wall with a few old books in, and cupboards underneath where we keep forms and papers. Two tatty old rugs on the floor. Heating, well the flue-pipe from the Rayburn comes up the wall there as you see, so that keeps it nice and warm. If there's three of us in here all wanting to watch the telly at once, the last man in has to see as best he can from behind the weight-tube. This room is about a hundred or a hundred and five feet above sea level. Spray sometimes up as high as the window, a bit now and again like now while I'm talking to you.

It's beginning to look as though it's building up for a good blow as a matter of fact. If it keeps up like this by the weekend we should have got a big swell on the sea; the waves'll start hitting the tower then, it'll be an experience for you.

So now we've been through the three rooms we live in: the kitchen, the bedroom and the sitting-room. As we go up to the next floor we're back again to the pattern of the open floors with the staircase round the wall.

Next is this one, the service room: we come into it through a double door like an air lock, only it's for fire and noise prevention. In here you can hardly move a foot, it's crammed with machinery: generator, stand-by generator, batteries and all the rest. A work bench, a store cupboard over there for spares for the light, and air-pressure tanks for the oil for the light. It's pumped up to here by hand, then it's vapourized and the vapour goes up to the burners above. That'll become clearer to you now as we go up the ladder from here to the light.

Here we are then; this is what it's all about, the light itself. That's all it is, a great big gas mantle. We light it with a match. It burns paraffin vapour pumped up from the tanks below. What gives the light its power is the lenses all round the platform we're on: they revolve round the light and magnify it into the beam. The rock light station where you were before had a beam of light that revolved itself, as opposed to this one which is a fixed point of light with lenses moving round it.

There are two gas mantles on platforms one above the other; the wall of lenses revolves round the pair of them. Somebody told me the total weight of these lenses is about eleven tons; they're on bearings in a bath of mercury, and they're so finely balanced you can push them round with one finger. Well two fingers. Well if I put both hands up and give a hefty shove. Doesn't make a sound when they move either. Fantastic.

In the middle among all the cog wheels and crankshafts underneath there, you'll see the most important single item on the station which is the Elsan toilet, commonly known as the thunder bucket. After you've used it you pour some water in from the container by the side of it, swill it around and then take it out through that low door there out on to the gallery and tip it over the side. The contents that is, not the bucket. We had an SAK out here last year and he threw the bucket over as well. That kind of thing tends to cause bad feeling; for some days afterwards Steve was for chucking him in the sea and not letting him come back again until he'd found it.

When you go out on the gallery to empty the bucket or contemplate the scenery, watch yourself with the door by the way; it's solid gun metal and bloody heavy, and it can easily swing to behind you and leave you stuck out there.

Finally we go out through it and here we are out on the gallery. This'll be about a hundred and eighty feet above sea level, and right bleeding wet and windy it is today too. You can see for miles but there's nothing to see but sea, apart from over there on the horizon where there's that island. Nothing of interest out here apart from fresh air, so let's go back inside.

Sometime if you ever want what you might call a psychedelic experience, you want to come up here when it's sunny and sit inside on one of the lens platforms and look out at the sea and the sky through them. That's something I couldn't describe in words, what it looks like and what the effect is. But it's an experience my handsome, you try it for yourself one day.

*

– The two things neither of those two other silly bastards have described for you are only the two most important things here, that's all. That'll give you some idea how unreliable they are and why I told you I was the only one who'd got anything worth while to say. The two things are the main reason for us being here in the first place, which is to light the light and sound the fog-gun. Are you technically minded? Well never mind, neither am I.

Lighting the light. You pump up the oil to the required pressure which is about seventy pounds to the square inch. Twenty minutes or so before you're due to put the light in, you light some meths in a small brass pan and put it in underneath to warm up the vapour to the outlet valve. When the whole thing's nicely brewed up, you turn that tap: the warm vapour comes out and goes up into the mantle and you light it. It's like a great big glowing ball of white about a foot in diameter. Whoever's on watch has to keep his eye on it through the night, check the pressure's keeping up and the burners aren't clogged. Then when the light's extinguished in the morning we clean out the burners, prick out the holes in them to make sure they haven't got sooted over, and then put them back again ready for the next night.

They didn't tell you either that during the day we hang

curtains up inside the lenses. This is because what they are is enormous magnifying glasses, so if you got the sun striking in through them on to the machinery it could cause a fire. Another thing Alex should've told you instead of all that crap about psychedelic experience is we spend half our lives polishing the lenses and keeping them clean. If he's up there contemplating the sea and the sky all the time, it's no wonder the lenses are always so bloody filthy when it's my turn to clean them. In addition we have to keep all the machinery clean and sparkling without a speck of dust or a smear or oil on it anywhere. This is because the PK is obsessional about cleanliness and can't think of anything else for us to do to prevent us disturbing him while he's trying to sleep.

The other important thing is the fog-gun, which is an antiquated jib outside on the gallery. When it's foggy you go out there, fix a couple of detonators and charges on the arms of it, and wind it up in the air so that it's over the top of the tower. Then you go back inside and sit on a chair inside the doorway and set the lever of the electric circuit for firing it. Once every five minutes you press the plunger to set off one of the charges. You wait another five minutes till the bell on the timing clock rings, then you fire the second one. When you've set two off, you have to go back out on the gallery, wind the jib down and reload it and wind it up again. Every ten minutes for however many hours the fog lasts, night or day, you go on firing; and a more boring occupation than sitting up there on your own and pressing the plunger every five minutes would be difficult to imagine.

I think you should now have got a picture of what everything's for and how it all works, and you won't need me to emphasize that it's all highly skilled work calling for years of training and experience; or to put it another way it's the sort of thing any half-wit could pick up in a week.

*

STEVE: I mean it's funny though isn't it, I mean seriously. Out here you use one kind of language all day long; you think nothing of it, all this effing and blinding. But at home you'd never think of it, would you? You wouldn't dream of getting up from the table after breakfast and saying 'I'm going to have a fucking shit'. You'd say 'I'm going upstairs', 'I must go to the toilet', something like that; only here it never crosses your mind to put it any other way, you say you're going to have a fucking shit. 'Pass the fucking sugar', 'Stop fucking about', 'What's on the fucking telly tonight?' that's your natural way of talking all the time, you don't think anything of it. If he's going to try and give an impression how we live, how we talk, I mean he'll have to put that in won't he? It won't bear any resemblance at all to what it's really like if he doesn't.

ALEX: No, no fucking resemblance at all.

STEVE: Exactly. That just exactly demonstrates it. Did you say it deliberately?

ALEX: Of course I said it deliberately you silly prick.

STEVE: Anyhow it still demonstrates it.

BARRY: What demonstrates it even clearer is you didn't hear what he just called you. I mean you heard it but it didn't register did it?

STEVE: What did he say?

BARRY: Don't you honestly know? Go on then, play that bit back.

STEVE: . . . Oh. Yes well Christ that's what I mean, isn't it? But that first evening after he'd come and we all did our little speeches, we laid it on a bit though didn't we?

ALEX: Some of us did, you speak for yourself.

STEVE: I know I did; I don't remember what I said exactly, but I know I did. Only why did I?

ALEX: I don't know you laid it on all that much.

BARRY: It was quite restrained for you, I thought you were making an effort to try and talk posh because you're the PK.

STEVE: Look this is supposed to be a serious fucking discussion;

for Christ's sake let's try and keep to the point he asked us to talk about which is why we use this fucking terrible language all the time.

ALEX: He's a fine bloody one himself anyway. It was the first thing I heard him say when he was swinging in towards the set-off on the rope and I was trying to catch him; I pulled him in a bit sharp and he hit his arm on the winch and he said 'Fucking hell'. I was very distressed about it frankly. I was shocked to think we were going to have someone who talked like that to stay with us.

STEVE: Look will you stop arsing about and stick to the fucking point? Any fucker'd say 'Fuck' if he nearly broke his fucking arm on the fucking winch, that's not what we're talking about. We're talking about using it in ordinary everyday conversation. When does it start?

BARRY: What do you mean when does it start, it never stops.

STEVE: I'm sorry, I'm doing my best with these ignorant uneducated bastards. I'll try again. When does it start? The sort of change into this kind of language, I mean? The day after you get here, the moment you set foot on the place, when?

ALEX: In the boat on the way out I suppose, really.

BARRY: No it's sooner than that; it's as soon as you get outside the front door when you've left home, I'd say. I remember once the taxi came to take me down to the boat, I got all my gear in it, I kissed Jean and the kids good-bye and got in, it was raining and the first thing I said to the taxi driver was something about it being a fucking horrible day.

ALEX: We're talking about civilized people, not uneducated oafs. Where I have trouble is the other way round mostly: two months out here, and then the first few days at home are bloody murder, I have to keep biting my tongue. I'm not kidding, I have to think twice every time before I speak.

STEVE: Christ that's terrible, I'm hopeless. We had the wife's mother with us last year; I wasn't thinking one day, she was doing something or other and I told her to stop fucking about. Very nicely you know, very politely, all my customary dignity and charm. She nearly fell through the fucking floor, I mean she nearly fell through the floor.

ALEX: I've done that, I told one of the neighbour's kids to fuck off once. It really upset June, she tore me off a strip afterwards. She said 'Is that how you talk out on the lighthouse?' What could I say? I said 'Yes, as a matter of fact it is'. Wait a minute, I haven't finished yet: she said 'What, in front of the PK?'

STEVE: Jesus.

BARRY: Anyway, get back to the point; what he asked us to talk about is why we do it.

ALEX: I don't think there's anything to discuss, I think we ought to tell him to get stuffed. We all do it, why shouldn't we; he does it himself too, it's natural, all men do it. It's what's called a natural phenomenon, you get a bunch of men together and they all do it; it doesn't mean anything, it's just natural behaviour.

STEVE: So what are you saying, when we're at home with our wife and kids and family and not talking like that we're not being natural?

ALEX: No I'm saying it's natural when we're here, it's natural for any all-male group.

BARRY: I bet parsons and vicars don't; I bet if you get a little group of them having coffee together they're not all effing and blinding.

ALEX: How do you know, you've never been in one.

BARRY: Fucking hell, you're not serious are you? Fuck me, he fucking is too.

STEVE: Don't be fucking stupid. Look, there you are, this is exactly what we're talking about, we're at it again. Why don't we say 'You're not serious are you, yes he is serious', why do we have to keep saying 'fucking' all the time, this is the whole point isn't it?

BARRY: Habit.

STEVE: Yes but why? Smoking's a habit, lots of things are a habit, but they've all got some sort of underlying reason. Smoking calms your nerves or whatever, but saying 'fucking' or 'shitting' and 'bastard' and all the rest of it, what does it do for you, I mean does it give you any pleasure or make you feel better? Why do you do it? I don't mean you personally, I mean you, me, him, all of us. What do we think it is, funny?

ALEX: No, why should we? I don't laugh every time you swear. I take it for granted. In fact if you stopped doing it I'd think there was something wrong with you.

BARRY: We expect it of each other you mean? That's absolute balls. I don't swear because you expect it of me, I swear because I feel like swearing that's all.

ALEX: That's just what I've been saying, isn't it? It's your natural way of talking when you're with a group of men.

STEVE: That's a typical bloody sweeping statement of yours, that is. It's not true, because it depends on who the men are and where they are and where the group is. Let's say there was a conference of lighthouse keepers, right? All up at Trinity House or somewhere like that. Two hundred of them in a room. When they're on their lighthouses they all carry on like we do, most of them. But they wouldn't be talking like that if you put them all in together. It's to do with the size of the group.

ALEX: When I was an SAK I was with a PK once, he didn't like swearing at all, he wouldn't let anybody swear.

BARRY: You and him must have got on a treat then.

ALEX: No, it was funny: mind you I was younger in those days, I had more respect for PKs.

BARRY: You got a better type of man being a PK.

ALEX: True, absolutely true. What I meant was funny was he didn't like swearing, so I restrained myself and so did the AK who was on the station as well.

STEVE: Oh yes that's right yes, blame it all on the PK. You daft prats, I've heard words from you I'd never heard before, what do you want out here then, a fucking Sunday School?

ALEX: Look, why don't you ever let me finish what I'm saying?

BARRY: Because it always takes you so long to get round to the point. Go on then, get on with it.

ALEX: He was a miserable sod; that's the point I'm trying to make. We restrained our language because he didn't like it – but he was a miserable sod and it was a miserable fucking station. We weren't being ourselves, we weren't being natural: that's the point I've been trying to make for the last ten fucking minutes only you're both too fucking stupid to see it.

STEVE: It doesn't mean anything, does it? Using bad language, putting it in every sentence just for emphasis like Alex did then, it's meaningless really, it's senseless.

BARRY: No I don't think you can dismiss it like that. I think it's useful, it's a sort of lubricant, it helps you to talk.

STEVE: Fuck me, you must have got into a right fucking state if you can't fucking talk without saying fucking this that and the other all the time.

BARRY: Perfect example, I couldn't have put it better.

ALEX: Anyway what are we all getting so apologetic about it for, and sort of feeling all the time we shouldn't do it really?

BARRY: Because we want to give a good impression, I suppose.

ALEX: Do we fuck.

STEVE: That's a different question. No, we don't want to give a good impression. We want to give a true impression. That's how we talk. There you are, Tony, we haven't really got anywhere about it, except for what it's worth we've recorded a bit of an example of the level of our conversation.

*

Today which is Monday or Tuesday; disorientation and loss of sense of time, and how it comes about.

Over a period of twenty-five days they have had eight middle watches each, when they were on duty from midnight until four o'clock in the morning. The best time for talking has been then, and they've seemed to be glad of company for all or part of the time on five or six of those occasions.

Sometimes staying up for the whole of the watch and going

to bed at five in the morning, other times staying up only until about two or half past. Sometimes waking at five and going down into the kitchen, getting involved in a chat or a game of chess with whoever was on morning watch; other times going to bed in the afternoon and getting up at ten-thirty or eleven at night. Sometimes in between having a day of waking at eight and not going to bed again until eleven-thirty or midnight. So it's the patternlessness which brings the confusion; but in this situation it's not particularly noticeable until an attempt at trying to decide whether it's Monday or Tuesday.

Another cause of disorientation.

You go to bed when you're tired. Undress, climb up the ladder to the bunk, draw the curtain, wriggle down into the sleeping-bag, switch the light off and eventually go to sleep; when you've had enough sleep you wake up again. But you've no idea if you've slept for one hour, eight hours, four hours or fourteen.

You put your hand up to the light switch to find out. Electricity comes from the generator which drives the machinery that revolves the lens; so if the light comes on it means the generator's running. And that means it's some time in the night. It must be some time in the night; but it might be ten o'clock, midnight or three in the morning. The light's bright above your eyes; so you switch it off again and lie and think. It works, so it's night: but what time did you go to bed? Was it morning, afternoon or evening? Have you been asleep an hour, five hours or twelve?

A watch isn't much help; all it says is it's eight o'clock or three o'clock or six: but not whether it's morning or night.

If you wake up and switch the light on and nothing happens, all you know is the generator is not running. So lying in the darkness and struggling to come awake you realize slowly it must be daytime, not night. You pull back the bunk curtain: there's no light in the room because the curtains are drawn across the other bunks and the door is shut. You fumble for the ladder, climb down it, feel your way round the weight-tube and open the door to the staircase. The daylight coming in through the small window opposite is usually no more than a grey half-light in winter: it might be early morning or it might be late afternoon.

You go down to the kitchen. What time is it, it's six o'clock my handsome, yes but six o'clock in the morning or six o'clock in the evening?

If it's Steve he pulls your leg and tries to convince you it's the opposite of what it is.

– You only just sneaked in, Steve said. He showed me the weather log-book. During the days before I came, in the Wind Force column every three hours from Saturday midnight until midday on Monday the wind had been recorded steady at Force 8. Unexpectedly on Monday afternoon it suddenly dropped for six hours down to Force 3 and 4. Sufficient for Amos to say it was worth trying to bring me out and get me on. By six o'clock that evening it started to rise again, by nine it was up to Force 7, by midnight back at 8. Tuesday, Wednesday, Thursday and thereonwards it went up to, and stayed at, 9 and 10 for another week.

Curious, and an example of what Amos was talking about when he said sometimes in winter there were long periods in which there might be only a day, and perhaps only one particular time on that one day even, when a relief could be done.

I remember it as up and down, up and down, over waves like mountains. Amos unperturbed, a small elderly man standing legs astride at the wheel of the open boat, heading it a slight angle towards each approaching wave. Most of the time it went like a steeplechaser up and down. He ignored the great cascades of spray flying past on each side. Sometimes one wave succeeding immediately after another came from a different direction too quickly for him to avoid meeting it head on; the prow sliced through it and the boat plunged and water came over everything.

Unconcerned, Amos wiped it out of his eyes and kept his attention focussed on the next wave ahead. Not a big talker, he said. As far as I recall, he spoke only once during the entire journey: in a mildly derogatory tone about the sea on an occasion it drenched him. 'Bit sloppy today,' he said.

Approached in the late afternoon in winter through a high bucking sea, there were only infrequent glimpses of the tower. It looked pale and forlorn against the lowering sky, with clusters of black clouds behind and above it; small in the distance almost diffidently modest. For long periods it couldn't be seen at all: the boat pointed in another direction and seemed to progress by sliding down the troughs of the waves. Then suddenly the tower was looming above, gigantic and arrogant, with the sea thundering round its base and plumes of water spouting angrily high in the air, the sea exploding like bombs.

Going up the rope, regarding yourself as a parcel. Amos and his assistants fix the harness, others winch you up, and one minute you're in the boat and the next you're up in the air. For a while you dangle and spin in space. Noisy; the continuous crashing of waves against the tower, the roaring of the wind. A bang on the knee on being jerked out of the boat, a crack on the shoulder on swinging hard into the set-off. Trying to make himself heard above the noise, Alex shouting and swearing to you to stand up properly after the buffeting so he can pull the harness away before the tightening rope drags you off again. The steep wet slippery cold rungs of the dog-steps in the blustering wind.

The bunk is very small and its ceiling very low: even sitting crosslegged with hunched shoulders and bowed head there is insufficient room to write in a notebook.

Bruises unnoticed made their presence felt uncomfortably and sleep was frequently disturbed the first night.

The wind has been blowing persistently at Force 8 and 9 for over a week; not dropping for five minutes, monotonously going on and on. As Alex said, it has built up a massively swelling sea: waves thump in against the tower. The entrance doors and the windows have to be kept shut; the atmosphere is hot and flaccid, the air lifeless and stale.

The sea rolls in from different directions. First one side of the tower takes a big wave, then a few minutes later the other. It vibrates and quivers. Because everything is closed up, the noise of the hits sounds distant and far away like the background crump crump crump of artillery in war films. Looking out from the window of the sitting-room there is nothing to be seen but a turmoil of green white-capped water below, and a gull struggling and ineffectively flapping its wings, trying to make headway against the wind.

Inside the pentagon of the lens on a bright morning: each wall of it is built like an enormous spider-web of thick and solid wide overlapping slats of glass. Some magnify and some reduce, some are clear and some refract; some are translucent, some are opaque, and others reflect. Through them can be seen a perpetually changing kaleidoscope of surging green sea foaming with white and a blue sky scattered with grey clouds; and the view is split and fractured into alternate bands, and across the rows of glass shimmering rainbows quiver in lines of prismatically fragmented light. On some levels hugely magnified waves appear to be rushing in at the lens to swamp it, until at slight movement of the head they change into minute ripples far below. On other levels the sea seems to be rolling and swaying above, upside down in the sky. A panoramic mingling and mixing and jumbling mosaic; that breaks and parts at another slight movement and then meets again in a different pattern of distorted images which re-form and enlarge and diminish, and shatter yet again and change and change.

When he comes down into the kitchen after a sleep Steve lumbers in and slumps down on the bench seat, where he sits propped up gazing vacantly into space with his eyes wide open. Someone puts a cup of tea on the table in front of him. After two or three minutes he reaches out for it without looking and begins to sip at it, his eyes still blank. He smokes a cigarette, inhaling deeply; then suddenly he shakes his head hard, screws up his eyes in a violent grimace and becomes wide awake.

Alex gropes his way into the room with his eyes half closed; he feels his way past the weight-tube to the sink, turns the rain-water tap full on and puts his head under it. Then he rubs his hair with a towel, brushes and combs it, and drinks three cups of coffee one after another before he speaks a word.

Barry comes through the door rubbing his hands briskly and flexing his shoulders, starting to talk as soon as he appears. He goes to the mirror, turning his head from side to side inspecting his face, then starts to wash it methodically and comprehensively.

The routine of lighthouse duty. Lighting the light at sunset, checking that it's functioning properly at approximately hourly intervals during the night, putting it out at dawn, servicing its machinery and cleaning the lenses during the day, doing the call-round test on the radio, and recording the details of the weather every three hours in the log.

There are two columns in the log-book for daily entry of the time at which the light is in Trinity House terminology 'exhibited' and 'extinguished'. But no one ever talks about 'exhibiting' it or even for that matter 'lighting' it; the phrase invariably used is 'putting it in'. On the other hand it is never 'put out' in the morning: then the only expression ever used is 'extinguished'.

Whoever is on watch at the time always refers to the light as though it was a personal possession; which, since he's solely responsible for it at that period, it is. Steve, as the afternoon begins to fade: 'I'd better start getting ready to put my light in' Alex later the same night: 'I'll go up top and see that everything's all right with my light'. Barry on the morning watch: 'It's looking like time I extinguished my light'.

The atmosphere is very different from on the rock. Three men live hugger-mugger on top of one another in a cramped confined space. Communal tumult, banging and barging about, physically and vocally; enjoyed proximity and involvement. Whoever has the spoon stirs the tea. Apart from the light from time to time nothing is 'mine'; everything is 'ours'.

Always high-spirited; perpetual criticising, mocking, guying, sending-up. The relationship beneath is strong enough to give and take anything and everything without offence.

Nothing strange to them about a tape-recorder; Steve's had one here frequently, no one's in any way unaccustomed to it or hesitant about speaking when it's switched on.

Quarter to eight at night, sitting round the kitchen table playing cards and drinking coffee out of saucerless cups. Because of the wind's constant roar the throb of the generator three floors above in the service room can only be heard faintly. Most of its power is used to drive the lenses; what's left is not enough to make the electric light bulb hanging from the ceiling shine brightly: it flickers dimly.

Barry yawns and scratches his head, studying his cards. Steve plays an ace, Alex puts a trump on it disdainfully, Steve scowls at him. A distant thud as though someone had swung a gigantic sledgehammer against the base of the tower. The electric light bulb twitches, the plates on the dresser rattle; coffee slops out of a full cup on to the table. Alex reaches behind him for the dish cloth and mops it up, and throws the cloth back in the sink.

– Here we go then, he says casually. Looks like she's building up again.

– You know what you are, says Steve. You're a lousy rotten shit, that's what you are.

Alex nods with self-satisfied agreement. Another thud; the light swings, plates rattle, more coffee spills on the table. Alex picks the trick up and wipes the table again, leaving the dish cloth on it.

– For Christ's sake get some of it drunk, says Steve. Don't let it go on doing that, how the bloody hell do you expect me to concentrate?

– Excuses, excuses, says Alex.

– Come on you two, get on with it, Barry says. It's me on the middle tonight, I want to get a couple of hours' kip in. He yawns again.

Outside the window a suddenly obliterating surge of creamy white, like a bucket of whitewash thrown against it. The crest of a wave breaking eighty-five feet above sea level.

*

Steve says he measures time by tins of peas. Every third day when he's cook he uses a tin of peas for dinner along with other vegetables. In one two-month spell of duty he knows he'll use eighteen or nineteen tins. He keeps them in a row along a shelf in his food cupboard so he can tell at a glance how many days as cook he's got left.

Whatever time you wake up there's always someone else awake because it's his turn on watch. Around four thirty in the morning: Steve had been on the middle, was still up in the kitchen drinking tea with Alex. A discussion about council housing, Steve saying high-rise blocks of flats conserve space but are psychologically bad for the occupants. Alex arguing that if urban development continued at the present rate, in a hundred years there'll be no countryside left. People needed space to live in, he said; they couldn't live on top of one another all the time. Steve agreed with that, and they went on discussing the important problem of people's need for living-space.

The wind dropped to 4 or 5; after three days the sea stopped throwing waves about and subsided into a sulky growling and splashing. Doors and windows were opened and the oppressively sultry atmosphere was replaced with draughts of cold damp air. Outside up on the gallery in the late afternoon, Barry looked at the overcast sky as the daylight began to disintegrate and fade. Five gulls flapped past in an untidy line; he watched them until they had almost disappeared.

– Peculiar, he said. You have to be peculiar to do this sort of job. Fancy standing watching seagulls from the top of a bloody great lump of granite sticking up out of the sea and thinking they look interesting.

Midnight, or nearly. Alex sitting in a chair in the sitting-room with his legs up on the table, wearing his working overalls and embroidering a traycloth; a roughly pencilled-in floral pattern at one corner stretched tightly in the circular wooden frame on his knee. Leaves outlined in blue on lime green stalks. A quietly satisfying hobby he said; you keep the cloth and the silks and needles in a shoe-box, it doesn't take up much room and isn't in anybody's way. 'I reckon to do one tablecloth or two trays cloths each turn off I'm here.' He doesn't like transfer patterns; he prefers making a design up for himself.

The daily domestic routine of cooking and cleaning. Steve has mopped the kitchen floor, scrubbed down the sink, wiped down the table and the cooker with a damp cloth, and after throwing the day's rubbish out of the window into the sea was giving the shelves of the dresser a flick over the with a duster.

– Now you see what we do all day, he said: light housework.

Books that Barry has been reading while I've been here. J. L. Hammond's *The Village Labourer*, *The Lore and Language of Schoolchildren* and a paperback by Margaret Drabble. I asked him what he thought of that, and he shrugged, opened the sitting-room window and threw it out into the sea.

Storms and gales. The wind howling and roaring, the waves crashing, spray flying past the window; the noise taken for granted and unremarkable and unremarked about for days. You go to bed, then some time later you wake up and are aware something's happened but you don't realize what. You lie awake in the dark; what is it, what's the matter, there's something odd. Oh yes I know what it is; the weather's dropped, everything's gone quiet. It's abnormal, you feel. A couple of days later the wind starts to blow up again; it brings back the heavy seas and a sense of everything being back to normal again.

Steve has false teeth. Once every few days he takes them out and puts them to soak in a plastic denture container which he keeps in the cupboard under the sink. This according to Alex is 'flash'. 'You ought to put them in a cup like everyone else does,' he said. Neither he nor Barry has false teeth.

By the end of the first week there was no more fresh meat. Towards the end of the month supplies of fresh vegetables are low, food stocks are dwindling and opportunities for variety in diet are restricted. For five days in succession the midday meal has been exactly the same: tinned sausages, tinned carrots, boiled potatoes, gravy and a tin of peas. After it has been eaten no one has ever omitted to say politely to whoever was cook for the day 'Nice meal, Barry, thank you', 'Thanks, Steve, that was good', 'Very enjoyable, Alex, thanks'.

On the radio call-round test this station is Oscar: because it's wild, said Barry. The voices from the other lighthouses are indistinct and atmospherics make reception poor. Whenever the rock light Alfa is heard, there are derogatory shouts of 'Butlin's holiday camp' for my benefit.

*

The store of pornographic books and magazines in the cupboards under the bench seat in the kitchen consists of a pile of old copies of *Amateur Gardening* and *Yachting World*, two faded back-numbers of *Reveille*, and a dog-eared paperbacked edition of *A Dictionary of Card Games*.

When he is offering you a cigarette Steve doesn't hold out the packet towards you; he takes a cigarette out and holds it between his finger and thumb and looks at you with lifted eyebrows. If you shake your head he puts it back again. I asked him why he did it. 'The wisdom of experience; if I offer the packet to either of those other two sods they help themselves to three at a time.'

Time passes enjoyably because there is always a lot to do: a conversation to be continued, a game of chess to be played, a football match to be watched on television, food to be prepared and eaten, coffee or tea to be drunk, clothes to be washed, books to be read, the sea to be looked at from the entrance door or out on the gallery, notes to be made, tape-recordings to be listened to, sleep to be slept. There's hardly time to do it all.

It has taken a long time to realize something; they are gentle men who move quietly despite the apparent talkativeness, the discussions and debates and arguments. That no conversation lasts longer than about twenty minutes at a time at the most. Then invariably one or other of the participants says off-handedly he must make himself something to eat, or have a sleep, or check something in the service room, or go up to the sitting-room and clean out his fridge. Anything trivial that gives him an excuse to go out of whatever room he's in. This is immediately accepted, the conversation promptly finishes; though the same one may start again half an hour later. A constantly recurring involvement-regulating break, accepted with unspoken recognition of the necessity for it.

The weather goes up and down; rough, calm, rough, calm.

– It's got to make up its mind for Friday, says Alex. Friday is his relief date, the day he's due to go ashore. As it approaches he listens to the shipping forecasts on the radio, watches the weather maps on the television, studies the pattern or lack of it in the log-book, pursing his lips. He says little about the subject in conversation to anyone, but frequently his eyes stray towards the window. Quite often too he glances at his watch.

I will be going ashore with him; regretfully.

In the middle watches, a man sits and talks: or sits in silence in the kitchen and thinks and then starts talking again, almost to himself and forgetting you're there. You're alone with him, he's alone with himself and you. The others are in bed and he has the promise the conversation is not going to be played back for the others to hear.

Four Men

i. *Barry Pennington*

– When I said you had to be peculiar, I meant you had to have
a certain kind of mentality. Different from most other jobs in
what it demands. It requires you to live two-thirds of your life
in one way, and the other third in another that's almost the
exact opposite. This is true of other jobs but there's more balance
in them somehow; you're not expected to be like you need to
be for this one for such a long period of time without a break.

I'm thinking of someone like a policeman. I've a friend who's
one: what I mean is that he acts like a policeman when he's on
duty, but when he's at home he's like any other ordinary man.
You need something in you to be a policeman, you've got to
have those certain qualities; I don't think they're particularly
nice ones myself but that's neither here nor there at the moment.
What I'm trying to say is you don't have to act like a policeman
for eight weeks at a stretch without a break, you get a chance to
drop it for a while once or twice a day.

You can't do that as a keeper though; while you're out on a
lighthouse there's no nipping home for a quick bit of normality
every few hours. That applies to soldiers too; but on the other
hand while they're on the job they come into contact with more
people all through the time; they've got recreational facilities,
being able to play football or go into pubs and mingle with
people.

We haven't, we live every minute of the day and night with two other men; we not only work with them but we have to be domesticated with them, set up home with them. It's a situation that's got homosexual undertones, that's what I'm trying to say: then at the end of your eight weeks you go back into normal existence, into heterosexual life.

There's not a lot of queerdom among keepers, at least I've not come across it; you get the occasional homosexual but no higher proportion of active ones than you would anywhere else. But we do live a very queer-like existence, we have to; so I think there must be quite a strong streak of it in us. Sometimes I wonder about it when I go ashore. It's got to be sex every night for at least a week and during the daytime as well if there's an opportunity; almost as if I'm trying to prove to myself that I am heterosexual, I'm not queer. Having to do it, prove it, I think it shows I must be worried about it. I've never had homosexual experience and I don't think I am a homosexual; but I don't know. Sometimes out here I wonder about it; you can't help wondering about it if you find yourself living contentedly with two other men and getting as fond of them as you're bound to do.

– It's this companionship that's the most attractive thing about the job to me. I'm not a good mixer, I don't like parties or crowds of people, I'm at my happiest when I'm here. But I'm not a loner either, I'm very dependent on Steve and Alex being around. It is Steve and Alex particularly, it won't be the same after you and Alex have gone ashore and the other keeper's come. He's all right, he's a decent enough chap; but I don't feel as close to him as I do to them. I'll be a bit resentful while I'm ashore about him being here with them instead of me.

I couldn't pinpoint it and say it was either Steve or Alex; in that sense it's not a personal attraction of one man towards one other. It's a dual thing. Obviously the major part of it's Steve, he's a man I admire and respect and look up to. But it's a fondness like a schoolboy for a master, I don't look on us as equals.

Whereas with Alex I do; we're both schoolboys in the same class together, Alex is like a school friend.

None of it means I don't love Jean and the kids; I do, perhaps more, perhaps equally, I don't know which. Now Nigel's growing up, when I'm ashore I don't have any doubts about being anything but an ordinary happy family man. Then as soon as I get back out here I start wondering: about this peculiar existence, about being so happy in it. The fact that having to shit in a bucket doesn't matter, having nothing but powdered milk for your tea and coffee doesn't matter. I wouldn't put up with those things at home, I'd be cursing and grumbling, I wouldn't tolerate them for a minute. It all makes me think.

– Another thing makes me think is the domesticity side of it. When I'm ashore at home I'm a really right lazy sod; I won't lift a finger in the house, I'd never even dream of dusting or washing up let alone cooking a meal. I won't make myself a cup of tea; I just sit back and let Jean do everything. She's more than willing to, she plays in with it; she says I've had to do everything like that for eight weeks without a break, I shouldn't do anything but let her look after me. I go along with it, I act the part of a man who's missed his home comforts; I let her think it's a relief to me not to have to do any housework. But the truth of the matter is I like doing it, at least when I'm out here I do. I'll spend hours cleaning something like a piece of machinery or dusting the lenses; not to fill the time in but because I enjoy doing it, I like to see it all spotless and clean.

The contrast between when I arrive home and when I arrive back off here; that's something else, that's another thing. When I go ashore I'm untidy, I leave all my things lying about; and I take it to the ultimate illogicality, I shout at Nigel if he makes crumbs on the carpet eating a biscuit say. But when I come back here I can't wait to get my gear unpacked and all my things folded away neatly in the drawers in my locker; then an hour later I'll be in the kitchen, Alex'll be eating a sandwich and breadcrumbs all over the place, I'll straight away be ready to wipe the table down without so much as giving it a second thought. This is my place; I look after it, I keep it clean and tidy: not on my own but with them, this is ours. I don't feel like that about my home ashore.

I've tried to talk with Jean about it but it's got to the state she doesn't like it even being mentioned. I can see her point of view; it's something she doesn't share, she can't understand and she couldn't be expected to. But the fact is when you come to think about it, this is more my home; I spend more time here than I do ashore. Jean says my home's ashore with her and the kids, but it isn't in practical terms; my home's really here, this is my place, our place, mine and Steve's and Alex's. And purely in terms of amount of time they're my main family. Jean'd go through the roof if I said anything like that so we tend to keep off the subject. I get a feeling when I'm at home she doesn't like to talk about what it's like here, she doesn't even want me to think about it.

That's natural for her to feel; but it doesn't make for a good situation between a husband and wife that you've got areas of mutual agreement not to talk about. That in itself makes things worse: I don't get that response from Alex and Steve, there's nothing we can't talk about if we want to. Politics, books, personal problems, daft made-up arguments just for the sake of arguing: the point is you can talk about anything, there's no constraint. Here I'm free to say what I like whereas at home I've got to watch my tongue.

I find it a difficult situation to be in that here I can be free and easy and relaxed, and at home I can't. That discussion we were having last week or whenever it was, I was thinking about it afterwards; about using bad language, why we use it here when we didn't at home. We were having a bit of fun about it, but I was surprised afterwards to find how much it'd disturbed me and made me think.

As I remember it Steve said something about Alex implying

we didn't behave naturally at home if we didn't use the same sort
of language there; I threw in something about parsons swearing
because it was starting to get a bit too near the truth for comfort
for me. I thought about it afterwards and I came to the conclusion
there was a lot in it. We're not natural at home, at least I'm not. I
said something about dropping back into it the moment I got
in the taxi outside the door on my way back. I think it is a
fact: I'm not as much at ease at home as I am away from it. At
home to a considerable extent I'm acting all the time: here I don't
act, I'm just me. I'm not saying it's good or bad, just stating the
fact.

It doesn't only apply to bad language either. I do a lot of kind
of 'me' things here that I don't do at home. Reading's one of them,
I do a hell of a lot here, chiefly due to Steve's influence. He's
always giving me things to read, political books chiefly; political
in the sense they make you think about what you might call
social things, inequalities in society. The point is they're about
ideas; the sort of subjects I'd never thought about before, that
open up your mind and make you think. Ashore I never read a
bloody thing except newspapers and magazines. Another thing
is playing chess; that again's a sort of mind-stretching thing
which I don't do at home. I'm happy to sit back there and be a
cabbage. So when I said to Jean this was my home, I meant it on
two levels: the domesticity of it, and the intellectually satisfying
part of it as well.

– You get very preoccupied with this world out here. You've
no choice, because you're stuck here, you're in it and you can't
get away. It's like looking down the wrong end of a telescope,
your attention's focussed entirely on this little bit; on yourself
and the other two people in it. It's a wrong perspective I know,
but it's a very seductive one. It's something you can't get out
of even if you want to; and I don't particularly want to.

I think I'll have to make some kind of choice before long. They
say if you stop in for ten years you'll never break away after that.

I've been in for just ten now. I don't know what other kind of job I could do; the service doesn't prepare you for any sort of other work in the way of giving you experience you could put to other better use. I'm not greatly worried about that, I think I could turn my hand to something else without much effort. It's the basic decision whether to stay in or not that has to be made first. I'll talk it over with Jean and I'll talk it over with Steve; but it sums up a big part of the problem when I say I know what he says'll be the more important.

– Those seagulls, they were stormy petrels, you know; they call them 'Mother Carey's chickens'. At night they fly out to the middle of the sea and roost there, then they come back towards land to find food during the day. That's where their home is, out in the middle of the ocean, floating about on the water; they're not belonging on land, only visiting it. That's a bit like how I feel it is with me.

*

ii. *Alex Merton*
– Oh in one word, satisfaction: complete and utter satisfaction, that's what I get out of it. Before I joined the service I was a milkman: a bit of a contrast, my handsome, that was no sort of job at all. But this one now, well I hardly know where to begin. Never crossed my mind, no one in the family, nothing like that; I'd lived on the coast all my life and always been fascinated by the sea, so I suppose it's only natural I should enjoy living out in the middle of it. I just suddenly woke up in the middle of the night one night, and there it was in my mind. Must have come from somewhere; something put it there, someone, God I suppose. I gave the wife a nudge, she was fast asleep; I woke her up and I said 'Hey June' I said, 'I know what I want to be – a lighthouse keeper.' 'Yes all right love' she said and then she went straight off back to sleep. Next morning we were

having breakfast and she suddenly looked at me and she said '*A what?*' So I said it again, and that was all there was to it.

I don't think she minds, but it's a pity you couldn't have met her and asked her yourself. I honestly don't think she does; whenever I've asked her about it she's always said the most important thing to her is to be married to a man who's happy. It's hard on her me going away all the time; but I think like most other keepers' wives she puts up with it because she knows one day we'll be together on a land light. I can't say I'll be glad when that happens but I won't say I'll be sad either. I won't: land lights, rock lights, tower lights, they're all the same to me. I hope I get a good crack at all of them, and then one day reach the dizzy heights of PK. It's better than staying a milkman; I mean Principal Milkman, that's nothing is it? But Principal Keeper of a lighthouse; there's only about fifty of those in the whole country. I'd sooner have that for a title than a knighthood or a lordship or anything else there is.

I'm not like Barry, I haven't got any educational standard of any kind. That's the great thing about this job, it doesn't matter if you've got book-learning or not; the only thing that counts is whether you're suitable for it and it's suitable for you. A matter of temperament, nothing else; the only way of finding out is to try. That's why I said to you that night we met in the pub it was a different world, I couldn't describe it, you'd have to come and find out for yourself. I reckon you've been with us long enough to have got a taste of it. But if you hadn't come you couldn't have got it, no one could, could they? A little world of its own; we make our own laws, we follow our own way of life. I think it's a good one because we all have an equal say. So long as you're on an enjoyable station, there can't be anything to beat it as a job that I can think of. It's Steve who does it, that must be obvious. When I'm a PK myself I only hope I'm half as good at it as him. I'd say he's the model PK, but that doesn't mean I think the sun shines out of his arse. He's got his faults and moods like we all have, he wouldn't be human if he didn't. If he was perfect he'd be impossible to get on with; but he's a terrific sort of person, the kind they don't come any better than.

He's a respecter. You feel you're a person who matters to him; and what matters to him is your individuality, you being you. Even though he's twenty years older than I am and a hundred times more experienced, he never makes me feel we're anything other than equal. I'll ask his opinion about something, and he'll ask mine: he gives just as much thought to the one as he does to the other. All day long we're swearing and arguing and disagreeing with each other, but it's all on the surface, none of it means anything. Underneath we all of us fundamentally get on, I don't think we'd carry on at one another like we do if we didn't.

Most of all what he respects is your privacy, your right to your own thoughts. He can see you're thinking about something, so he never tries to catch your attention then to what he's saying. He'll go babbling on although he knows bloody well you're not listening. He doesn't mind, he won't criticize you for not listening, he won't even say anything that'll indicate he's noticed it. It's a gift; I hope as I get older I'll be able to do the same.

– You switch off, you have to. You separate yourself from the other two in your mind, you go out of the room and go somewhere else for a time. That's why this one is the best, the middle watch; it's the time when you really are on your own and you can let your thoughts wander. A bit lonely sometimes and you're glad of someone to talk to: but I think loneliness is something you should feel, it's part of living. You miss your wife, you want her in bed with you; you should feel that it's good to feel like that. I think it's good for me; I'll never take June for granted. She'll always be the first person I'll want to see when I go ashore and the last person I want to leave. We're very close together sometimes, out here I mean; I talk to her, there's moments she'll be right beside me in the room. I'm not eating my heart out about it, that's the job; but if you know how I mean in my mind she's with me. That's what's important in a relationship between a man and a woman, that they carry a bit of each other round inside.

– I don't have the slightest difficulty at all when I go ashore, putting this place behind me. The moment I'm off the boat I never give it any more thought. I have a hell of a time ashore, I enjoy every single minute. With June and the baby, we go out for walks, go shopping, all the everyday things other people take for granted. It gives them an extra sort of depth; but not with a sad feeling about it having to come to an end. It doesn't, only for a bit: it's waiting again for next time I'm ashore. I hope she feels that; we talk about it often, when she says she does I believe her. A lot must be to do with her and the sort of person she is. Because she's like she is about it, I'm a very happy man.

Being with June and being out here; those are both happy times. Very different obviously, and this is another thing about the life that appeals to me. It is all so different, your home and your job; so you can look forward to them equally in turn. Out here there's so many times that are enoyable in different ways. Dinner time, I always like that; going to bed and going to sleep; my day for being cook; the arguments and discussions; sitting on my own doing my embroidery; being on morning watch and seeing the sunrise; going up inside the lens and looking out through it at all the different colours and shapes. Those are all times I'm really happy and enjoy.

– To pick out one time as the best of all, I'd say it's definitely when I'm on the middle watch. I go up out on the gallery sometimes in the middle of the night, and look down and listen to the sea. It has a lot to say to you if you listen to it, does the sea. When there's a big storm on and it's battering away at the bottom of the tower, it's like it's lost its temper. It's saying 'I'm angry, look at me, I'm big and strong and I'm going to hammer you tonight, I'm going to thump you, I'm going to try and smash you to bits.' It puts on this performance for you to show you how strong it is; it's like it's saying 'They don't know, those people who live on land; they've never seen me like this in a storm miles and miles out from shore. People on ships, they don't know me either because I'm tossing them about from side to side and they're getting wet and falling about and can't see. But you're all right up there Alex, this is a private performance for you, you watch this.' It goes crashing about, it's a stupendous sight, terrific; there's not many people can ever have had that sort of grandstand view of it when it's in that mood. It's not a bit frightening; you know it couldn't ever knock the place down because it's stood here so long against everything the sea can throw at it. So you just stand there and enjoy it; I say 'That's right sea, go on boy, go on, I know how you feel, let's be seeing you then, come on.'

Or another night I'll go up and it'll perhaps be moonlight and calm; the sea's as flat as a tabletop, it's just lapping round the foot of the tower. Then it's saying 'I feel tired tonight, I feel all gentle and peaceful, I just want to flop around'. It sort of gives a hissing sound, like it was whispering to me: 'I'm tired tonight, Alex, I can't be bothered with anything, all I want to do's have a bit of a quiet chat and then I'm going to sleep'. I say 'That's all right sea, I'm tired too, I've had a hard day like you, let's both take it easy tonight.' It's very peaceful then, you take your own mood from it, it's very beautiful.

But these are things you couldn't really talk of with anyone could you? I mean if you told them the sea talked to you and you said things back, they'd think you were out of your mind. You keep it to yourself; you know it's like that, that's all that matters really. I've often thought I'd like to try and tell somebody about it but you can't, how could you? It's not anything you can put into words.

*

iii. *Steve Collins*

– I said I'd been in the service since I was born, only I should've put it the other way round. I was born when I came into the service, that was more how it was. The war, you know, all that; I'd been in the Army, I'd been fighting in the Far East, I'd been killing men. I think it was the atom bomb business, Hiroshima, Nagasaki; I thought Christ no, slaughtering people, what are we doing, what am I part of, it's all wrong. I wanted to do something; I wanted to be part of something I'd no qualms about doing, no one could turn it round against other people. It'd got to be regulated, it'd got to be ordered because that sort of existence suited me; but it'd got to be something harmless at the same time.

I don't want it to sound like a vocation or calling; it was nothing like that about it appealed to me. The nearest I could get to it would be innocence; an innocent harmless occupation, you aren't going round doing good to people but no one could say you were doing harm. Lighthouses don't do anything: they only stand there serving a purpose like street lamps, useful if people want to make use of them but nothing more. They don't generate strong feelings in people, nobody's either for or against them, they're taken for granted. I'm not putting it well, it's a long time since I had to think about it. But I was a young man, I think it was something vague like that which was in my mind.

Nan, she's my wife, I hadn't met her long before; I was sick about Hiroshima and she knew it. I wanted to get away from the world but not turn my back. I didn't want to have any more part in destruction but there was nothing as a person I could create. 'Don't just do something, stand there'; that was about the mark. There was that feeling people who went around doing things were doing terrible things with the best of intentions. The scientists who discovered things, Jesus, look what happened, how people used what they found out. The one who gave them the start to split the atom, Rutherford, what would he have done to himself if he'd known where it was going to lead?

When you're a young man you know how it is, you feel things, you should do too. I was raw, I felt like I'd been stripped of my skin; it was feeling all the way through, I felt like hell. She was marvellous, Nan; this was her idea. Pay back something somehow, make a penance; almost like taking Holy Orders only that's indulging yourself, going round doing good to other people is using them for the benefit of your own soul.

A right load of bullshit that must sound; I'm struggling you see, trying to remember how it was. I can't get any nearer to it, it was something like that. It was then; not now, Christ I'm not burdened with feeling guilty, I've worked through all that. But that' show it started; then I got into the habit of it of, the job, and I went on and I'll go on a few more years yet.

– I like it. That's not the same as I love it: I like it, it's all right, it suits me. Not bitter and twisted and resigned to it and wishing I could do something else; but not starry-eyed and romantic about it either. I like it: I like it: just said like that, nice and level, no more no less. Contented enough to keep on doing it but not self-satisfied enough to sit on my arse about it and think no more. You've got to keep thinking; you've got to keep yourself alive. In this kind of job that could be hard to do if you let it. Let's face it, it's not a let's face it sort of job. Try and push yourself, make that bit extra effort so you don't get to the state where you don't think any more.

– How do they do it? With some of them that's what beats me. You meet these fucking terrible old men; Principal Keepers, dead from the toes up, Christ I've served under some of them. You can't hate them, all you can do for them is weep. The men who lived for Trinity: dead men, they died twenty years ago, the terrible thing about them is they don't know. The only time they've got any feeling is when they shouldn't have; if the weather's bad and the relief gets overdue. They can't go ashore, they're fretting and bad tempered and shitting themselves; then when it's the other way round and they're at home they start doing the same thing because they can't get back. Apart from in between those two times they're like pillars of stone. Jesus what a state; they've forgotten what life's about, that it's about people not relief dates. What an insult to their wives they get like that when they're ashore; or on the light what bloody insult to the men. Say all right, if I'm stuck out here with you a few days longer that's all right, I don't mind, you're good company: I'd sooner be with you than on some lonely bloody railway platform somewhere waiting for a train. Or at the other end, you're my wife I'm happy with you; I'm not suffering I can't get away.

They take themselves so seriously, they take life seriously. They want you to do the same, they get bloody furious about it if you don't. Look here you, I'm a miserable bugger; while I'm around you're going to be miserable buggers too. What do they think they are then, God? They think they've a right to tell another man or woman how they should feel and influence them into feeling it. They shouldn't be in this job if they think that's what it's for, to give them power.

– What is it really? There's only one way to look at it to me; none of it makes sense so you get what you can out of it. Life is hard, it's fucking terrible at times, but what does it add up to in the end? You go through it in misery or you get as much enjoyment from it as you can. It'll make no difference, when it's done it's done, that's the end of it. I don't believe in heaven or hell, they're here; you choose which one you're going to be a lodger in. It's up to you to laugh about it or feel sorry for yourself. It has to be a bit of a forced laugh sometimes, you've got to force it; but if you didn't you might as well pack it in.

Escapism, sure: this life here is escapism, I don't think there's any argument. So what, all life's escapism in some form, why not choose the one you like best? With these two lads I've got here life's all right, I'll settle for this. If they were my boys, my sons, I'd be proud of them; two fine young men, I'd like to have thought my own would have turned out to be the same. But there you are, he died when he was seven, he had leukaemia. I've got four daughters and I look at Alex and Barry and I think if you can't have everything at least you've got other things instead. Nan took it hard. But she thinks the same, there's a million haven't got a tenth of what's in life for us.

– A hard man, has it made me a hard man, that's what I ask myself? The lighthouse service, is that what it's made me, hard? Nan says no, she's the one whose opinion matters. So I say keep talking, don't bottle it in. I've known men poison themselves in this job with their own acid; if the roof fell in they'd sit there and look at it and not say a word. I'll fight to stop it happening to me or anyone with me, we're not going to join up with the army of the living dead.

Say it, that's what I try to get over to them all the time. It doesn't matter what, sense or nonsense, say it, get it out and said and done. It's words; keep it going, talk about belting people is all right. But don't go off on your own thinking about murdering people; you're not harming them, you're killing yourself. Lighthouses could be powder kegs if you didn't communicate; or they'd be hiding places for hermits. I wouldn't be in charge of a production line turning out grey men.

– I'm a revolutionary, a communist, an anarchist. Someone who's in this job, how can you be a revolutionary, going off and leaving the world, it'd be a fair question. I've no time for all the bullshit about running a station for a start. If you want to keep it clean, if you like pottering about polishing things like Barry does, all right. That's what he likes to do, that's fine. But you don't order men to do it; you don't lay a finger on them to make them. They do it if they want to, to make themselves happy. This is their home for two months, you let them run it their own way. Your job as PK's to see the light's shown when it should be, not let it dazzle you so you can't see anything else. These are men here, give them freedom to be as they are. Christ knows it's an odd way of life they've chosen; no women, no sex, it's hard for the younger ones. For me it's a desexing experience; but I've been married twenty-six years, I'm not bothered by it. Nan and I've adjusted to regulating our sex-life. But for these younger ones, sometimes I wonder if it's right they should be here.

– Two months at a time is too long to be on a light. Trinity's beginning to see that at last; next year they'll be putting us on to one month off and one month ashore. That's as it ought to be, you'll get more of a variety in keepers then, it'll be quite a good life. The atmosphere of the towers, the air; it'll be fresher, there'll be more life in it to breathe. You won't get men going ashore pasty-faced in colour and pasty-faced inside. They'll be more human both ways round, when they're off on the light and when they're ashore.

Younger men, too; they'll have more chance of promotion, it'll stop all this rubbish about one PK to a station, and make it two. 'My tower', no one should be able to say that. I do, but it's wrong, it's not mine. I have to check myself not to go along with the great paternalism that's Trinity House. Benevolent paternalism maybe, but it's out of date. Two hundred years behind the rest of society; it's got to change to keep up with the times.

There's got to be keepers who don't toe the line; their job's to encourage others to carry on the same way. When I was younger I was always playing tricks, doing stupid things, anything for a laugh. Don't do so much of it now, all it meant was I was getting a reputation as a funny man. Inside I'm not; I'm a serious man.

– This thing is about human beings getting on with each other. In small confined places like this, in a way that tries not to spoil them for living when they're ashore. I hope it's an experience of that. When you go yourself with Alex whenever it is, Friday or whatever day after that the relief's done: try and take back some sort of impression of ordinary human beings rubbing along.

Appendix

FROM: The Public Relations Officer, The Corporation of Trinity House, Tower Hill, London E.C.3.

Dear Tony,

Thank you for showing me the manuscript of your book, which I have now read with great interest and enjoyment. You have certainly covered the subject, and my only comments about it are as follows:–

1) I have always felt that because of our longstanding reputation for being a silent service, most of the references to Trinity House in what books are available never fully describe its Corporate aspect in an acceptable way. In an attempt to rectify this we have ourselves recently produced a booklet on the subject which at the same time shows that the Corporation is a modern and forward-looking organization. Copies are available free from the above address.

2) A point which needs to be emphasized is that since the war, Trinity House has been involved in a continuing process of major modernization of all aids to navigation, particularly lighthouses: where possible these are increasingly being fitted with automatic or semi-automatic equipment which cuts out many of the keepers' former time-consuming and menial tasks. But in the case of off-shore lighthouses modernization schemes have never been easy, taking into account difficulties of access, weather conditions, limited working space and the need to work to a carefully controlled budget. For instance the modernization of one tower lighthouse took over three years to complete at a cost of more than £100,000: the scheme included electrification, and the modernization of the keeper's quarters by, among other things, the removal of the curved bunks and the fitting of standard beds. There are very few lighthouses remaining with poor amenities and in due course these will be modernized.

3) Five years ago the first regular helicopter service for exchanging keepers on off-shore lighthouses was introduced; it has been extended since then and now the majority of off-shore lighthouses are relieved

in this manner. This has greatly reduced the travelling time for keepers going to and coming off duty; and more importantly has cut down the frequency of 'overdue' reliefs which was so often the case with those carried out by boat. At the present time we are carrying out an experiment using a helicopter for the relief of a tower light; if this proves successful in due course the remaining tower lights could be integrated into the scheme.

4) Reference is made to rates of pay and hours of duty. As far as rates of pay and allowances are concerned, these are kept under regular review, and I would hate to feel that readers would be led to believe that the rates referred to still apply. They do not: they are now higher and they will of course continue to be adjusted from time to time. As for hours of work and length of spells of duty, after long discussion with the Unions a basic 40-hour working week has been introduced now. This means that for all off-shore lighthouses the tour of duty has become one month off followed by one month ashore, and a similar reduction has been made in the working hours of keepers at land lights. To achieve this we are involved in a major recruiting campaign so that we can double the number of personnel stationed at all rock lighthouses.

5) You may be interested to know that Trinity House has recently appointed a Welfare Officer to the Lighthouse Service, to improve communications between Head Office and members of the Service on all matters appertaining to the welfare of personnel. He is in fact an ex-lighthouse keeper himself, and he travels extensively, making himself readily available to assist keepers and their families with any problem affecting their welfare. There is also now a Safety Adviser: he investigates and advises on all aspects of safety throughout the Service, has been visiting all installations and will continue to make periodic inspections of them.

I hope you will find this information useful and that you will be able to incorporate some of it in the book.

>With all good wishes,
>
>Yours sincerely,
>
>[signed] George
>
>*G. S. Thomson*

Acknowledgements

To have written such a book as this would obviously have been impossible without the eventual permission of the Elder Brethren of Trinity House; to say I am grateful to them is an understatement. The two men with whom I came into contact most frequently during the period in which it was being compiled – Don Henry, Principal of the Lights Department, and George Thomson the Public Relations Officer – extended unstinted co-operation and unlimited assistance. They always granted me every facility I asked for, and complied with every request no matter how inconvenient. To them too I cannot adequately express my thanks.

I am also grateful to the Arts Council of Great Britain for financial assistance to me while I was preparing the book; to my publisher Harold Harris of Hutchinson for waiting patiently for the manuscript; to Simon Scott, also of Hutchinson, for his extensive help with the editing; and to my wife Margery, not only for her hours of arduous work in typing it but as always for her love and support.

The people to whom I'm most grateful of all however are those who provided the material of which the book consists. Over a period of six months I stayed on a number of lighthouses in several different parts of the country; the descriptions of the three types – a land light, a rock light and a tower – are composite pictures, and not descriptions of specific stations. Innumerable lighthouse keepers, keepers' wives, and others connected in other ways with the service all talked willingly and without reservation; and in return had the assurance they would not be identified. For that reason I have altered all personal details, and obscured the localities and changed the locations in which they talked.

Additionally the interviews themselves are composites of conversations with different people, transcribed from tape-recordings. But this is what was said; and I hope it conveys some impression of the world of those in the lighthouse service. It is one I shall always feel greatly privileged to have been allowed to enter.

Previously published by
ELAND BOOKS

MEMOIRS OF A
BENGAL CIVILIAN

JOHN BEAMES
**The lively narrative of a Victorian
district-officer**

With an introduction by Philip Mason

They are as entertaining as Hickey . . . accounts like
these illuminate the dark corners of history.
Times Literary Supplement

John Beames writes a splendidly virile English and
he is incapable of being dull; also he never hesitates
to speak his mind. It is extraordinary that these
memoirs should have remained so long unpublished
. . . the discovery is a real find.
John Morris, The Listener

A gem of the first water. Beames, in addition to being
a first-class descriptive writer in the plain Defoesque
manner, was that thing most necessary of all in an
autobiographer – an original. His book is of the
highest value.
The Times

This edition is not for sale in the USA

*If you wish to receive details of forthcoming publications,
please send your address to
Eland Books, 53 Eland Road, London SW11 5JX*

Previously published by
ELAND BOOKS

A VISIT TO DON OTAVIO

SYBILLE BEDFORD
A Mexican Journey

I am convinced that, once this wonderful book becomes better known, it will seem incredible that it could ever have gone out of print.
Bruce Chatwin, Vogue

This book can be recommended as vastly enjoyable. Here is a book radiant with comedy and colour.
Raymond Mortimer, Sunday Times

Perceptive, lively, aware of the significance of trifles, and a fine writer. Applied to a beautiful, various, and still inscrutable country, these talents yield a singularly delightful result.
The Times

This book has that ageless quality which is what most people mean when they describe a book as classical. From the moment that the train leaves New York. . .it is certain that this journey will be rewarding. When one finally leaves Mrs Bedford on the point of departure, it is with the double regret of leaving Mexico and her company, and one cannot say more than that.
Elizabeth Jane Howard

Malicious, friendly, entertaining and witty.
Evening Standard

This edition is not for sale in the USA

*If you wish to receive details of forthcoming publications,
please send your address to
Eland Books, 53 Eland Road, London SW11 5JX*

Previously published by
ELAND BOOKS

THE DEVIL DRIVES

A Life of Sir Richard Burton.

FAWN M. BRODIE

Richard Burton searched for the source of the Nile,
discovered Lake Tanganyika, and, at great risk,
penetrated the sacred cities of Medina and Mecca.
But he was much more than an explorer:
he was also an amateur botanist, swordsman,
zoologist and geologist. He wrote forty-three books,
translated erotica, and spoke forty languages and
dialects. His life is probably the most fascinating
and outlandish of all the Victorians.

A model of what a life of Burton should be.
Philip Toynbee, Observer

No one could fail to write a good life of Sir Richard
Burton (not even his wife), but Fawn Brodie has
written a brilliant one. Her scholarship is wide and
searching, and her understanding of Burton and
his wife both deep and wide. She writes with clarity
and zest. The result is a first class biography of an
exceptional man…Buy it, steal it, read it.
J. H. Plumb, New York Times

*If you wish to receive details of forthcoming publications,
please send your address to
Eland Books, 53 Eland Road, London SW11 5JX*

TRAVELS WITH MYSELF AND ANOTHER

MARTHA GELLHORN

Must surely be ranked as one of the funniest travel books of our time — second only to *A Short Walk in the Hindu Kush* . . . It doesn't matter whether this author is experiencing marrow-freezing misadventures in war-ravaged China, or driving a Landrover through East African game-parks, or conversing with hippies in Israel, or spending a week in a Moscow Intourist Hotel. Martha Gellhorn's reactions are what count and one enjoys equally her blistering scorn of humbug, her hilarious eccentricities, her unsentimental compassion.
Dervla Murphy, Irish Times

Spun with a fine blend of irony and epigram. She is incapable of writing a dull sentence.
The Times

Miss Gellhorn has a novelist's eye, a flair for black comedy and a short fuse . . . there is not a boring word in her humane and often funny book.
The New York Times

Among the funniest and best written books I have ever read.
Byron Rogers, Evening Standard

*If you wish to receive details of forthcoming publications,
please send your address to
Eland Books, 53 Eland Road, London SW11 5JX*

Previously published by
ELAND BOOKS

THE
WEATHER
IN
AFRICA

MARTHA GELLHORN

This is a stunningly good book.
Victoria Glendinning, New York Times

She's a marvellous story-teller, and I think
anyone who picks up this book is certainly not
going to put it down again. One just wants to go
on reading.
Francis King, Kaleidoscope, BBC Radio 4

An authentic sense of the divorce between Africa
and what Europeans carry in their heads is
powerfully conveyed by a prose that selects its
details with care, yet remains cool in their
expression.
Robert Nye, The Guardian

This is a pungent and witty book.
Jeremy Brooks, Sunday Times

*If you wish to receive details of forthcoming publications,
please send your address to
Eland Books, 53 Eland Road, London SW11 5JX*

Previously published by
ELAND BOOKS

A STATE OF FEAR

ANDREW GRAHAM-YOOLL
Memories of Argentina's nightmare

For ten hair-raising years Andrew Graham-Yooll
was the news editor for the Buenos Aires Herald.
All around him friends and acquaintances were
'disappearing'; and as an honest and brave
reporter he was under constant suspicion from all
sides in Argentina's war of fear.

Because of the author's obvious honesty and
level-headedness, we get an especially frightening
picture of life in a society where the slightest
deviation may cause you to disappear for ever.

'It is the story of trying to do two contradictory
things: write honestly and keep alive . . .
Gripping.'
Andrew Thompson, Guardian

'Will become a classic document about 20th
century Argentina . . . It is a small masterpiece.'
Hugh O'Shaugnessy, Financial Times

If you wish to receive details of forthcoming publications,
please send your address to
Eland Books, 53 Eland Road, London SW11 5JX

MOROCCO
THAT WAS

WALTER HARRIS

With a new preface by Patrick Thursfield

Both moving and hilariously satirical.
Gavin Maxwell, Lords of the Atlas

Many interesting sidelights on the customs and characters of the Moors. . .intimate knowledge of the courts, its language and customs. . .thorough understanding of the Moorish character.
New York Times

No Englishman knows Morocco better than Mr W. B. Harris and his new book. . .is most entertaining.
Spectator (1921)

The author's great love of Morocco and of the Moors is only matched by his infectious zest for life. . . thanks to his observant eye and a gift for felicitously turned phrases, the books of Walter Harris can claim to rank as literature.
Rom Landau, Moroccan Journal (1957)

His pages bring back the vanished days of the unfettered Sultanate in all their dark splendour; a mingling of magnificence with squalor, culture with barbarism, refined cruelty with naive humour that reads like a dream of the Arabian Nights.
The Times

*If you wish to receive details of forthcoming publications,
please send your address to
Eland Books, 53 Eland Road, London SW11 5JX*

Previously published by
ELAND BOOKS

FAR AWAY
AND LONG AGO

W. H. HUDSON
A Childhood in Argentina

With a new preface by Nicholas Shakespeare

One cannot tell how this fellow gets his effects; he writes as the grass grows.
It is as if some very fine and gentle spirit were whispering to him the sentences he puts down on the paper. A privileged being
Joseph Conrad

Hudson's work is a vision of natural beauty and of human life as it might be, quickened and sweetened by the sun and the wind and the rain, and by fellowship with all other forms of life. . .a very great writer. . .the most valuable our age has possessed.
John Galsworthy

And there was no one – no writer – who did not acknowledge without question that this composed giant was the greatest living writer of English.
Far Away and Long Ago is the most self-revelatory of all his books.
Ford Madox Ford

Completely riveting and should be read by everyone.
Auberon Waugh

*If you wish to receive details of forthcoming publications,
please send your address to
Eland Books, 53 Eland Road, London SW11 5JX*

Previously published by
ELAND BOOKS

HOLDING ON

A Novel by
MERVYN JONES

This is the story of a street in London's dockland
and of a family who lived in it. The street was built in
the 1880s, and the Wheelwright family (originally
dockers) lived there until its tragic demolition in
the 1960s, when it was replaced by tower blocks.
  As a social document, the book rings with truth,
but it is much more than that: its compelling
narrative brings the reader right into the life of the
Wheelright family and their neighbours.

Moving, intelligent, thoroughly readable…
it deserves a lot of readers.
Julian Symons, Sunday Times

A remarkable evocation of life in the East End of
London…Mr Jones fakes nothing and blurs little…
It is truthful and moving.
Guardian

Has a classic quality, for the reader feels
himself not an observer but a sharer in the life of
the Wheelwrights and their neighbours.
Daily Telegraph

*If you wish to receive details of forthcoming publications,
please send your address to
Eland Books, 53 Eland Road, London SW11 5JX*

Previously published by
ELAND BOOKS

THREE CAME HOME

AGNES KEITH
A woman's ordeal in a Japanese prison camp

Three Came Home should rank with the great imprisonment stories of all times.
New York Herald Tribune

No one who reads her unforgettable narrative of the years she passed in Borneo during the war years can fail to share her emotions with something very like the intensity of a personal experience.
Times Literary Supplement

This book sets a standard which will be difficult to surpass.
The Listener

It is one of the most remarkable books you will ever read.
John Carey, Sunday Times

*If you wish to receive details of forthcoming publications,
please send your address to
Eland Books, 53 Eland Road, London SW11 5JX*

GOLDEN EARTH

NORMAN LEWIS

Travels in Burma

Mr Lewis can make even a lorry interesting.
Cyril Connolly, Sunday Times

Very funny . . . a really delightful book.
Maurice Collis, Observer

Norman Lewis remains the best travel writer alive.
Auberon Waugh, Business Traveller

The reader may find enormous pleasure here without knowing the country.
Honor Tracy, New Statesman

The brilliance of the Burmese scene is paralleled by the brilliance of the prose.
Guy Ramsey, Daily Telegraph

*If you wish to receive details of forthcoming publications,
please send your address to
Eland Books, 53 Eland Road, London SW11 5JX*

Previously published by
ELAND BOOKS

THE HONOURED SOCIETY

NORMAN LEWIS
The Sicilian Mafia Observed

New epilogue by Marcello Cimino

One of the great travel writers of our time.
Eric Newby, Observer

Mr Norman Lewis is one of the finest journalists
of his time. . .he excels both in finding material
and in evaluating it.
The Listener

It is deftly written, and every page is horribly
absorbing.
The Times

The Honoured Society is the most penetrating book
ever written on the Mafia.
Time Out

*If you wish to receive details of forthcoming publications,
please send your address to
Eland Books, 53 Eland Road, London SW11 5JX*

NAPLES '44

NORMAN LEWIS

As unique an experience for the reader as it must have been a unique experience for the writer.
Graham Greene

Uncommonly well written, entertaining despite its depressing content, and quite remarkably evocative.
Philip Toynbee, Observer

His ten novels and five non-fiction works place him in the front rank of contemporary English writers : . . here is a book of gripping fascination in its flow of bizarre anecdote and character sketch; and it is much more than that.
J. W. Lambert, Sunday Times

A wonderful book.
Richard West, Spectator

Sensitive, ironic and intelligent.
Paul Fussell, The New Republic

One goes on reading page after page as if eating cherries.
Luigi Barzini, New York Review of Books

This edition is not for sale in the USA

If you wish to receive details of forthcoming publications, please send your address to Eland Books, 53 Eland Road, London SW11 5JX

Previously published by
ELAND BOOKS

A VIEW
OF THE WORLD

NORMAN LEWIS
Selected Journalism

Here is the selected journalism of Norman Lewis,
collected from a period of over thirty years. The
selection includes ten of the best articles from *The
Changing Sky*, eight more which have never been
collected within a book, and two which have
never previously been published.

From reviews of *The Changing Sky*:

He really goes in deep like a sharp polished
knife. I have never travelled in my armchair so
fast, variously and well.
V. S. Pritchett, New Statesman

He has compressed into these always
entertaining and sophisticated sketches material
that a duller man would have hoarded for half a
dozen books.
The Times

Outstandingly the best travel writer of our age, if
not the best since Marco Polo.
Auberon Waugh, Business Traveller

*If you wish to receive details of forthcoming publications,
please send your address to
Eland Books, 53 Eland Road, London SW11 5JX*

Previously published by
ELAND BOOKS

A YEAR IN
MARRAKESH

PETER MAYNE

A notable book, for the author is exceptional both in his literary talent and his outlook. His easy economical style seizes, with no sense of effort, the essence of people, situations and places . . . Mr Mayne is that rare thing, a natural writer . . . no less exceptional is his humour.
Few Westerners have written about Islam with so little nonsense and such understanding.
Times Literary Supplement.

He has contrived in a deceptively simple prose to disseminate in the air of an English November the spicy odours of North Africa; he has turned, for an hour, smog to shimmering sunlight. He has woven a texture of extraordinary charm.
Daily Telegraph

Mr Mayne's book gives us the 'strange elation' that good writing always creates. It is a good book, an interesting book, and one that I warmly recommend.
Harold Nicolson, Observer

*If you wish to receive details of forthcoming publications,
please send your address to
Eland Books, 53 Eland Road, London SW11 5JX*

Previously published by
ELAND BOOKS

KENYA DIARY (1902–1906)

RICHARD MEINERTZHAGEN

With a new preface by Elspeth Huxley

Those who have only read the tranquil descriptions of Kenya between the two Wars may be surprised by Meinertzhagen's often bloodthirsty diaries. They do not always make pleasant reading, but they offer an unrivalled and startlingly vivid account of life during the early days of the colony.

One of the best and most colourful intelligence officers the army ever had.
Times, Obituary

This book is of great interest and should not be missed
New Statesman

One of the ablest and most successful brains I had met in the army.
Lloyd George, Memoirs

Anybody at all interested in the evolution of Kenya or the workings of 'colonialism' would do well to read this diary.
William Plomer, Listener

*If you wish to receive details of forthcoming publications,
please send your address to
Eland Books, 53 Eland Road, London SW11 5JX*

Previously published by
ELAND BOOKS

JOURNEYS OF A
GERMAN IN ENGLAND

CARL PHILIP MORITZ
A walking-tour of England in 1782

With a new preface by Reginald Nettel

The extraordinary thing about the book is that the writing is so fresh that you are startled when a stage-coach appears. A young man is addressing himself to you across two centuries. And there is a lovely comedy underlying it.
Byron Rogers, Evening Standard

This account of his travels has a clarity and freshness quite unsurpassed by any contemporary descriptions.
Iain Hamilton, Illustrated London News

A most amusing book. . .a variety of small scenes which might come out of Hogarth. . .Moritz in London, dodging the rotten oranges flung about the pit of the Haymarket Theatre, Moritz in the pleasure gardens of Vauxhall and Ranelagh, Moritz in Parliament or roving the London streets is an excellent companion. We note, with sorrow, that nearly two centuries ago, British coffee was already appalling.
Alan Pryce-Jones, New York Herald Tribune

*If you wish to receive details of forthcoming publications,
please send your address to
Eland Books, 53 Eland Road, London SW11 5JX*

Previously published by
ELAND BOOKS

TRAVELS INTO THE
INTERIOR OF AFRICA

MUNGO PARK

With a new preface by Jeremy Swift

Famous triumphs of exploration have rarely engendered outstanding books. *Travels into the Interior of Africa*, which has remained a classic since its first publication in 1799, is a remarkable exception.

It was a wonder that he survived so long, and a still greater one that his diaries could have been preserved . . . what amazing reading they make today!
Roy Kerridge, Tatler

The enthusiasm and understanding which informs Park's writing is irresistible.
Frances Dickenson, Time Out

One of the greatest and most respected explorers the world has known, a man of infinite courage and lofty principles, and one who dearly loved the black African.
E. W. Bovill, the Niger Explored

Told with a charm and naivety in themselves sufficient to captivate the most fastidious reader . . . modesty and truthfulness peep from every sentence . . . for actual hardships undergone, for dangers faced, and difficulties overcome, together with an exhibition of virtues which make a man great in the rude battle of life. Mungo Park stands without a rival.
Joseph Thomson, author of Through Masailand

If you wish to receive details of forthcoming publications,
please send your address to
Eland Books, 53 Eland Road, London SW11 5JX

Previously published by
ELAND BOOKS

A CURE FOR SERPENTS

THE DUKE OF PIRAJNO
An Italian doctor in North Africa

The Duke of Pirajno arrived in North Africa in 1924. For the next eighteen years, his experiences as a doctor in Libya, Eritrea, Ethiopia, and Somaliland provided him with opportunities and insights rarely given to a European. He brings us stories of noble chieftains and celebrated prostitutes, of Berber princes and Tuareg entertainers, of giant elephants and a lioness who fell in love with the author.

He tells us story after story with all the charm and resource of Scheherazade herself.
Harold Nicolson, Observer

A delightful personality, warm, observant, cynical and astringent. . .Doctors who are good raconteurs make wonderful reading.
Cyril Connolly, Sunday Times

A very good book indeed. . .He writes a rapid darting natural prose, like the jaunty scutter of a lizard on a rock.
Maurice Richardson, New Statesman

Pirajno's book is a cure for a great deal more than serpents.
The Guardian

In the class of book one wants to keep on a special shelf.
Doris Lessing, Good Book Guide

If you wish to receive details of forthcoming publications, please send your address to
Eland Books, 53 Eland Road, London SW11 5JX

Previously published by
ELAND BOOKS

NUNAGA

DUNCAN PRYDE

Ten years among the Eskimos

Duncan Pryde, an eighteen-year-old orphan, an ex-merchant-seaman, and disgruntled factory worker left Glasgow for Canada to try his hand at fur-trading.

He became so absorbed in this new life that his next ten years were spent living with the Eskimos. He became part of their life even in its most intimate manifestations: hunting, shamanism, wife-exchange and blood feuds.

This record of these years is not only an astonishing adventure, but an unrivalled record of a way of life which, along with the igloo, has vanished altogether.

He tells us stories, which he seems to have been born to do.
Time

One of the best books about Arctic life ever written . . . A marvellous story, well told.
Sunday Times

If you wish to receive details of forthcoming publications,
please send your address to
Eland Books, 53 Eland Road, London SW11 5JX

Previously published by
ELAND BOOKS

A FUNNY OLD QUIST

The Memoirs of a Gamekeeper

EVAN ROGERS

EDITED BY CLIVE MURPHY

An octogenerian gamekeeper tells us his story.
He has worked for sixty-eight years on the same
Herefordshire estate, and can remember the time
when wooden clogs were worn and young women
gave birth in the fields while gathering stones for a
shilling a ton.

Although he is a downright traditionalist who
dislikes new-fangled ways, he doesn't pretend that
life was always easy, and he is sometimes sharply
critical of his former masters. From this truthful
and vivid account, we get an unsentimental picture
of life on a semi-feudal estate – a way of life that
has almost completely disappeared.

A refreshing and informative book, a social
document of permanent value, as well as a
good read.
Times Literary Supplement

Extraordinary is the proper word for it.
Country Life

*If you wish to receive details of forthcoming publications,
please send your address to
Eland Books, 53 Eland Road, London SW11 5JX*

Previously published by
ELAND BOOKS

THE LAW

A novel by
ROGER VAILLAND

With a new preface by Jonathan Keates

The Law is a cruel game that was played in the taverns of Southern Italy. It reflects the game of life in which the whole population of Manacore is engaged. Everyone from the feudal landowner, Don Cesare, to the landless day-labourers are participants in the never-ending contest.

Every paragraph and every section of this novel has been carefully cast and seems to be locked into position, creating a structure which is solid and formal, yet always lively. . .while we are reading the novel its world has an absolute validity. . . *The Law* is an experience I will not easily forget.
V. S. Naipaul, New Statesman

The Law deserves every reading it will have. It is and does all that a novel should – amuses, absorbs, excites and illuminates not only its chosen patch of ground but much more of life and character as well.
New York Times

One feels one knows everyone in the district. . .every page has the texture of living flesh.
New York Herald Tribune

A full rich book teeming with ambition, effort and desire as well as with ideas.
Times Literary Supplement

If you wish to receive details of forthcoming publications,
please send your address to
Eland Books, 53 Eland Road, London SW11 5JX